SELECTED
WRITINGS
OF
JOAQUIN
MILLER

Joaquin Miller in his forties

SELECTED WRITINGS

OF

JOAQUIN MILLER

Edited with Introduction and Notes by Alan Rosenus

DRAWINGS BY JOAQUIN MILLER

Urion Press • 1977

Library of Congress Catalog Number 73-88918
ISBN 0-913522-05-8

Printed in U.S.A.

First Edition

Library of Congress Cataloging in Publication Data

───

Miller, Joaquin, 1837-1913.
    Selected writings of Joaquin Miller.

    "A Urion primary source book."
    I. Title.
PS2396.R6   813'.4   76-25508
ISBN 0-913522-05-8

TABLE OF CONTENTS

LIST OF JOAQUIN MILLER'S DRAWINGS
FROM HIS CALIFORNIA DIARY

LIST OF PHOTOGRAPHS

Acknowledgements

I owe a special debt of gratitude to Alice Schlichter, Department of Linguistics, the University of California, Berkeley, for her translations of the Wintu portions of Joaquin Miller's *California Diary*. I also wish to express my thanks to Jean Beckner of the Honnold Library whose personal interest in Joaquin Miller has been encouraging and helpful. Acknowledgement must also be made to the head of Special Collections at the Honnold Library, Ruth Hauser; and to the Honnold Library itself, my sincere gratitude for permission to photograph Joaquin Miller's drawings and use previously unpublished material in this volume. For similar reasons, I wish to thank Pherne and Earl K. Miller, niece and nephew of Joaquin Miller, whose well wishes are deeply appreciated. The negatives of Miller's drawings—obtained under somewhat restricted conditions—were greatly improved by the careful printing of Grey Crawford.

A.R.

Sources of the Texts

"Notes From an Old Journal," "An Elk Hunt in the Sierras," "The Pit River Massacre," "In the Land of Clouds," "The New and the Old," " 'Idahho,' " "An Old Oregonian in the Snow," and "John Brown—Joseph De Bloney" were taken from *Memorie and Rime* (New York: Funk and Wagnals, 1884). "A Bear on Fire," "The Great Grizzly Bear," "As a Humorist," "The Grizzly as Fremont Found Him," "Bill Cross and His Pet Bear," and "Treeing a Bear" come from *True Bear Stories* (Chicago and New York: Rand McNally & Co, 1900). "A Ride Through Oregon" first appeared in the *Overland Monthly*, VIII (April 1872), 303-310. "Rough Times in Idaho" was published in the *Overland Monthly*, V (September 1870), 280-286. *The California Diary* first appeared as *Joaquin Miller: His California Diary*, ed. John S. Richards (Seattle: F. McCaffrey at his Dogwood Press, 1936); additional material and Joaquin Miller's drawings are published here for the first time, courtesy of the Honnold Library. The chapters from *Overland in a Covered Wagon* are published as they appeared in *Overland in a Covered Wagon: An Autobiography*, ed. Sidney G. Firman (New York and London: D. Appleton, 1930). "Utopia" comes from *The Californian*, II (December 1880), 557-563. "The Battle of Castle Crags" is from a small booklet, *The Battle of Castle Crags* (San Francisco: The Traveler, 1894).

introduction

Joaquin Miller was already an exceptional writer of prose when he became famous in London as the "Poet of the Sierra" in 1871; after his great success, he did not always reveal the naked Adam of himself with the same candor and spirit found in the selections included in this volume — many of which were written prior to his remarkable London journey. After the English acclaimed him as America's most important writer, his American audience — and critics especially — were unable to "see" him. Miller himself wrote later on, "...it really seems to me that from the day I was suddenly discovered and pointed out in London I have been an entire stranger in my own land....As for that red-shirted and hairy man bearing my name abroad and 'standing before Kings,' I never saw him, never heard of him until on returning to my own country, I found that this unpleasant and entirely impossible figure ever attended and even overshadowed my most earnest work."[1] By the time Miller wrote these words, he had forgotten the style in which he had charmed the whole English nation — a performance, sometimes helped along by red shirt, on other occasions by correct English attire, which certainly guaranteed that his work would never be properly valued at home. The transition from obscure Judge of Grant County, Oregon, to the man who had gathered into his following Browning, Tennyson, and Rossetti, was so crucial to his later development that I have placed his own account of the London journey at the beginning of the present collection of his prose. Here, in "Notes from an Old Journal," we appreciate the strength of his diction; and we also get hints of why some of his contemporaries in frontier Oregon thought of this man of action as someone who was excessively sensitive. Somewhere, mixed in with his worship of beauty, his great ambition, and simple trust were the invisible resources that went to overturn the laws of probability.

But if we compare the early portions of the journal written prior to his London "discovery" with the "remembered account" of the Rossetti dinner—composed after he was back in America—we find that the spontaneity of language and the naked Adam have disappeared in a flash. The acclaimed Miller now anticipates the feelings of an audience he knows is going to contemplate every word. No longer does he walk the streets of London responding as quickly and unconsciously as a mirror.

Outwardly, Miller never gave much consideration to London's literary conventions, and this made some of his contemporaries uncomfortable.[2] Joaquin was hurt by the scepticism of his American friends. Couldn't they understand? That was the way the literary world *had* to be treated. He had seen enough to convince him that the creation of wonderful names was a joke. His attitude was all the more incomprehensible because Miller was not a satirist. A transcendentalist who emphasized the divinity of the physical world (its imperfections as well as its beauty), he was actually a sort of believer. Unlike Bret Harte, Bierce, and Twain, Miller had little scorn or contempt for the citizens of the West, and none for the land or its native people. He kept this faith and respect even while—as some thought—he betrayed it with his other face.

Later in his career, the number of Joaquin Millers seemed to multiply. The unexpected Victorian prodigy of the anti-poet with curled mustachios who received the Bay Area Women's Press Club dressed only in the skin of a wildcat and recited "Mary Had a Little Lamb" to Bay

Area savants as an example of "ideal poetry" sometimes gave way to another personality, the Miller his public wanted him to be: their longings are evident in many of the magazine articles of the period: an unfailing bearded seer, a Tennysonian creation in marble. Another (perhaps more enduring) Miller drove down from the hills in Oakland and directed the planting of hundreds of thousands of trees. In 1886 he established Arbor Day in California. Miller once declared, "I am afraid of the man who does not love beauty,"[3] and trees were a part of the indestructible world of natural value he believed in. Though he shared in his age's enthusiasm for new inventions, he could see no sane future for America except in an agrarian program.

Joaquin was also stabilized by his relations with powerful women. It is unfortunate we do not get detailed (rather than idealized) portraits of them in his work, for he knew some of the more beautiful and influential women of his age.

Joaquin's generation made a mistake by not acknowledging him as a writer of prose. Once he was called, the "Poet of the Sierra," everyone assumed the matter had been decided. Miller, however, preferred to write prose; he thought some of it was superior to anything he had done in poetry, and his more observant critics have agreed in this.[4] In collecting what I consider to be the best of his stories and journals, I have simply kept my ear tuned for the qualities that contributed to Miller's originality. His style — with its disparate elements of humor and idealism, its instinctual base and powerful feeling — extended the tone and range of transcendental intimacy. In many cases — especially where Miller was not too worried about being correct — his words have a sound and feel that make him our contemporary. Compatible with the most congenial portraits of the forested New

World of Oregon and California, the language is also able to reveal a psyche in conflict with itself as overwhelming forces negate some of his most precious ideals.

Regarding the "embroidered Miller" sometimes objected to: indeed, much of the best of Miller's writing is embroidered. In this volume, both factual and fictionalized accounts of Miller's life are presented. They are in no conclusive way superior or inferior to each other as pieces of writing; but they make handy tools for gaining insights into Miller himself and for studying the manner in which raw material from experience is molded into works of the imagination. For instance, it is interesting to compare the wholly accurate *California Diary* account of his Mt. Shasta elk hunt with the later fictionalized version, "An Elk Hunt in the Sierras." The story has been altered by an aesthetic; it has been given an epic "feel." But the original in the *Diary* has the cold, the discomfort, and the necessity that create epic material in the first place.

In viewing Miller's total performance as a prose writer, the paradox is discovered that although in many ways he was ahead of his contemporaries, in other respects he was a man of the past. As a helpless victim of his own flawed feelings, as a pioneer ecologist, as a champion of minority races, he was in advance of this time. To understand the extent to which he was held by ties in the remote past, we have to look again at his first piece of writing, *The California Diary,* and then study his later books. The birth of Miller's consciousness and what was enduring in his work can be found in the *Diary*. At first, it is merely an account book, then it becomes a more full record of his life with the Indians and miners in the Mt. Shasta region. Before he turns twenty, Miller begins to feel that human folly, shame, perhaps even the Fall itself, are as much a creation of church-going Christianity as they are the inevitable results of the nature of things.[4a] It is here, too, that we see the birth of the sometimes treacherous and hopelessly confused Miller: a young man whose sympathies and ties are so complex they become unmanageable. Unable to satisfy the conflicting sides of his nature, he frequently resorts to violence.

If we place *The California Diary* in historical perspective, it is discovered that when Miller began keeping his record in 1855, another dozen years would pass before Mark Twain would publish his first collection of sketches; Bret Harte had just moved from New York to San Francisco, and the *Overland Monthly* would not appear for another fourteen years. Melville's *Piazza Tales* had not yet been published; Walt Whitman had yet to distribute his unwanted volume of *Leaves of Grass* to New York City bookstores; and an important political sidelight: the Missouri Compromise had recently been repealed, which gave Lincoln's anti-slavery speeches a new immediacy. Miller was viewed by a far different world when, in 1871, he became a famous man. In the interim, he had completed at least one draft of *Unwritten History: Life Among the Modocs* (he had a copy of it with him to show to his friend, Ina Coolbrith, when he arrived in San Francisco in 1870), and he had also drafted a number of his best sketches, though they wouldn't be published until much later. If we look at Miller from the point of view of when his work was composed and when it was actually published, we are viewing him through a sort of time-warp. He had done most of his serious grappling with himself in the late 1850's and 1860's. Certain transformations later on took place in his writing that might be called experimental, but his duel with the city of New York in *The Destruction of Gotham* fell short of being the victory it should have been, and *The Building of the City Beautiful*—despite its many fine passages—

suffers from Miller's tendency to idealize. Joaquin's own personal failings, and the detailed characterizations of the faults of others that made his early work so immediately affecting, do not appear in the majority of his later books.

If, however, Miller's best writing is a reliable guide to his genuine loyalties, we find that his allegiances at the end of his career were attached to an even more remote past than the early events he had recorded in his first journal. By far the most interesting book of his late period is *Overland in a Covered Wagon,* presented here in selection, which was begun as an autobiographical introduction to the complete edition of his poetry and was later published in revised form. Along with *True Bear Stories,* it proves that Miller retained his skill as a prose writer until the end of his career. The autobiography has a richness of tone and fidelity to detail only possessed by writers who have an unusual sense of the past. Miller's "looking back" was actually a look to the future—for the world of permanent value was there for him in an age that had disappeared—and his memories held many of the qualities that were—and still are—unique in American experience.

On the other hand, if we are searching for a late piece of creative self-discovery, we are not likely to find it. The key to Miller's lack of follow-through as a writer after he had unfolded himself so splendidly in *Unwritten History: Life Among the Modocs* may be found in his frequent references to the scorn with which poets were held. Another clue is suggested by the simple statement in the Preface to his very first book of poems, *Specimens,* "I anticipate your disapproval." [5] Despite his remarkable powers of forgiveness and self-forgiveness, Miller, whom Ambrose Bierce called "the greatest-hearted man I ever knew," quite possibly never forgave himself for being a writer.

Thankfully, we are not denied the best fruits of Miller's tremendous prose output, which—even after careful selection—yield an impressive body of work. His documentation of the land and its spirit, his narrative accomplishments (and humorous imperfections), the anatomies of senseless shame; his wondrous balancing feats, tenderness, relaxed philosophy and exuberant heroism show the naked Adam—in essence—as not vitally harmed by its failings.

Recognizing that each of the pieces in this volume deserves to be appreciated in greater detail, I am making this a brief introduction since I have written at length on Miller elsewhere.[6] Other material relevant to the text can be found in the Notes. Fortunately, in a note which precedes his London journal, Joaquin himself provides a little introduction to the book.

July, 1976

ALAN ROSENUS

NOTES FROM AN OLD JOURNAL

NOTES FROM AN OLD JOURNAL

Tired of carting around the world a mass of manuscript once called a journal, but now worn almost to a circle, and yet not willing to leave it for strangers to trouble over, I have copied out these extracts and burned the rest of it. Whether or not I should have cremated the whole crude heap is a question I am quite prepared to hear decided in the affirmative by the reader. Yet to have destroyed it entirely would have been like forgetting one's first love. Besides that, these bits of the journal, you see, pave the way to words of others worth hearing. And so it is I have kept these few extracts, taking care, as you must credit me, to leave out all names or allusions that might cause pain or displeasure to even the most sensitive. Yet I half suspect that I have, with them, left out much of the heart and life of the thing. —J.M.

in new york

Reached New York to-day, August 17th, 1870, after seven days' and seven nights' incessant ride from San Francisco, and fourteen from Eugene City, Oregon. Pandora's box! New York at last! Now I shall write home and tell them I am on this side the Rocky Mountains. At Eugene I wrote a letter and left it behind me, telling my parents I was going to "Frisco." Once safely there I wrote them I was going East. And now I shall give them the first hint of going to Europe. Taken in pieces, it will not be so hard for them. And oh! but this is a tough town! And the time I had in landing on this island! I have fought many battles with Indians, I have seen rough men in the mines, but such ruffians as assailed me on landing from the Jersey ferry I have never encountered before. Two of these literally hauled me into a coach. I cried out: they shouted to the crowd and police that I was drunk; and another "tough," who said he was my friend, helped them hustle me in, and held the door till they dashed away. By and by they stopped, and one got down, and holding the door meekly asked me to tell him again what hotel I said I wanted to go to! At the door of the hotel—the Astor House—the only name I could think of or was familiar with, they demanded five dollars. I paid it. But what makes me mad—mad at myself as well as them—they gave me a Confederate five-dollar bill in change! How could they know I came from a land where they use only gold, and we can't tell one kind of green, greasy paper from another? Ah, I see: this Confederate is white—or was white. Well, I am going to cut off my hair the first thing, and get me a new hat.

August 18. Shaved and shorn! Now, let them come after me! . . . Great event to-day. My brave, good brother, who heard the roar of war away out yonder by the sounding Oregon, and came on here to see it through, is with me. He is dark-haired and very handsome. He dresses and looks just like these other fellows, though, and, like Chinamen, one can hardly tell them apart. But, dear, brave boy, he is not like these other fellows a bit. And how he and I once quarrelled over this war business! True, I can remember, when we were both little lads and father talked to us about the slaves, how we planned together to steal the poor negroes and help them away to the North. But when the war came, and the armies went down desolating the South, then, with that fatality that has always followed me for getting on the wrong side, siding with the weak, I forgot my pity for the one in my larger pity for the other. And so my brother John shouldered his gun, we shook hands, and I never saw him

4

any more till to-day. His name is on the rolls of New Jersey, a lieutenant only. We do not mention the war. His side won. But, as with many another noble fellow, it has cost him his life I fear. I can see death on his pale, gentle face. His deep blue eyes have lost their glory. What will mother say?

going

August 19. I shall get out of this town at once. . . . At Central Park to-day I wanted to rest under a tree, a cool, clean tree, that reached its eager arms up to God, asking, praying for rain, and a policeman, club in hand, caught hold of me and shook me, and told me to keep off the grass. "Keep off the grass!" There was no grass there. New York, if you will come to Oregon you may sit untroubled under the trees, roll in grass that is grass, and rest forever . . . . I must put my pants inside my boots. Then I am sure they won't know me, and get after me everywhere I go . . . . If I was living in this town I would make those policemen give up their clubs. Are the people here a lot of dogs, that these fellows have to use clubs? Take away their clubs, and give them pistols and swords. If a man must be killed, let him be killed like a gentleman, not like a dog. I am going to get out of this town quick. I do not fit in here. . . . Bought my ticket, $65, second class, ship Europa, Anchor Line, to land at Glasgow; and off to-morrow. . . . Have tried so hard to get to see Horace Greeley. But he won't see me. Maybe he is not here. But I think he is . . . . Went over and tried to see Beecher;[7] found a door by the pulpit open, and went in. The carpenters were fixing up the church, but they looked so hard at me that I did not ask for Mr. Beecher. I went up on the platform and sat down and peeled an apple, and put the peelings on the little stand. Then I heard a man cough away back in the dark, and he came and climbed up the little ladder, and took those peelings in his thumb and finger—long, lean, bony fingers, like tongs—and backing down the ladder he went to the door and threw them away with all his might. Then he coughed again, but all the time did not let on to see me. I felt awful, and

5

got down and left soon. However, I got some leaves from a tree by the door to send to mother. . . . Two handsome, well-dressed gentlemen spoke to me to-day, the only people who have spoken to me since I have been here — except to bully me; said they knew me in Texas, but could not recall my name.

in ayr, scotland

September 4, 1870. What a voyage!Cold? Cold seas and cold seamen. I don't think I spoke a dozen words in the whole desolate fourteen days. A lot of Germans going home to fight filled the ship; a hard, rough lot, and they ate like hogs. . . . Saw an iceberg as big as Mount Hood in the middle of the ocean. . . . And why may there not be people on these broken bits of the great sealed-up North? Fancy Sir John Franklin's ship frozen fast and all in trim, he there stiff and silent, glass in hand, his frozen men all about him at their posts — fancy all this drifting away to the friendly warm waves of the South, on one of these great islands of ice. . . . Saw Ireland on the north; green as the green sea; dotted with cottages, crossed by stone fences like a checker-board. It is a checker-board: the white cottages are the chessmen. What games shall be played? Who play them? And who win? . . .

September 10. God bless these hale and honest Scotch down here at peaceful Ayr! Did not stop an hour in Glasgow. It looked too much like New York. But here I have come upon the edge of Godland; mountains and rivulets and cold, clear skies. It looks like Oregon. Only I miss the trees so much. A land that is barren of trees is old and ugly, like a bald-headed man, and ought to get ready to die. . . . I have made lots of friends. One man showed me more than one hundred books, all by Ayrshire poets, and some of them splendid! I have not dared tell any one yet that I too hope to publish a book of verse. . . .

I go every day from here to the "Auld Brig" over the Doon, Highland Mary's grave, and "Alloway's auld haunted kirk!" . . . Poetry is in the air here. I am now working like a beaver, and shall give up my journal. If my mind is not strong enough to hold what I see, or if my thoughts and notions are not big and solid enough to stick together and stay with me, let them go. . . . Heigho! what a thing is the mind: a sieve, that catches all the ugly things, stray and wreck and castaway, all that is hard and hideous. But lo! our sieves will not hold the sweet pure water. . . .

September 12. Am going from here to Byron's tomb in Nottingham very soon now. I have a wreath of laurel, sent by a lady from San Francisco, for the great poet's grave, and I go to place it there. Shall take in Scott's home and tomb . . . . Good-by, Burns, brother. I know you, love you. Our souls have wandered together many a night this sweet autumn-time by the tranquil banks of the Doon. . . .

September 16. They say Carlyle lives near here, on a farm. I like Carlyle—that is, the parts of him which I don't understand. And that is saying that I like nearly all of Carlyle, I reckon.

September 18. In the sunset to-day, as I walked out for the last time toward the tomb of Highland Mary, I met a whole line of splendid Scotch lassies with sheaves of wheat on their heads and sickles on their arms. Their feet were bare, their legs were bare to the knees. Their great strong arms were shapely as you can conceive; they were tall, and their lifted faces were radiant with health and happiness. I stepped aside in the narrow road to enjoy the scene and let them pass. They were going down the sloping road toward some thatched cottages by the sea; I toward the mountains. How beautiful! I uncovered my head as I stepped respectfully aside. But giving the road to women here seems unusual, and one beautiful girl, with hair like the golden sheaves she carried, came up to me, talked and laughed and bantered in words that I could not understand, much as I wanted to. . . . And then the beautiful picture moved on. O Burns, Burns, come back to the banks of bonny Doon! It is worth while.

> How beautiful she was! Why, she
> Was inspiration. She was born
> To walk God's summer-hills at morn,
> Nor waste her by the cold North Sea.

What wonder, that her soul's white wings
Beat at the bars, like living things?

I know she sighed, and wandered through
The fields alone, and ofttime drew
Her hand above her head, and swept
The lonesome sea, and ever kept
Her face to sea, as if she knew
Some day, some near or distant day,
Her destiny should come that way.

in the ruins of melrose abbey

The Royal Inn, September 20. Waded the Tweed
yesterday, and looked over Sir Walter Scott's "poem in
stones," as he called it. So beautiful, and so sad. Empty as
a dead man's palm is this place now. Wet and cold, I
walked on to Melrose Abbey, three miles distant. Was let
in through a great gate by a drunken old woman. The
sun was going down; the place of buried kings seemed
holy — too holy at least to have a drunken and garrulous
and very ugly woman at my elbow. I gave the old creature
a half-crown and told her to leave me. She did so, and I
rested on the tombs; still warm they were with sunshine
gone away. Then a sudden fog drew up the Tweed past
Dryburg, where the great wizard is buried, and I began to
grow chill. I got up and groped about in the fog among
the tombstones and fallen arches. But in a very little time
I found the fog so dense that together with the night it
made total darkness. I hurried to the great gate. It was
closed. The wretched old woman had got still more drunk
on my half-crown, and I was there for the night. And
what a night I passed! It would have killed almost any
other man. As it is, my leg is so stiff I can hardly hobble
down-stairs.

AT LORD BYRON'S TOMB

O master, here I bow before a shrine;
  Before the lordliest dust that every yet
Moved animate in human form divine.
  Lo! dust indeed to dust. The mould is set
  Above thee, and the ancient walls are wet,

8

And drip all day in dark and silent gloom;
As if the cold gray stones could not forget
Thy great estate shrunk to this sombre room,
But learn to weep perpetual tears above thy tomb.

September 25. Something glorious! The old man, John Brown by name, took the wreath for Byron's tomb—and a sovereign—and hung it above the tablet, placed on the damp and dingy wall by his sister. Well then, the little old people who preside over the little old church did not like it—you see my bargain with the old man is that he is to have a sovereign a year to keep the wreath there as long as he lives (or I have sovereigns)—and he faithfully refused to take down the wreath, but nailed it to the wall. Then the little-souled people appealed to the Bishop. And what has the Bishop done? What has the Bishop said? Not a word. But he has sent another wreath to be nailed alongside of my wreath from California!

O my poet! Worshipped where the world is glorious with the fire and the blood of youth! Yet here in your own home—ah well! The old eternal truth of Christ. . . . but why say the truth of Christ? Better say the words of Christ; and that means eternal truth. . . . I have not told any one here that I write verses. . . . Byron sang in the voice of a god: and see what they say of him. But they may receive me. "No prophet is without honor, *save in his own land*," is the language of the text I believe.

September 28. Have written lots of stuff here. I have been happy here. I have worked, and not thought of the past. But to-morrow I am going to go down to Hull, cross the Channel, and see the French and Germans fight. For I have stopped work and begun to look back. . . . I see the snow-peaks of Oregon all the time when I stop work—the great white clouds, like hammocks swinging to and fro, to and fro, as if cradling the gods: maybe they are rocking and resting the souls of great men bound heavenward.... And then the valley at the bottom of the peaks; the people there; the ashes on the hearth; the fire gone out....there is no one there to rekindle it....Stop looking back, I say. Get back to the Bible truths: the story of Lot and his lost. . . . Never look back. A man, if he be a real

9

man, has his future before him and not behind him. The old story of Orpheus in hell has its awful lesson. I, then, shall go forward and never look back any more. Hell, I know, is behind me. There cannot be worse than hell before me . . . . Yet for all this philosophy and this setting the face forward, the heart turns back.

in a christian's war

Calais, France, October 30, 1870. Been to the war! Brutes! Shuttlecocked between the two armies, and arrested every time I turned around. I am sure the Germans would have shot me if I could have spoken a word of French. I am doubly certain the French would have sabred me if I had been able to speak one word of German. As I knew neither tongue, nothing about any language except Modoc — although I am trying to pick up the English — they contented themselves by tumbling all my manuscript — which they could not read — and sending me out of the country. And such heartlessness to each other! By the road one day I found a wounded soldier. He had got out into the hedge: hundreds passed — soldiers, citizens, all sorts. He was calling to all, any one. I got out of the mass of fugitives and tried to help him. Then, when it was seen that some one was at his side, others came up, and he was cared for, I reckon. . . . Everybody running away! I running faster than ever cripple ran before. This would not sound well in Oregon. I must put it in better form: I will merely say I came on in haste. . . . I am no great talker, but do like to be in a land where I can talk if I want to. . . . I found a wounded horse on a battlefield one day trying to get on his feet. I helped him. He was bleeding to death, and soon sank down again. But I tell you he looked at me like a human being. Poor horses! I am more sorry for them than the men.

in london

London, November 2, 1870. Am at last in the central

10

city of this earth. I was afraid to come here, and so it was I almost went quite around this boundless spread of houses before I entered it: saw all these islands and nearly all the continent first. But I feel at home almost, even now, and have only been here three days. Tired though, so tired! And then my leg bothers me badly. There is a bit of lead in there about as big as the end of my thumb. But ever since that night in Melrose Abbey it has felt as big as a cannon-ball. And then I have been rather active of late. Active! The Oregonians ought to have seen me running away from the French, the Germans—both at once. But you see they took my pistols away from me before I had a chance to protest or even suspected what they were going to do. Ah well! I am safe out of it all now, and shall, since I am too crippled to get about, sit still and write in this town. When I came in on the rail from Dover, I left my bag at the station; paid two pence—great big coppers, big as five of America's—and took a ticket for it, and so set out to walk about the city. And how delightfully different from New York!

Now, I want to note something strange. I walked straight to Westminster Abbey—straight as the crooked streets would let me; and I did not ask any one on the way, nor did I have the remotest idea where it was. As for a guide-book, I never had one in my life. But my heart was in that Abbey, going out to the great spirits, the immortal dust gathered there, and I walked straight to where my heart was. . . . And this encourages me very much. . . . As if by some possible turn of fortune or favor of the gods I—I may really get there, or at least set out upon the road that these silent giants have journeyed on....

settled down in london

After keeping on my feet till hardly able to stand, I left the Abbey and walked up Whitehall, up Regent Street, down Oxford Street toward St. Paul's. Then I broke down, and wanted to find a place to stop. But I must have looked too tired and wretched as I dragged myself along. I told a woman finally, who had rooms to let, that

11

I was ill and must stop. She shut the door in my face, after forcing me out of the hall. New cities, cities new to me, of course, have new ways. If one does not know their ways one frightens the honest folk, and can't get on with them at all.

A public-house here is not a tavern or an inn. I tried to get to stop at two or three of these reeking gin-mills. They stared at me, but went on jerking beer behind the counter, and did not answer. At one place I asked for water. All stopped and looked at me—women with great mugs of beer half way to their brutal big red mouths; a woman with a baby in one arm, wrapped tightly in a shawl along with herself, and a jug of beer in the other, came up and put her face in mine curiously; then the men all roared. And then one good-natured Briton paid for a pewter mug full of beer for me. But as I had never tasted beer, and could not bear the smell of it, I was obliged to refuse it. I was too tired to explain, and so backed out into the street again and hobbled on. I did not get the water. I now learn that one must not ask for water here. No one drinks water here. No public-house keeps it. Well, to one from Oregon, the land of pure water, where God pours it down from the snowy clouds out of the hollow of His hand—the high-born, beautiful, great white rain, this seems strange. . . .

All drinking-shops here—or rather "doggeries," as we call them in Oregon—are called "publics." And a man who keeps one of these places is called a publican. Now I see the sense and meaning of the Bible phrase, "publicans and sinners."

When I reached Aldersgate Street that first day, I saw the name "Little Britain" to my left, and knowing that Washington Irving had dwelt there, I turned aside to follow where he had been, in the leaves of the Sketch Book. But I could go but a little way. Seeing the sign of the Young Men's Christian Association close at hand, I climbed up the long crooked stairs, and soon was made quite at home and well refreshed by a cup of coffee and a roll at three half-pence; also a great deal of civility and first-class kindness for nothing at all. I had bed and breakfast at the same reasonable rate; and the next

12

morning, leaving my watch and money here, I went to Mile End by bus, to see where Mr. Bayard Taylor had lived when here.

I lost my way in one of the by-streets, and asked how to get out. People were kind and good-natured, but they spoke with such queer accent that I could not understand. At last a little girl of a dozen years, very bright and very beautiful, proposed to show me the way to the main street. She was a ray of sunlight after a whole month of storms. . . . She was making neckties, she said, and getting a sixpence a day; five pence she paid to a Mrs. Brady, who lived at 52 New Street, and this left her a penny a day to dress and enjoy life upon!

"And can I live with Mrs. Brady for five pence a day?"

"Maybe so. Mrs. Brady has a room; maybe you can get it. Let us go and see."

We came, we saw, and settled! I give Lizzie a shilling a day to run errands, for my leg is awful. She went to the station and got my bag, and she keeps my few things in perfect shape. I think she has some doubts about my sanity. She watches me closely, and I have seen her shake her head at this constant writing of mine. But she gets her shilling regularly, and oh! she is so happy—and so rich! Mrs. Brady is about six feet high, and very slim and bony. She has but one eye, and she hammers her husband, who drives a wagon for a brewery, most cruelly. He is short and stout as one of his beer-barrels, and a good hearted soul he is too. He loves his old telegraph-pole of a wife, however, and refuses to pound her back when she pounds him, although he assured me yesterday, in confidence, that he was certain he could lick her if he tried.

November 8. Mrs. Brady must be very old or a very great liar. Last night she assured me that her father used to shoe Dick Turpin's [8] horses. She went into detail to show how he would set the shoes on hind side before to look as if he was going away from London, when, in fact, he was coming this way. As if I did not know anything about horses, and how that all this was impossible. I expect she will next develop that she had some intimate relations with Jack Sheppard,[9] or, most likely, some of his descendants . . . .

13

November 20. Lizzie is a treasure, but she will lie like sixty. Yet she is honest. She goes out and brings me my coffee every morning. Mrs. Brady acts as a sort of mother, and is very careful of her in her coarse, hard way. I must find out who she is, and get her to school if I get on. She tells me her people live over on the "Surrey side," wherever that is. But I have already found that, like Mrs. Brady, she does not like to tell the truth about herself if she can get around it. How odd that poor people will lie so! Truth, the best and chiefest thing on this earth, is about the only luxury that costs nothing; and they ought to be persuaded to indulge in it oftener. New Street! It is the oldest street, I should say, in this part of London. This house we are in is cracked, and has been condemned. The reliable Mrs. Brady says it has only a few months more to stand; that the underground railroad or something runs under it. So I must get out, I guess.

cowley house, cowley street, westminster

February 14, '71. From Mile End to old Westminster! I am right back of the Abbey. From my garret window I can see the Virginia creepers, which they say were planted by Queen Elizabeth. The walls are high; but this garret of mine is still higher. They call it the poet Cowley's house. As if any poet ever had money enough to build so big a house, or ever had such bad taste as to build such an ugly one.

I hear all the bells of Westminster here, and of Parliament, big Ben, and all. And I hear perpetual pounding and hammering about the Abbey — all the time building or repairing. Not a good place to sleep or to rest, O immortal poets! Such an eternal pounding and pecking of stones and rasping of trowels and mortar no one ever heard. I had rather rest in Oregon.

hunting for a publisher

February 27, '71. I have nearly given up this journal to get out a book. I wanted to publish a great drama called "Oregonia," but finally wrote an easy-going little thing

14

which I called "Arizonian," and put the two together, and called the little book "Pacific Poems." It has been ready for the printer a long time. But here one cannot get a publisher at all unless one pays for it. And my money is out, my watch at my Uncle Rothschild's, and I have nothing to pay with. My brother is slow about sending me money. I am so afraid he is seriously ill. But the book must come out, if I even have to publish it without a publisher!

March 12. What a time I have had tramping about this city with my printed "Pacific Poems" under my arm. I think I have called upon or tried to call upon every publisher in this city. I had kept Murray, son of the great Murray, Byron's friend, to the last. I had said to myself: "This man, whatever the others may do, will stand up for the bridge that brought him over. If all others fail I will go to the great Murray . . . . All others failed, and I went, or rather I tried to go, but only tried, the first time or two. I at first marched stiffly and hastily up Albermarle Street, past the great publishing house. I then went home. I had slept well here in the gloomy old Cowley House at the head of Cowley Street, and next day boldy entered the great publishing house, and called for Mr. Murray. The clerk looked hard at me. Then, mentally settling the fact that I really had business with the great publisher, he said: "Mr. Murray is in. Will you send up your card?"

My heart beat like a pheasant in a forest. For the first time I was to meet a great publisher face to face. "No, no, thank you; not to-day. I will come to-morrow—to-morrow at precisely this time." And I hurried out of the house, crossed the street, took a long look at it, and went home the happiest man in London.

I came next day an hour before my time, but I did not enter. I watched the clock at the Piccadilly corner, and came in just as I had agreed. I think the clerk had forgotten that I had ever been there. For my part, I had remembered nothing else. The great Murray came down—a tall, lean man, bald, with one bad eye, and a habit of taking sight at you behind his long, thin forefinger, which he holds up, as he talks excitedly, and

15

shakes all the time, either in his face or your own; and I was afraid of him from the first, and wanted to get away.

He took me up-stairs, when I told him I had a book all about the great West of America; and there he showed me many pictures of Byron — Byron's mother, among the rest, a stout, red-faced woman, with awful fat arms and low, black curls about a low, narrow brow.

I ventured to say she looked good-natured.

"Aye, now, don't you know, she could shie a poker at your head, don't you know?" And the great Murray wagged his finger in her face, as he said this quite ignoring me, my presence, or my opinion. Then he spun about on his heel to where I stood in the background, and taking sight at me behind his long, lean finger, jerked out the words:"Now, young man, let us see what you have got."

I drew forth my first-born and laid it timidly in his hand. He held his head to one side, flipped the leaves, looked in, jerked his head back, looked in again, twisted his head like a giraffe, and then lifted his long finger:

"Aye, now, don't you know poetry won't do? Poetry won't do, don't you know?"

"But will you not read it, please?"

"No, no, no. No use, no use, don't you know?"

I reached my hand, took the despised sheets, and in a moment was in the street, wild, shaking my fist at that house now and then, as I stopped in my flight and turned to look back with a sort of nervous fear that he had followed me.

my first book

March 20, '71. Published! And without a publisher! No publisher's imprint is on my little book; a sort of illegitimate child, I have sent it forth to the press for a character. The type still stands, and if this goes well I can get a hearing and shall have a lot more of my rhymes set up, make a big book, and fire it right at the head of these stolid Britons.

March 26. Eureka! The *St. James Gazette* says "Arizonian" is by Browning!

16

Walter Thurnbury, Dickens's dear friend, and a better poet than I can hope to be, has hunted me up, and says big things of "Pacific Poems" in the London *Graphic*. Two splendid Irish enthusiasts from the Dublin University are at my side, stanch and earnest in their love. Now, the new book must come out! Yesterday I submitted a list of names for it—nine names—and one of my Irish friends settled on "Songs of the Sierras." And that it is agreed, shall be the name of the new baby. Good! Good! I see a vast new sun shouldering up in the east over the dense fog of this mighty town. . . . I have met————, the society poet of this city. I met him through Tom Hood. And he is a character—a sweet, gentle character, but so funny. Yet here I am on forbidden ground. The decent custom of Europe, which forbids mention of men in channels such as this, cuts out nearly all that is of interest in journals. But this one man stands out like a star in his quaint and kind originality. He gave me letters to almost everybody, and I in turn gave him the manuscript of "Arizonian," written mostly on old letters and bills, for it was written in one night and at a single sitting—and I got out of paper. But I think this generous-hearted gentleman half regretted giving me the letters; and I shall not present all of them. He has already taken me to see Dean Stanley, and it is more than hinted that if I get on I am to meet Her Majesty the Queen at the Dean's in the Abbey some evening at tea. . . .

Dear, dear; you should have seen him last night as he stood with his back to the fire, fluttering his long, black coat-tail with one hand, while his other hand swung his eyeglass in a dizzy circle before his eyes. And he tiptoed up and he fluttered and swung as he said, with a final high flourish of his long black coat, "Yes, yes; I—I—I like the Americans. I must say that I never found an American yet that was really vi-vi-vicious. I have found some that I thought were d-d-dreadful fools. But I never found one that I though was really vi-vi-vi-vicious!"

the end of the journal in london

April 19. The book came out; and in the whirl of

17

events that followed, the "notes" were neglected. It was a great day—a great year. Such a lot of favors and countless courtesies! For example, I had three letters in succession come to me signed "Dublin." I could not answer or even read all my letters, and so was not particularly disturbed or elated to find these letters from "Dublin," whoever "Dublin" might be. But one of my young Irish friends discovered these letters one day, and fairly caught his breath! "His Grace, the Archbishop of Dublin! He wants you to breakfast with him. Why, your fortune is made!" The doors of all social London are wide open. But somehow I am too full of concern about home to be very happy.

London, May 3. I find here among the Pre-Raphaelites one prevailing idea, one delight—the love of the beautiful. It is in the air. At least I find it wherever the atmosphere of the Rossettis penetrates, and that seems to be in every work of art—beautiful art. I am to dine with Dante Rossetti! All the set will be there. I shall hear what they say. I shall listen well, for this love of the beautiful is my old love—my old lesson. I have read it by the light of the stars, under the pines, or away down by the strange light on the sea, even on the peaks of the Pacific—everywhere. Strange that it should be so in the air here. And they all seem intoxicated with it, as with something new, the fragrance of a new flower that has only now blossomed after years of waiting: a sort of century plant—a quarter of a century plant, maybe. For, nearly twenty-five years ago, I am told, these Pre-Raphaelites began to teach this love of the beautiful.

back in america.

Easton, Pa., August 3. At "Dublin's" breakfast, I met Robert Browning, Dean Stanley, Lady Augusta, a lot more ladies, and a duke or two, and, after breakfast, "Dublin" read to me—with his five beautiful daughters grouped about—from Browning, Arnold, Rossetti, and others, till the day was far spent. When I went away he promised to send me his books. He did so. I put them in

18

my trunk, and did not open them till I got to America. Fancy my consternation as well as amazement and delight to find that this "Dublin" was Trench, the author of "Trench on Words." Ah! why didn't he sign his name Trench? for I knew that book almost by heart.

Yes, back to America With the cup raised to my lips I was not permitted to drink. I knew bad news would come. I felt a foreshadowing of it all the time. . . . My brother wrote that our family circle, for the first time, was broken. My only sister was dead. And in that same letter my brother wrote with but a feeble hand. He asked me to come and stand by his side, for the sands were crumbling under his feet. And so I left London, went down to the sea, and took the first boat, sailing from Southampton, where poor Artemus[10] died, and so stood by my dying soldier brother, who had never yet grown strong again after the war. And here, while praise and abuse of my new book went on, I saw and knew nothing of it all, but watched by my best friend, the gentlest man I ever knew, at this little town in Pennsylvania.

O boy at peace upon the Delaware!
O brother mine, that fell in battle front
Of life, so braver, nobler far than I,
The wanderer who vexed all gentleness,
Receive this song: I have but this to give.
I may not rear the rich man's ghostly stone;
But you, through all my follies loving still
And trusting me . . . nay, I shall not forget.

A failing hand in mine, and fading eyes
That look'd in mine as from another land,
You said:"Some gentler things; a song for Peace.
'Mid all your songs for men, one song for God."
And then the dark-brow'd mother, Death, bent down
Her face to yours, and you were borne to Him.

recollections of the rossetti dinner

There is no thing that hath not worth;
There is no evil anywhere;
There is no ill on all this earth,
If man seeks not to see it there.

September 28. I cannot forget that dinner with Dante
Gabriel Rossetti, just before leaving London, nor can I
hope to recall its shining and enduring glory. I am a
better, larger man, because of it. And how nearly our feet
are set on the same way. It was as if we were all crossing
the plains, and I for a day's journey and a night's
encampment fell in with and conversed with the captains
of the march.

But one may not give names and dates and details over
there as here. The home is entirely a castle. The secrets of
the board and fireside are sacred. And then these honest
toilers and worshippers of the beautiful are shy, so shy
and modest. But I like this decent English way of keeping
your name down and out of sight till the coffin-lid hides
your blushes—so modest these Pre-Raphaelites are that I
should be in disgrace forever if I dared set down any
living man's name.

But here are a few of the pearls picked up, as they were
tossed about the table at intervals and sandwiched in
between tales of love and lighter thoughts and things.

All London, or rather all the brain of London, the
literary brain, was there. And the brain of all the world, I
think, was in London. These giants of thought,
champions of the beautiful earth, passed the secrets of all
time and all lands before me like a mighty panorama. All
night so! We dined so late that we missed breakfast. If I
could remember and write down truly and exactly what
these men said, I would have the best and the greatest
book that ever was written. I have been trying a week in
vain, I have written down and scratched out and revised
till I have lost the soul of it, it seems to me; no
individuality to it; only like my own stuff. If I only had set
their words down on paper the next day instead of
attempting to remember their thoughts! Alas! the sheaves

have been tossed and beaten about over sea and land for days and days, till the golden grain is gone, and here is but the straw and chaff.

The master sat silent for the most part; there was a little man away down at the other end, conspicuously modest. There was a cynical fat man, and a lean philanthropist—all sorts and sizes, but all lovers of the beautiful of earth. Here is what one, a painter, a ruddy-faced and a rollicking gentleman, remarked merrily to me as he poured out a glass of red wine at the beginning of the dinner:

"When travelling in the mountains of Italy, I observed that the pretty peasant women made the wine by putting grapes in a great tub, and then, getting into this tub, barefooted, on top of the grapes, treading them out with their brown, bare feet. At first I did not like to drink this wine. I did not think it was clean. But I afterward watched these pretty brown women"—and here all leaned to listen, at the mention of pretty brown women—"I watched these pretty brown women at their work in the primitive winepress, and I noticed that they always washed their feet—after they got done treading out the wine."

All laughed at this, and the red-faced painter was so delighted that he poured out and swallowed another full glass. The master sighed as he sat at the head of the table rolling a bit of bread between thumb and finger, and said, sitting close to me: "I am an Italian who has neven seen Italy. *Belle Italia!*" . . .

By and by he quietly said that silence was the noblest attitude in all things; that the greatest poets refused to write, and that all great artists in all lines were above the folly of expression. A voice from far down the table echoed this sentiment by saying:"Heard melodies are sweet; but unheard melodies are sweeter." "Written poems are delicious; but unwritten poems are divine," cried the triumphant cynic. "What is poetry?" cries a neighbor. "All true, pure life is poetry," answers one. "But the inspiration of poetry?" "The art of poetry is in books. The inspiration of poetry in nature." To this all agreed.

Then the master very quietly spoke: "And yet do not despise the books of man. All religions, said the Chinese philosophers, are good. The only difference is, some religions are better than others, and the apparent merit of each depends largely upon a man's capacity for understanding it. This is true of poetry. All poetry is good. I never read a poem in my life that did not have some merit, and teach some sweet lesson. The fault in reading the poems of man, as well as reading the poetry of nature, lies largely at the door of the reader. Now, what do you call poetry?" and he turned his great Italian eyes tenderly to where I sat at his side.

"To me a poem must be a picture," I answered.

Proud I was when a great poet then said: "And it must be a picture—if a good poem—so simple that you can understand it at a glance, eh? And see it and remember it as you would see and remember a sunset, eh?" "Aye," answered the master, "I also demand that it shall be lofty in sentiment and sublime in expression. The only rule I have for measuring the merits of a written poem, is by the height of it. Why not be able to measure its altitude as you measure one of your sublime peaks of America?"

He looked at me as he spoke of America, and I was encouraged to answer:"Yes, I do not want to remember the words. But I do want it to remain with me—a picture—and become a part of my life. Take this one verse from Mr. Longfellow:

> "'And the night shall be filled with music,
>   And the cares that infest the day
> Shall fold their tents like the Arabs,
>   And as silently steal away.'"

"Good!" cried the fat cynic, who, I am sure, had never heard the couplet before, it was so sweet to him; "Good! There is a picture that will depart from no impressible clay. The silent night, the far sweet melody falling on the weary mind, the tawny picturesque Arabs stealing away in the darkness, the perfect peace, the stillness and the rest! It appeals to all the Ishmaelite in our natures, and all the time we see the tents gathered up and the silent children of the desert gliding away in the gloaming."

22

A transplanted American, away down at the other end by a little man among bottles, said: "The poem of Evangeline is a succession of pictures. I never read Evangeline but once." "It is a waste of time to look twice at a sunset," said Rossetti, *sotto voce*, and the end man went on: "But I believe I can see every picture in that poem as distinctly as if I had been the unhappy Arcadian; for here the author has called in all the elements that go to make up a perfect poem."

"When the great epic of this new, solid Saxon tongue comes to be written," said one who sat near and was dear to the master's heart, "it will embrace all that this embraces: new and unnamed lands; ships on the sea; the still deep waters hidden away in a deep and voiceless continent; the fresh and fragrant wilderness; the curling smoke of the camp-fire; action, movement, journeys; the presence — the inspiring presence of woman; the ennobling sentiment of love, devotion, and devotion to the death; faith, hope and charity, — and all in the open air."

"Yes," said the master thoughtfully, "no great poem has ever been or ever will be fitted in a parlor, or even fashioned from a city. There is not room for it there."

"Hear! hear! you might as well try to grow a California pine in the shell of a peanut," cried I. Some laughed, some applauded, all looked curiously at me. Of course, I did not say it that well, yet I did say it far better. I mean I did not use the words carefully, but I had the advantage of action and sympathy.

Then the master said, after a bit of reflection: "Homer's Ulysses, out of which have grown books enough to cover the earth, owes its immortality to all this, and its out-door exercise. Yet it is a bloody book — a bad book, in many respects — full of revenge, treachery, avarice and wrong. And old Ulysses himself seems to have been the most colossal liar on record. But for all this, the constant change of scene, the moving ships and the roar of waters, the rush of battle and the anger of the gods, the divine valor of the hero, and, above all, and over all, like a broad, white-bosomed moon through the broken clouds, the splendid life of that one woman; the shining faith, the constancy, the truth and purity of Penelope — all these

23

make a series of pictures that pass before us like a panorama, and we will not leave off reading till we have seen them all happy together again, and been assured that the faith and constancy of that woman has had its reward. And we love him, even if he does lie!"

How all at that board leaned and listened. Yet let me again and again humbly confess to you that I do him such injustice to try thus to quote from memory. After a while he said: "Take the picture of the old, blind, slobber-mouthed dog, that has been driven forth by the wooers to die. For twenty years he has not heard the voice of his master. The master now comes, in the guise of a beggar. The dog knows his voice, struggles to rise from the ground, staggers toward him, licks his hand, falls, and dies at his feet."

Such was the soul, heart, gentleness of this greatest man that I ever saw walking in the fields of art . . . .

STORIES OF CALIFORNIA, OREGON, AND IDAHO

THE BATTLE OF CASTLE CRAGS

At what date Mountain Joe located Lower Soda Spring Ranch, now known as Castle Crag Tavern, I am not certain. Col. Hastings was the first proprietor—1844. Hastings was the first man to open a permanent trail up the Sacramento River, and pass with a pack train and a band of Spanish cattle from California to Oregon by this route; though McCloud, a Hudson's Bay trapper, after whom the McCloud River was named, was here before him—1841.

Hastings was so charmed with Soda Springs, and so delighted with the waters, that he built a small fort or barracks on the north side of the little valley opposite the springs, and, Mountain Joe said, applied for a grant, which was to include Mount Shasta, then known as Chaste Butte. I have heard this old barracks spoken of as Fremont's Fort. Fremont was not here at all in the early days. He lost nearly half his force in a night battle with the Klamath and Modoc Indians east of here, on the other side of Mount Shasta, in 1846, and but for Kit Carson would have been annihilated.

In his reports to the Government, published in the first volume of his memoirs, which he sent me shortly before his death, there is no mention of this place, and all know that he was very elaborate and exact. The scene of his operations lay entirely to the east and southeast side of the great snow pyramid, and was full of battles. He concludes his report to Congress of the fatal night attack in these words: "I have since fought these Indian nations from one end of their possessions to the other."

He complains bitterly of the British traders for furnishing the Klamath Indians with steel points for arrows, saying, "Kit Carson pronounces them the most beautifully warlike arrows ever made."

True, Fremont and Kit Carson did their hard fighting not far away from what is now Castle Crag Tavern, and you could reach their battle-grounds easily any day now; but you must bear in mind that in those days there were no roads, and men had to keep compactly together and out of dangerous passes or perish. Besides, I have heard Mountain Joe, who served under Fremont through the Mexican War, and was also much with him on the plains, say that it was Hastings, not Fremont, who built the old pine log barracks in the little valley across from Soda Springs, at the base of the hill.

Whether it was the winter snows, the solitude or the savages that drove out the first proprietor of Soda Springs, no one can say; but it was doubtless the latter. Down on the south side of Castle Creek stands, or stood a few years ago, a white-oak tree with this bit of history cut in shapely letters on its widening bark, "Killed with Hastings, 1844." A mile or so further down the old pack-trail is, or was, another oak, telling, with its lone cross, where a whole party with its laden pack-train perished at the hands of the red men.

It is equitable to set Mountain Joe down as the first earnest and permanent proprietor of all this region round about here, for he tilled the soil, built some houses, and kept a sort of hotel, and guided people to the top of Mount Shasta, to say nothing of his ugly battles with the Indians for his home.

I first saw this strange man at his own campfire when a school-lad at home in Oregon, where he had camped near our place with his pack-train. He told us he was in the habit of going to Mexico for half-wild horses, driving them up to Oregon, and then packing them back to California, by which time they were tamed and ready for sale. He told my brother and me most wondrous tales about his Soda Springs, Mount Shasta, the Lost Cabin, and a secret mine of gold. He talked to us of Fremont till the night was far spent, and father, with the schoolteacher, had to come out after us. But what won my heart entirely was the ease with which he reached his left hand, and taking "Di Bella Galica" from my father, divided "Gaul in three parts" in the ashes of the campfire as he read and translated the mighty Roman by the roaring Oregon. He was a learned foreigner, of noble birth, it was said, certainly of noble nature. I could not forget Mountain Joe and his red men, and his Mexicans and mules and horses; and so, in the fall of 1854, I ran away from school and joined him at Soda Springs, now Castle Crag Tavern.

He was my ideal, my hero. You will find him in one character or another, for he had many characters, in nearly all my work. I cannot say certainly as to his hidden treasures, though he always seemed to have pots of gold to draw on in those days; but I can frankly confess that I have drawn on him and his marvelous stories, making them my own, of course, for all these years, — a veritable mine, indeed, to me.

I found him fortressed in the old Hastings barracks, before mentioned, though the place had been nearly destroyed by fire in his absence. We guided a few parties here and there, taking the first party to the top of the mountain that ever reached that point with ladies, I believe, and then returned to Yreka for the winter, going back to Lower Soda over the spring snowbanks with a tremendous rush of miners that Mountain Joe had worked up by his stories of the Lost Cabin and mysterious gold mines.

Thousands on thousands of men! The little valley of Soda Creek back of Castle Crag Tavern was a white sea of tents. Every bar on the Sacramento was the scene of excitement. The world was literally turned upside down. The rivers ran dark and sullen with sand and slime. The fishes turned on their sides and died. But the enraged miners found almost nothing. Mountain Joe disappeared. Men talked of hanging "Mountain Joe's boy." The game disappeared before the avalanche of angry and hungry men. The Indians had vanished at their first approach, and were starving in the mountains.

The tide went out as it came in—suddenly, savagely. Deeds of cruelty to Mexicans and half-tamed Indians who tried to be friendly and take fish in the muddied waters were not rare, as the disgusted miners retired from the country either up or down the river, leaving trails of dead animals, camp *debris* and cast-iron oaths behind. As they went Joe came, and the Indians came, furious! We treated them well, tried to make friends of them once more, but they would have none of it.

By the end of June, 1855, the last miner had left our section; and soon the last Indian left us to go on the warpath. Mountain Joe and I were now utterly alone, with not even a Mexican to take care of the pack-train and do the cooking. But we kept on. We had quite a garden, but it was needing water; so Joe and I took our guns each day, leaving the store or trading-post to care for itself, and went up the creek to work on a ditch.

Meantime, ugly stories were afloat; and ugly sullen Indians came by now and then—Modocs on their way across to the Trinity Indians, by the pass up little Castle Creek. They would not sit down, nor eat, nor talk. They shook their heads when we talked, and assumed to not know either the Shasta or Chinook dialect. The Trinity Indians were in open revolt beyond Castle Crags, and Captain Crook from Fort Jones, near Yreka, the famous General Crook, was in the field there. He drove them up Trinity River to Castle Crags, but had no decisive battle.

One hot morning, while we were at work on the ditch, Joe suddenly dropped his pick and caught up his gun. A horse went plunging up the valley past us with an arrow quivering in his shoulder; and smoke began to curl above the pines from the burning trading-post. We hastened down, but did not see a single Indian, nor did we see another horse or mule. All had silently disappeared in the half hour we had held our faces to the earth in the ditch.

Blotches of flour from torn sacks here and there made a white trail up over the red foothills on the brown, sweet-smelling pine-quills, and, without a word, Joe led cautiously on, I at his heels. The savages divided soon, the party with the horses going to the right, toward the Modoc country, the party with the stores, leaving a trail of flour, to the left, toward Castle Crags. This latter Joe followed, crossing the river at a ford, and going up the left bank of little Castle Creek. The canyon shuts in very close after a time. In a narrow pass the spilt flour was suspiciously plentiful, and Joe led across the spurs of the mountain toward what is now Sisson. It was called Strawberry Valley then, and was kept by two brothers by the name of Gordon. We were desperately worn and hungry, and they treated us well.

As said before, there were and had for some time been rumors of coming trouble. Joe and I turned back from Sisson to give the alarm and get help along the river. Portuguese Flat, which it took us two days to reach through the mountains, as we dared not take the trail, was the nearest post. Dog Creek, the ghost of which may be dimly seen in Delta now, was then a prosperous camp, and full of men. Judge Gibson, then the only magistrate in the country, had married an influential chief's daughter, and, by a wise and just course, had gained great authority, and had kept this tribe, the Shastas, from taking part in the great uprising which finally spread all over the Coast. The Indians had determined on a war of extermination. It ended in the utter extinction of many tribes in Oregon and some in California.

Courage was not lacking in those days, but coolness and experience in Indian warfare were wanting. Gibson had all these. So had Mountain Joe; but Joe had lost an eye by an arrow, and the other eye was not good. So he deferred to Gibson. Major Dribelbies, then sheriff, and Ike Hare, each took active part in trying to keep down the uprising of savages, and also in getting up an expedition against those in revolt, while Joe and I went back, and, with such friends as we could gather, waited at the base of Castle Crags for Gibson and his men.

Amazing as it may seem, he brought but about fifty, all told, Indians and white; and yet he was the only man who could have done as well. The miners were already more than disgusted with the country; and Indians rarely fight Indians in a general uprising like this. Mountain Joe could raise but ten men of his own.

Gibson led straight up Big Castle Creek, as if avoiding Catle Crags and the savages entrenched there. He kept himself almost entirely with his Indians, and hard things were said of him by the worn and discouraged white volunteers. They suspected that he was afraid to make the fight, and was trying to join the regulars under Crook in the Trinity Mountains.

At last, when our shoes and moccasins, as well as patience, were worn out, he turned sharply to the right, making the entire circuit of the Castle. We rested by a deep, dark lake which the Indians call the abode of their devil, Ku-ku-pa-rick, and they refused to approach its grassy, wooded shores.

Here Gibson, leaving his Indians for the first time, passed from man to man as they crouched under the trees. He told them that there was to be a fight, and a fight to a finish; that the hostiles were not an hour distant, and that no one could turn back and live, for if we did not kill them they would kill us. He told us that they had come down out of the Castle to kill deer, and so their arrows were not poisoned, and that we could swim.

He broke us up in parties, putting good and bad together, with Indians at the head of each. He told me to go with Joe, whom he sent to make a show of attack on the side next to Soda Springs. When near the hostiles Joe put me behind a tree on the edge of a small open place, and told me to stay there. Then he went on, creeping through the dense brush, to place the other men. I put some bullets into my mouth so as to have them handy, but I do not know what I did with them. I fired a few shots after Joe opened the fight, but hit only brush and rocks I reckon. And now pandemonium! Indians do not often yell in battle; but on both sides of us now the yelling was simply fiendish. They yelled from the top of the Castle to the bottom, it seemed to me.

We had taken the enemy entirely unawares, asleep, most of them, after the morning's chase, and our first shots brought down their dozing sentinels on the rocks. Finally there was some parleying, and the yelling, the whiz of arrows and the crack of rifles stopped. Then some Indian women came out and across the little gorge to Joe and his men, and I, thinking they had all surrendered, walked out into the open. Gibson called from the rocks ahead of me and to my right: "Boys, the fight now begins, and we've got to git them or they git us. Come on! Who will go in with me?" I answered that I would go, for it was all a picnic so far as I had yet seen, and I ran around to him. But there was blood on his hands and blood on his face, blood on all of his Indians, and most of the white men were bloody and hot.

The enemy used arrows entirely. They could tell where we were, but we knew where they were only when we felt their sting. Gibson led, or rather crept, hastily on, his head below the chaparral. No one dared speak. But when we got in position, right in the thick of it, our men opened. Then the arrows, then the yelling, as never before! The women and children prisoners down with Joe set up the death song, as if it was not already dismal enough. The savages bantered us and bullied us, saying we were all going to be killed before the sun went down; that we were already covered with blood, and that they had not lost a man. I had not yet fired a shot since joining Gibson, and, rising up to look for a target, he told an Indian to "pull the fool down by the hair," which he promptly did.

The battle had lasted for hours. The men were choking, and the sun was near going down. We must kill or be killed, and that soon. We must do our work before dark. The white man has little show with an Indian in battle at night.

Gibson gathered all who could or would go, and took still another place by storm. Then Lane fell, mortally hurt by an arrow in the eye. I saw Gibson's gun fall from his hand from the very deluge of arrows; then all was blank, and I knew no more of that battle.

The fight was over when I came to my senses, and it was dark. A young man by the name of Jameson was trying to drag me through the brush; and it has always seemed to me that a good many people walked over me and trod on me. I could hear, but could not see. An arrow had struck the left side of my face, knocked out two teeth, and had forced its point through at the back of my neck. I could hear, and I knew the voices of Gibson and Joe. They cut off the point of the arrow, and pulled it out of my face by the feather end. Then I could see. I suffered no pain, but was benumbed and cold as we lay under the pines. Joe held my head all night expecting that I would die. Gibson had the squaw prisoners carry his wounded down to the pack-trail on the banks of the Sacramento. They laid us down under some pines and pretty juniper trees on the west side of the swift, sweet river. And how tender and how kind these heroic men were! I was as a brother to them now, — their boy hero. Only the day before I had been merely "Mountain Joe's boy."

Gibson's loss in killed was considerable for so small a number engaged, — several Indians, though only one white man. Indians never give their loss, because of encouragement to the enemy; and Mountain Joe and Gibson, for a like reason, always kept their list of killed and wounded as low as possible, and spoke of the battle of Castle Crags as a trifling affair. Yet General Crook, in his letter to Captain Gibson, marveled that he ever got out with a single man.

I had promised to mark the grave of Ike Hare with a fragment of granite from Castle Crags, so that those who pass up and down the pleasant walks around Castle Crag Tavern might look with respect on the resting-place of a brave man and an honest legislator of two States. But my little tablet would seem so pitiful in the mighty presence of Mount Shasta. And it is Crook's monument, and Dribelbies' and Mountain Joe's. The finger of the Infinite traces and retraces in storm or sun the story and the glory of their unselfish valor here while the world endures. It is enough. There are those who care to read of savage incidents in these border battles, but such things should be left to obscurity, and I shall set down but two here. The first of these was the treatment of the dead Modoc chief, Docas Dalla, by the chief of our Indian allies. When the body was dragged before him, where he stood in the heat and rage of battle directing his men, he threw off his robe, and, nearly naked, leaped on the naked body (for it had already been stripped and scalped), and there danced and yelled as no fiend of the infernal regions could have danced and yelled. He called his fallen foe by name, and mocked and laughed, and leaped up and down on the dead till the body was slippery with blood which gushed from its wounds, and he could no longer keep his footing. Yet after all it was only the old Greek and Trojan rage, — the story of Homer in another form of expression; and Castle Crag was Troy above the clouds.

One more incident, as described to me by the son of this same furious chief on revisiting the battleground: This son of the chief was but a lad at the time, and so was left by his father with two Indians and a few white men, who were too lame and worn out to rush into the fight, in charge of the blankets, supplies and so forth. They were left in the little depression or dimple in the saddle of the mountain a few hundred feet above and to the south of Crook's or Castle Lake, and in the Modoc pass or trail.

When Gibson forced the fighting as night came on, the hostiles separated, some going down the gorge as if to reach their stores of arrows in the caves of Battle Rock (for their supply must have been well nigh spent by this time), while others stole off up the old Modoc trail that winds up above and around the lake, and in which the son of the chief and other Indians, as well as some whites, lay concealed. And here in this dimple on the great granite backbone that heaves above and about the lake, here above the clouds, amid drifts and banks and avalanches of everlasting snow, the wounded fugitives, with empty quivers, and leaving a red path as they crawled or crept on and up over the banks and drifts of snow, were met by their mortal enemies face to face.

If you will stand here facing Battle Rock to the south, and with your back to the lake, which lies only a few hundred feet to the rear, though far below, you will see how impossible it was for the wounded savages to escape down the rugged crags to the left, or up and over the crescent of snow to the right. They could not turn back; they could not turn to the left nor to the right; and so they kept on. Two of them got through and over the ridge and onto the steep slope of snow, and slid down almost to the lake, where they lay for a few moments concealed in the tall grass. But their relentless red enemies followed their crimson trail, found and tomahawked and scalped them where they lay, and threw their bodies into the lake.

Like all decisive battles with swift-footed savages, this

35

one covered a large field. The fighting, or at least the dead, and the blood on the rocks and snow, reached from the south shore of Crook's Lake to the north base of Battle Rock. The cross cut in the white spruce tree by the hand that writes this, and not far from the northernmost bank of the lake, may be set down as the outer edge of the battle-ground in that direction!

You will find small stone cairns set up here and there on heads of granite rocks that break above the snow. It is the custom for an Indian, when passing the scene of some great disaster, especially if alone, to place in a conspicuous position a stone by the way in memory of his dead. He never rears his monument at one time, as does the white man. He places but one stone, often a very small one, and leaves the rest to time and to other hands.

Mountain Joe, Jameson (now of Port Gable, Washington) and others have published accounts of this fight, so that I must say no more. But I will add Captain Gibson's story of it from his own trembling hand:

GIBSON'S SWITCH, Sacramento River, July 25, 1893.

In the year 1855, there being a great rush of miners here, the Sacramento River and other streams became muddy, and thereby obstructing the run of fish. The Indians became very indignant on account of it stopping the run of fish, which was their principal living. They commenced making preparations for hostilities by getting into strongholds, the principal one being the Castle Crags. Captain Crook came to the east fork of the Trinity about twelve miles from here with a company of regulars, and went out to Castle Crags with a view to break up the band, but failed to engage them.

I sent him a letter telling him that the way I was situated, so that, by raising some men, I could destroy them. His answer was to do so, which I did. We had a severe fight, — some men killed and a number wounded. We also found that the arrows were Modoc arrows, also amongst the dead two Modoc chiefs. I sent word of the battle to Captain Crook, and he gave it his hearty approval, and thanked me.

We had and have every reason to believe that the Indians intended to consolidate and make a general outbreak, as the Modocs did soon after do; and there is no doubt but they would have done it had it not been for that battle as aforesaid at Castle Crags. Captain Crook was afterward a famous Indian fighter, General Crook. I was enabled to reach these Indians, which Crook could not, through my father-in-law, Wielputus, the chief of the Shastas. We took twenty-nine of his men with us. R. P. Gibson

This, you note, is of recent date. It is, in fact, a dying

36

man's last utterance. Finding himself near the edge, he called on the survivors to meet him once more on the old battle-field on the thirty-eighth anniversary. The mayor of Oregon City answered, answered from the cemetery there for Mountain Joe. Major Dribelbies, the old sheriff of Shasta, is buried in Oregon. Ike Hare, his associate, lies buried within a stone's throw of Castle Crag Tavern. Years after the battle, when we met in the north, and when the new country was organized, the Shasta men there who had known us of old, in their loyalty and in memory of our battle days, made one of us a judge, one of us a sheriff, and one of us a senator.

Gibson and I went on the battle-ground alone at this last roll call, for only Jameson beside survives, and he is very ill. We marked with a Greek cross on a white spruce tree the spot where we had rested above and beyond the lake, and then followed the line of stone mounds or cairns to the south and above the lake, past the lesser lake in the saddle of the ridge that divides the waters of Castle Lake from those of Castle Creek. The battle was fought directly under the highest crag in the northwest corner of the great Castle, although on the other side of Little Castle Creek. This battle-rock is conspicuous above all other spires of rocks of Castle Crags for hours on the way around the spurs of Mount Shasta to the north.

Fires have swept the country here time and again since the Indians perished, and it is not nearly so well wooded as of old. Castle Lake, probably from this devastation, is not half so broad and deep as when we first found it hidden in its dense banks of verdure. We thought ourselves the first white men to look down into Castle Lake; but General Crook, with whom I served a year later as interpreter at old Fort Crook, east of Mount Shasta, told me that he had pursued the Modocs to that point, and had set up a small mound of white marble stones near there. So that it is Crook's Lake.

Wintun Nancy is about the only surviving member of her tribe. She has her home under the shadows of the crags not far from Castella. She is old and industrious, and is about the only authority now left on Indian habits and customs.

AN ELK HUNT IN THE SIERRAS

When it was discovered that gold did not exist in great paying quantities on the head-waters of the Sacramento River, the thousands there who had overrun the land and conquered the Indians melted away. But I had been kindly treated by the Indians, partly perhaps because I was the only white boy in the country at that time, and partly maybe because I had been badly wounded in a battle against them, and was still weak and helpless after a sort of peace was patched up; and so I went freely among them. The old chief's family was strangely kind to me. He had a very beautiful daughter. But I needed the services of a surgeon, and as the summer passed I set out for the settlements, a hundred miles down the Sacramento River to the south.

Early in the fall of 1855 I reached Shasta City, in my slow journey from Soda Springs, after the battle of Castle Rocks, and there had the services of an Italian doctor, who quite healed my wounds and set me once more on my feet. We became greatly attached, and this new friend of the Old World seemed resolved to be my friend indeed. He had a cabin and a mining claim near Shasta City, and was counted rich in gold dust. In this cabin he established me, set me to reading all sorts of books, and began to teach me Italian and Spanish. But my heart was not always in that cabin or with my books. Often and often I climbed the highest mountain looking away toward Mount Shasta to the north. Somebody was waiting up there, I knew. I knew that two dark eyes were peering through the dense wood toward the south; two soft brown hands parting the green foliage, looking out the way that I should come, certain that I would come at last. My friend and benefactor had furnished me with a fine horse and the finest saddle that the place could furnish; besides, he had armed me like a brigand, clad me in a rich, wild fashion, and filled my purse with gold dust. Great plans he had for our future—going to the Old World and resting all the years in Italy. I was not strong enough or yet quite content enough to work much, and so was often absent, riding, dreaming, planning how to get back to the north and not hurt the kind heart of my new friend. One night when I was absent thus he and his partner were both murdered in their cabin and robbed of their gold. When I returned the cabin was cold and empty.

When the spring came tripping by from the south over the chaparral hills of Shasta, leaving flowers in every footprint as he passed, I set my face for Mount Shasta, the lightest-hearted lad that ever mounted horse. A hard day's ride brought me to Portuguese Flat, the last new mining camp and the nearest town to my beloved Mount Shasta. Here I found my former partner in the Soda Springs property, Mountain Joe, and together we went up to Mount Shasta.

The Indian chief, Blackbeard, gave me a beautiful little valley, then known as Now-ow-wa, but now called by the euphonious (?) name of Squaw Valley, and I built a cabin there. As winter settled down and the snow fell deep and fast, however, the Indians all retreated down from out the spurs of Mount Shasta and took refuge on the banks of the McCloud River. I nailed up my cabin, and on snowshoes recrossed the fifteen miles of steep and stupendous mountains, and got down to winter at my old home, Soda Springs. But a new Yankee partner had got his grasp about the throat of things there, and instead of pitching him out into the snow, I determined to give it all up and set my face where I left my heart, once more, finally and forever, with the Indians. Loaded down with arms and ammunition, one clear, frosty morning in December I climbed up the spur of Mount Shasta, which lay between me and my little valley of snow, and left the last vestige of civilization behind me. It was steep, hard climbing. Sometimes I would sink into the snow to my waist. Sometimes the snow would slide down the mountain and bear me back, half buried, to the place I had started from half an hour before. A marvel that I kept on. But there was hatred behind, there was love before—elements that have built cities and founded empires. As the setting sun gilded the snowy pines with gold I stood on the lofty summit, looking down into my unpeopled world of snow.

An hour of glorious gliding, darting, shooting on my snowshoes, and I stood on the steep bluff that girt above and about my little valley. A great, strange light, like silver, enveloped the land. Across the valley, on the brow of the mountain beyond, the curved moon, new and white and bright, gleamed before me like a drawn cimeter to drive me back. Down in the valley under me busy little foxes moved and shuttle-cocked across the level sea of snow. But I heard no sound nor saw any other sign of life. The solitude, the desolation, the silence, was so vast, so actual, that I could feel it—hear it. A strange terror came upon me there. And oh, I wished—how devoutly I wished I never shall forget—that I had not ventured on this mad enterprise. But I had burned my ship. It had been as impossible for me to return, tired, hungry, heartsick as I then was, as it had been for me to lay hold of the bright cold horns of the moon before me. With a sigh I tightened my belt, took up my rifle, which I had leaned against a pine, and once more shot ahead. Breaking open my cabin door, I took off my snowshoes and crept down the steep wall of snow, and soon had a roaring fire from the sweet-smelling pine wood that lay heaped in cords against the walls. Seven days I rested there, as lone as the moon in the cold blue above. Queer days! Queer thoughts I had there then. Those days left their impression clearly, as strange creatures of another age had left their foot-prints in the plastic clay that has become now solid stone. When the mind is so void, queer thoughts get into one's head; and they come and establish themselves and stay. I had some books, and read them all through. Here I first began to write.

On the eighth day my door darkened, and I sprang up from my work, rifle in hand. Two Indians, brave, handsome young fellows, one my best and dearest friend in all the world, stood before me. And sad tales they told me that night as I feasted them around my great fireplace. The tribe was starving over on the McCloud! The gold-diggers had so muddied and soiled the waters the season before that the annual run of salmon had failed, the Indians had for the first time in centuries no stores of dried salmon, and they were starving to death by hundreds. And what was still more alarming, for it meant the ultimate destruction of all the Indians concerned, I was told that the natives of Pit River Valley had resolved to massacre all the settlers there. After a day's rest these two Indians, loaded with flour for the famishing tribe, set out to return. Again I was left alone, this time for nearly three weeks. The Indians returned with other young men to carry flour back to the famishing, while we who were strong and rested prepared for a grand hunt for a great band of elk which we knew wintered near the warm springs, high up on the wood slopes of Mount Shasta. Perhaps I might mention here that this cabin full of provisions had remained untouched all the time of my absence. I will say further that I believe the last Indian would have starved to death rather than have touched one crumb of bread without my permission. These Indians had never yet come in contact with any white man but myself. Such honesty I never knew as I found here. As for their valor and prowess, I can only point you to the Modoc battle-fields, where the whole United States Army was held at bay so long nearly twenty years after, and pass on.

After great preparation, we struck out steeply up the mountain, and for three days wallowed through the snow in the dense, dark woods, when we struck the great elk trail. A single trail it was, and looked as if a saw-log had been drawn repeatedly through the snow. The bottom and sides of this trail were as hard and smooth as ice. Perhaps a thousand elk had passed here. They had been breaking from one thicket of maple and other kinds of brush which they feed upon at such times, and we knew they could not have gone far through this snow, which reached above their backs. We hung up our snowshoes

41

now, and, looking to our arms, shot ahead full of delightful anticipation. At last, climbing a little hill, with clouds of steam rising from the warm springs of that region, we looked down into a little valley of thick undergrowth, and there calmly rested the vast herd of elk. I peered through the brush into the large, clear eyes of a great stag with a head of horns like a rocking-chair. He was chewing his cud, and was not at all disconcerted. It is possible we were not yet discovered. More likely their numbers and strength gave them uncommon courage, and they were not to be easily frightened. I remember my two Indians looked at each other in surprise at their tranquillity. We lay there some time on our breasts in the snow, looking at them. The Indians observed that only the cows were fat and fit to kill. Some of the stags had somehow shed their horns, it seemed. There were no calves. So the Indians were delighted to know that there was yet another herd. We fell back, and formed our plan of attack at leisure. It was unique and desperate. We did not want one or two elk, or ten; we wanted the whole herd. Human life depended upon our prowess. A tribe was starving, and we felt a responsibility in our work. It was finally decided to go around and approach by the little stream, so that the herd would not start down it — their only means of escape. It was planned to approach as closely as possible, then fire with our rifles at the fattest, then burst in upon them, pistol in hand, and so, breaking their ranks, scatter them in the snow, where the Indians could rush upon them and use the bows and arrows at their backs.

Slowly and cautiously we approached up the little warm, willow-lined rivulet, and then, firing our rifles, we rushed into the corral, pistols in hand. The poor, helpless herd was on its feet in a second, all breaking out over the wall of snow, breast high on all sides. Here they wallowed and floundered in the snow, shook their heads and called helplessly to each other. They could not get on at all. And long after the last shot and the last arrow were spent I leisurely walked around and looked into the eyes of some of these fat, sleek cows as they lay there, up to their briskets, helpless in the snow. Of course the Indians had no sentiment in this matter. They wanted only to kill and secure meat for the hungry, and half an hour after the attack on the corral of elk they were quartering the meat and hanging it up in trees secure from the wolves. In this way they hung more than a hundred elk, not taking time to skin or dress them in any way. The tallow was heaped about our camp-fire, to be defended against the wolves at night. And such a lot of wolves as came that night! And such a noise, as we sat there feasting about the fire and talking of the day's splendid work. The next morning, loaded with tallow, my two young friends set out on the long, tedious journey to the starving camp on the McCloud River. They were going to bring the whole tribe, or, at least, such of them as could make the trip, and the remainder of our winter was to be spent on Mount Shasta. I was once more left alone. But as our ammunition at hand was spent, I was in great fear and in real danger of being devoured by wolves. They drew a circle around that camp and laid siege to it like an army of well-drilled soldiers. They would sit down on their haunches not twenty steps away, and look at me in the most appetizing fashion. They would lick their chops, as if to say, "We'll get you yet; it's only a question of time." And I wish to put it on record that wolves, so far as I can testify, are better behaved than the books tell you they are. They snarled a little at each other as they sat there, over a dozen deep, around me, and even snapped now and then at each other's ears; but I saw not one sign of their eating or attempting to eat each other. By day they kept quiet, and only looked at me. But it was observed that each day they came and sat down a little bit closer. Night, of course, was made to ring with their howls both far and near, and I kept up a great fire.

At last—ah, relief of Lucknow!—my brave boys came back breathless into camp. And after them for days came stringing, struggling, creeping, a long black line of withered, starving, fellow-creatures. To see them eat! To see their hollow eyes fill and glow with gratitude! Ah, I have had some few summer days, some moments of glory, when the heart throbs full and the head tops heaven; but I have known no delight like this I knew there, and never

43

shall. Christmas came and went, and I knew not when, for I had now in my careless happiness and full delight lost all reckoning of time. But, alas, for my dream of lasting rest and peace with these wild people of Mount Shasta! As the birds of spring began to sing a bit, and the snow to soften about our lofty camp, a messenger came stealing tiptoe over from the Pit River Valley. And lo! the Indians had risen, starved and desperate, and murdered every white man there. And I knew that I should be accused of this.

THE PIT RIVER MASSACRE

The English spell the name of this river with an additional letter, as if after the name of an eminent stateman. But I think the above is right, as the name is certainly derived from the deep and dangerous pits that once made this whole vast region here — Pit River Valley — very dangerous ground for strangers. These pits, dug in trails and passes by squaws who carried the dirt away in baskets, were from ten to twenty feet deep, jug-shaped and covered with twigs and reeds and leaves. At the bottom lay sharpened elk and deer antlers, and sometimes sharpened flints and spears, pointed up to receive the victim. Even if one was not disembowelled on first falling into the pit, the ugly shape of it made it not only impossible for man but for even the most savage and supple wild beast to climb again to the light; and darkness and a lingering death were the inevitable end. These pits of course made the land a terror, and it was not until as late as 1856 that this most lovely valley in all California was fairly possessed by settlers. Once in possession, the white man of course soon found out the secret pits, and they gradually filled up as they fell into disuse. Yet in the Pit River war, which follwed the massacre, I know that one man and several horses were disembowelled by these dreaded pits; for after the Indians again got possession they attempted to restore this curious means of defence against invasion.

The buds were beginning to swell and birds to sing in the sunniest places about my Indian camp on the southern slope of Mount Shasta as the news came of the Pit River massacre. I was the only white person left in all the country round. And I knew at once that I would be

45

accused of having advised and directed the massacre. For all knew that I sympathized with the Indians. I cannot enter into detail to show how the Indians had been wronged; how they had been driven to this; how their men had been shot down for no other offence than that of having wives which the gold hunters and gamblers desired; how that, after one year of this bloody work, they found themselves starving and dying and desperate; how they rose up and swept away every white man into eternity, and fed their little ones on the thousand cattle. But I take the responsibility of saying that the Indians were entirely in the right. Politic it was not, it meant their final annihilation. But they died finally not without some revenge. Nor will I trouble myself with any detailed denial of complicity in the massacre. If I had had any part in it at all, I certainly should not hesitate to say so frankly. For after a quarter of a century, looking at the matter with maturer sense, and from all sides and in all lights, I do not see how the Indians could have done anything else and retain a bit of self-respect. And I do not see how the white men could have expected anything else in the end. The rape of the Sabines was as nothing compared to the ruthless way in which these men had seized upon the handsomest Indian women of the valley and murdered their fathers, brothers, husbands, who dared protest or even ventured to beg about their doors as the winter went past, while they housed in comfort in the snowy valley and fed their fattened herds in half a dozen great corrals made of ricks of hay. This hay was fired simultaneously in the half-dozen barracks scattered over the valley, generally by the hand of a captive squaw; and as the white men fled out over the snow they were shot down by the Indians. And this is the story of the massacre as it came to me at my camp early in the spring of 1857. Two white men only had escaped. They had not been pursued; but they were known to be at that time trying to make their way through the snow to Yreka, three days' travel away to the north-west. As I knew their line of retreat would be not far from my camp, I had bonfires set on a cliff of rocks overlooking the country, in hope that they might be guided to my camp and be fed. But they made their way to Yreka without finding me, and there gave the world the first news of the destruction of the settlement. Of course I did not know of their final escape, but thinking to give the first information of the deplorable event, and desiring to be quite certain of my report, I set out at once for Pit River Valley, sixty miles distant, and far below my camp on the spurs of Mount Shasta.

Blackbeard, the chief of the tribe I had cast my fortunes with, did not say much. He advised me, however, to keep away and out of the whole affair. But I had an image all the time of those two men struggling through the snow in death, and terror ringing in their ears, and I wanted to meet and help them. And then we had been shut up in camp so long, were so full of rest, that restraint was hard to bear. I resolved, however, to go no nearer than the great bald mountain overlooking the valley, from which I could see with my glass and be able to say positively whether or not the last hay fort had been burned. My two favorite young Indians were permitted to go with me. But the chief told me that he should lead his people still deeper into the fastness of Mount Shasta, try to keep his young men from taking sides in the coming war, and wait to see what might happen. I do not think the old chief doubted my devotion to him or questioned the sincerity of my cherished purpose of establishing my Indian republic, or sort of Indian territory, with Mount Shasta for its geographical centre and he for its head chief. But I think he gravely doubted my judgement, as well he might at that time, and so he did not give me his confidence at all. In fact, so far from trusting me, he deceived me. For I could see busy preparation for battle going on all about me. The morning I set out with my two young followers, with the promise to go no farther than the great bald mountain overlooking the valley, I missed several of our best warriors from the camp. They had, like Job's war-horse, "sniffed the battle from afar," and had gone like true gentlemen to champion their color and their kind, and to battle for the right, as it was given them to see the right, and—die!

After such a swift day's run over the snow as seems

almost incredible, we stood in the sunset on the summit of the bald mountain overlooking Pit River Valley. No smoke curled any more against the cold blue sky that rounded above the vast valley. The stillness of death hung over it. Where the great hay-ricks had been drawn around the herds of cattle in secure corrals, with the houses in the centre, only black spots were to be seen. The snow had disappeared from the valley, and instead of the weary and eternal white that had met my eyes everywhere for so many months, I witnessed the welcome green of spring spread like a carpet beneath me. I could almost smell the flowers. Far beyond and across the two great rivers that cleave the glorious valley I could see a boundless field of blue. This was the camas blossom. This flower sweeps over and purples all Oregon in the early spring. Civilization has laid hand on it, named it the hyacinth, and grows it in single stems from bulbs carefully kept in windows and warm places in the spring-time.

How I wanted to go down and gather a handful of flowers! What gift would be so precious for some one waiting for my return back in the camp of snow and woods? I know this sentence and this sentiment read absurdly, and my only excuse for it is its absolute truth. I knew quite well that away down there in each of those dark spots dead men lay unburied, and that the beautiful valley before me, another Eden from which man had been newly expelled, was soon to be the scene of bloody war; that my own life was in peril from both races and in all places now; and yet all this, all these perils were as nothing compared to my desire, my determination to have a handful of flowers.

As we stood there the stars came out—they came out shyly, timidly, as on tiptoe. I saw them come out while it was yet day, twinkle a bit and then go back, as if afraid. By and by they trooped out in armies, and all heaven was ablaze with the biggest stars this side of Syria. They stood out above the gleaming snow-peaks about us so near and clear that you might almost fancy you heard them clink against their fronts of icy helmets. The stillness was like a song, an immortal melody. We listened, we leaned and listened; the stars leaned out of heaven listening. No sound of life. No sound of strife now. Eden was as still on the day before the fashioning of man. Should I turn back as I promised? Perhaps if I had not promised so certainly I had not so madly resolved to see more. Yet I could have resisted all the temptation to slide down that steep mountain of snow and see and know all, had it not been for the flowers. Oh, the mad glory of going down there and grasping the summer in my hand and taking her back to winter in the wilderness!

Pretty soon Indian camp-fires began to gleam about the green and wooded girdle of the valley. Fate set one of these camp-fires almost at our feet. Seven miles distant and one mile perpendicular! We looked each other in the face as we stood there on the starlit summit of snow and saw the camp-fire gleam through the green pine tops at our feet. That light down there was death to any moth that might flutter too closely about it. But it was irresistible. And then the flowers!

I tightened my belt. The Indians did the same. Then with but a single word we bounded down that steep mountain of snow with a wild and savage delight that I defy any mortal to feel inside the pale of civilization. That night was our friend. With her protecting arms about us, her mantle shutting us in from the sight of unfriendly eyes, we would look in upon the Indian camp, we would hear their speeches about the council fire, see their wild, splendid gestures! Ah, we would have something to tell when we returned. And then the flowers!

I dare not say how soon we reached that camp, nor have I time to enter into detail. What narrow escapes of discovery as we lay on our bellies under the sweet-smelling pines and listened to the stirring eloquence of the nearly naked warriors. How the blood tingles at such times! What a spice peril like this gives to life!

Soon the feasting began. Then the tempting smell of roasted beef was too much for our hungry stomachs to bear longer, and as we could hear nothing more and could really do nothing at all, we passed on around the camp and went still on till we came to the level valley and

49

the warm naked earth with flowers at her breast and girdle.

I snatched these flowers from the hand of nature that reached them up from the south, and then, with a little detour where we saw a nude dead man — a mute, unchallenged witness of the massacre — we began, weak and hungry, to climb the mountain on our return.

Day dashed in upon us like troopers long before we knew it. We had forgotten the stars in the dial-plate above in the intense excitement before us, and before we had quite left the edge of the open valley we were in the full light.

Suddenly we met two old women. They were attached to an outpost which we had passed in the night, and were on their way to the camp we had been spying out. We took them with us, and ran up the hills as fast as our weak and worn legs would carry us. When quite in the woods and well up the mountain-side, the Indians wanted to kill the women, fearing that they might escape and give the alarm. I protested. The old women listened and understood all that was said. They of course took sides with me. The young Indians seemed very much set on this notion of theirs, and finally, odd as it may seem, we deliberately sat down there on the steep and snowy mountain-side and argued the thing quite a while, the old women taking a very active part in the argument, as you may well believe.

Finally one of them broke away and escaped. Then of course we set the other loose and dashed ahead with all the strength that desperation could lend us. A hundred swift fellows would be at our heels in an hour, we knew right well.

As we climbed one hill, with a great hollow behind us, we could see the trees alive on the ridge behind us and across the steep, deep hollow. But they were too far away to shoot at us yet. One more hill before us! As we finally struggled to the summit of the old bald mountain, where we had stood in the twilight of the day before, I being literally borne and dragged between my two companions, we saw the base of the hill black with savages. And I could scarcely stand! It was decided to descend the

50

mountain to the left and cross the McCloud. The Indians tore off some tough cedar bark from a dead trunk, tied me in this hollowed cradle, and so dragging me darted down the hill toward the McCloud River on a swift run. Once safely near the river we began to feel relieved. On the bluff above the river they took me out, stood me between them and rushed down the steep wooded hill to the water's edge. The enemy stopped on the steep bluffs above and overlooking the river. They were within pistol-shot behind the trees scattered about the brow of the hill. But they knew too much to follow us into the thicket. No, they preferred to pick us off at their leisure as we attempted to swim the river.

But swim that river, swift and strong and cold as death, I could not. So my two Indian friends rolled a light dry log into the water as we lay close under the bank hidden from the enemy above, who were waiting to see us plunge into the stream before us. I lay down on this log, one of the Indians taking charge of my arms. Then they came into the water with me. They pushed the log down the river under the steep bank, unseen by those on the hill, and both clung to it as the swift current bore us away. This was our escape! Before the Indians on the bluff suspected it, we were a mile away down the river and climbing the bank on the other side. They did not follow us further. The two brave fellows left me and went on for help when certain we were not followed. And so I finally reached camp, barely alive, and with no sign of summer or sweet flowers in my feeble hand.

A BEAR ON FIRE

It is now more than a quarter of a century since I saw the woods of Mount Shasta in flames, and beasts of all sorts, even serpents, crowded together; but I can never forget, never!

It looked as if we would have a cloudburst that fearful morning. We three were making our way by slow marches from Soda Springs across the south base of Mount Shasta to the Modoc lava beds — two English artists and myself. We had saddle horses, or, rather, two saddle horses and a mule, for our own use. Six Indians, with broad leather or elkskin straps across their foreheads, had been chartered to carry the kits and traps. They were men of means and leisure, these artists, and were making the trip for the fish, game, scenery and excitement and everything, in fact, that was in the adventure. I was merely their hired guide.

This second morning out, the Indians — poor slaves, perhaps, from the first, certainly not warriors with any spirit in them — began to sulk. They had risen early and kept hovering together and talking, or, rather, making signs in the gloomiest sort of fashion. We had hard work to get them to do anything at all, and even after breakfast was ready they packed up without tasting food.

The air was ugly, for that region — hot, heavy, and without light or life. It was what in some parts of South America they call "earthquake weather." Even the horses sulked as we mounted; but ther mule shot ahead through the brush at once, and this induced the ponies to follow.

The Englishmen thought the Indians and horses were only tired from the day before, but we soon found the whole force plowing ahead through the dense brush and over fallen timber on a double quick.

Then we heard low, heavy thunder in the heavens. Were they running away from a thunder-storm? The English artists, who had been doing India and had come to love the indolent patience and obedience of the black people, tried to call a halt. No use. I shouted to the Indians in their own tongue. "Tokau! Kisa! Kiu!" (Hasten! Quick! Quick!) was all the answer I could get from the red, hot face that was thrown for a moment back over the load and shoulder. So we shot forward. In fact, the horses now refused all regard for the bit, and made their own way through the brush with wondrous skill and speed.

We were flying from fire, not flood! Pitiful what a few years of neglect will do toward destroying a forest! When a lad I had galloped my horse in security and comfort all through this region. It was like a park then. Now it was a dense tangle of undergrowth and a mass of fallen timber. What a feast for flames! In one of the very old books on America in the British Museum — possibly the very oldest on the subject — the author tells of the park-like appearance of the American forests. He tells his English friends back at home that it is most comfortable to ride to the hounds, "since the Indian squats (squaws) do set fire to the brush and leaves every spring," etc.

But the "squats" had long since disappeared from the forests of Mount Shasta; and here we were tumbling over and tearing through ten years' or more of accumulation of logs, brush, leaves, weeds and grass that lay waiting for a sea of fire to roll over all like a mass of lava.

And now the wind blew past and over us. Bits of white ashes sifted down like snow. Surely the sea of fire was coming, coming right on after us! Still there was no sign, save this little sift of ashes, no sound; nothing at all except the trained sense of the Indians and the terror of the "cattle" (this is what the Englishmen called our horses) to give us warning.

In a short time we struck an arroyo, or canyon, that was nearly free from brush and led steeply down to the cool, deep waters of the McCloud River. Here we found the Indians had thrown their loads and themselves on the ground.

They got up in sulky silence, and, stripping our horses, turned them loose; and then, taking our saddles, they led us hastily up out of the narrow mouth of the arroyo under a little steep stone bluff.

They did not say a word or make any sign, and we were all too breathless and bewildered to either question or protest. The sky was black, and thunder made the woods tremble. We were hardly done wiping the blood and perspiration from our torn hands and faces where we sat when the mule jerked up his head, sniffed, snorted and then plunged headlong into the river and struck out for the deep forest on the farther bank, followed by the ponies.

The mule is the most traduced of all animals. A single mule has more sense than a whole stableful of horses. You can handle a mule easily if the barn is burning; he keeps his head; but a horse becomes insane. He will rush right into the fire, if allowed to, and you can only handle him, and that with difficulty if he sniffs the fire, by blindfolding him. Trust a mule in case of peril or a panic long before a horse. The brother of Solomon and willful son of David surely had some of the great temple-builder's wisdom and discernment, for we read that he rode a mule. True, he lost his head and got hung up by the hair, but that is nothing against the mule.

As we turned our eyes from seeing the animals safely over, right there by us and a little behind us, through the willows of the canyon and over the edge of the water, we saw peering and pointing toward the other side dozens of long black and brown outreaching noses. Elk!

They had come noiselessly, they stood motionless. They did not look back or aside, only straight ahead. We could almost have touched the nearest one. They were large and fat, almost as fat as cows; certainly larger than the ordinary Jersey. The peculiar thing about them was the way, the level way, in which they held their small, long heads—straight out; the huge horns of the males lying far back on their shoulders. And then for the first time I could make out what these horns are for—to part the brush with as they lead through the thicket, and thus save their coarse coats of hair, which is very rotten, and could be torn off in a little time if not thus protected. They are never used to fight with, never; the elk uses only his feet. If on the defense, however, the male elk will throw his nose close to the ground and receive the enemy on his horns.

Suddenly and all together, and perhaps they had only paused a second, they moved on into the water, led by a bull with a head of horns like a rocking-chair. And his rocking-chair rocked his head under water much of the time. The cold, swift water soon broke the line, only the leader making the bank directly before us, while the others drifted far down and out of sight.

Our artists, meantime, had dug up pencil and pad and begun work. But an Indian jerked the saddles, on which the Englishmen sat, aside, and the work was stopped. Everything was now packed up close under the steep little ledge of rocks. An avalanche of smaller wild animals, mostly deer, was upon us. Many of these had their tongues hanging from their half-opened mouths. They did not attempt to drink, as you would suppose, but slid into the water silently almost as soon as they came. Surely they must have seen us, but certainly they took no notice of us. And such order! No crushing or crowding, as you see cattle in corrals, aye, as you see people sometimes in the cars.

And now came a torrent of little creeping things: rabbits, rats, squirrels! None of these smaller creatures attempted to cross, but crept along in the willows and brush close to the water.

They loaded down the willows till they bent into the water, and the terrified little creatures floated away without the least bit of noise or confusion. And still the black skies were filled with the solemn boom of thunder. In fact, we had not yet heard any noise of any sort except thunder, not even our own voices. There was something more eloquent in the air now, something more terrible than man or beast, and all things were awed into silence — a profound silence.

And all this time countless creatures, little creatures

and big, were crowding the bank on our side or swimming across or floating down, down, down the swift, wood-hung waters. Suddenly the stolid leader of the Indians threw his two naked arms in the air and let them fall, limp and helpless at his side; then he pointed out into the stream, for there embers and living and dead beasts began to drift and sweep down the swift waters from above. The Indians now gathered up the packs and saddles and made a barricade above, for it was clear that many a living thing would now be borne down upon us.

The two Englishmen looked one another in the face long and thoughtfully, pulling their feet under them to keep from being trodden on. Then, after another avalanche of creatures of all sorts and sizes, a sort of Noah's ark this time, one of them said to the other:

"Beastly, you know!"

"Awful beastly, don't you know!"

As they were talking entirely to themselves and in their own language, I did not trouble myself to call their attention to an enormous yellow rattlesnake which had suddenly and noiselessly slid down, over the steep little bluff of rocks behind us, into our midst.

But now note this fact — every man there, red or white, saw or felt that huge and noiseless monster the very second she slid among us. For as I looked, even as I first looked, and then turned to see what the others would say or do, they were all looking at the glittering eyes set in that coffin-like head.

The Indians did not move back or seem nearly so much frightened as when they saw the drift of embers and dead beasts in the river before them. But the florid Englishmen turned white! They resolutely arose, thrust their hands in their pockets and stood leaning their backs hard against the steep bluff. Then another snake, long, black and beautiful, swept his supple neck down between them and thrust his red tongue forth as if a bit of the flames had already reached us.

Fortunately, this particular "wisest of all the beasts of the field," was not disposed to tarry. In another second he had swung to the ground and was making a thousand graceful curves in the swift water for the further bank.

The world, even the world of books, seems to know nothing at all about the wonderful snakes that live in the woods. The woods rattlesnake is as large as at least twenty ordinary rattlesnakes; and Indians say it is entirely harmless. The enormous black snake, I know, is entirely without venom. In all my life, spent mostly in the camp, I have seen only three of those monstrous yellow woods rattlesnakes; one in Indiana, one in Oregon and the other on this occasion here on the banks of the McCloud. Such bright eyes! It was hard to stop looking at them.

Meantime a good many bears had come and gone. The bear is a good swimmer, and takes to the water without fear. He is, in truth, quite a fisherman; so much of a fisherman, in fact, that in salmon season here his flesh is unfit for food. The pitiful part of it all was to see such little creatures as could not swim clinging all up and down and not daring to take to the water.

Unlike his domesticated brother, we saw several wild-cats take to the water promptly. The wild-cat, as you must know, has no tail to speak of. But the panther and California lion are well equipped in this respect and abhor the water.

I constantly kept an eye over my shoulder at the ledge or little bluff of rocks, expecting to see a whole row of lions and panthers sitting there, almost "cheek by jowl" with my English friends, at any moment. But strangely enough, we saw neither panther nor lion; nor did we see a single grizzly among all the bears that came that way.

We now noticed that one of the Indians had become fascinated or charmed by looking too intently at the enormous serpent in our midst. The snake's huge, coffin-shaped head, as big as your open palm, was slowly swaying from side to side. The Indian's head was doing the same, and their eyes were drawing closer and closer together. Whatever there may be in the Bible story of Eve and the serpent, whether a figure or a fact, who shall say? — but it is certainly, in some sense, true.

An Indian will not kill a rattlesnake. But to break the charm, in this case, they caught their companion by the shoulders and forced him back flat on the ground. And there he lay, crying like a child, the first and only Indian

57

I ever saw cry. And then suddenly boom! boom! boom! as if heaven burst. It began to rain in torrents.

And just then, as we began to breathe freely and feel safe, there came a crash and bump and bang above our heads, and high over our heads from off the ledge behind us! Over our heads like a rocket, in an instant and clear into the water, leaped a huge black bear, a ball of fire! his fat sides in flame. He sank out of sight but soon came up, spun around like a top, dived again, then again spun around. But he got across, I am glad to say. And this always pleases my little girl, Juanita. He sat there on the bank looking back at us quite a time. Finally he washed his face, like a cat, then quietly went away. The rattlesnake was the last to cross.

The beautiful yellow beast was not at all disconcerted, but with the serenest dignity lifted her yellow folds, coiled and uncoiled slowly, curved high in the air, arched her glittering neck of gold, widened her body till broad as your two hands, and so slid away over the water to the other side through the wild white rain. The cloudburst put out the fire instantly, showing that, though animals have superhuman foresight, they don't know everything before the time.

"Beastly! I didn't get a blawsted sketch, you know."

"Awful beastly! Neither did I, don't you know."

And that was all my English friends said. The Indians made their moaning and whimpering friend who had been overcome by the snake pull himself together and they swam across and gathered up the "cattle."

Some men say a bear cannot leap; but I say there are times when a bear can leap like a tiger. This was one of the times.

THE GREAT GRIZZLY BEAR

The Indians with whom I once lived in the Californian Sierras held the grizzly bear in great respect and veneration. Some writers have said that this was because they were afraid of this terrible king of beasts. But this is not true. The Indian, notwithstanding his almost useless bow and arrow in battles with this monster, was not controlled by fear. He venerated the grizzly bear as his paternal ancestor. And here I briefly set down the Modoc and Mount Shasta Indians' account of their own creation.

They, as in the Biblical account of the creation of all things, claim to have found the woods, wild beasts, birds and all things waiting for them, as did Adam and Eve.

The Indians say the Great Spirit made this mountain first of all. Can you not see how it is? they say. He first pushed down snow and ice from the skies through a hole which he made in the blue heavens by turning a stone round and round, till he made this great mountain; then he stepped out of the clouds onto the mountain-top, and descended and planted the trees all around by putting his finger on the ground. The sun melted the snow, and the water ran down and nurtured the trees and made the rivers. After that he made the fish for the rivers out of the small end of his staff. He made the birds by blowing some leaves, which he took up from the ground, among the trees. After that he made the beasts out of the remainder of his stick, but made the grizzly bear out of the big end, and made him master over all the others. He made the grizzly so strong that he feared him himself, and would have to go up on top of the mountain out of sight of the forest to sleep at night, lest the grizzly, who, as will be seen, was much more strong and cunning then than now,

59

should assail him in his sleep. Afterwards, the Great Spirit, wishing to remain on earth and make the sea and some more land, converted Mount Shasta, by a great deal of labor, into a wigwam, and built a fire in the center of it and made it a pleasant home. After that, his family came down, and they all have lived in the mountain ever since. They say that before the white man came they could see the fire ascending from the mountain by night and the smoke by day, every time they chose to look in that direction. They say that one late and severe springtime, many thousand snows ago, there was a great storm about the summit of Mount Shasta, and that the Great Spirit sent his youngest and fairest daughter, of whom he was very fond, up to the hole in the top, bidding her to speak to the storm that came up from the sea, and tell it to be more gentle or it would blow the mountain over. He bade her do this hastily, and not put her head out, lest the wind should catch her in the hair and blow her away. He told her she should only thrust out her long red arm and make a sign, and then speak to the storm without.

The child hastened to the top and did as she was bid, and was about to return, but having never yet seen the ocean, where the wind was born and made his home, when it was white with the storm, she stopped, turned and put her head out to look that way, when lo! the storm caught in her long red hair, and blew her out and away down and down the mountain side. Here she could not fix her feet in the hard, smooth ice and snow, and so slid on and on down to the dark belt of firs below the snow rim.

Now, the grizzly bears possessed all the wood and all the land down to the sea at that time, and were very numerous and very powerful. They were not exactly beasts then, although they were covered with hair, lived in caves and had sharp claws; but they walked on two feet, and talked, and used clubs to fight with, instead of their teeth and claws, as they do now.

At this time, there was a family of grizzlies living close up to the snows. The mother had lately brought forth, and the father was out in quest of food for the young, when, as he returned with his club on his shoulder and a young elk in his left hand, under his arm, he saw this little

60

child, red like fire, hid under a fir-bush, with her long hair trailing in the snows, and shivering with fright and cold. Not knowing what to make of her, he took her to the old mother, who was very learned in all things, and asked her what this fair and frail thing was that he had found shivering under a fir-bush in the snow. The old mother grizzly, who had things pretty much her own way, bade him leave the child with her, but never mention it to anyone, and she would share her breast with her, and bring her up with the other children, and maybe some great good would come of it.

The old mother reared her as she promised to do, and the old hairy father went out every day, with his club on his shoulder, to get food for his family, till they were all grown up and able to do for themselves.

"Now," said the old mother Grizzly to the old father Grizzly, as he stood his club by the door and sat down one day, "our oldest son is quite grown up and must have a wife. Now, who shall it be but the little red creature you found in the snow under the black fir-bush." So the old father Grizzly kissed her, said she was very wise, then took up his club on his shoulder and went out and killed some meat for the marriage feast.

They married and were very happy, and many children were born to them. But, being part of the Great Spirit and part of the grizzly bear, these children did not exactly resemble either of their parents, but partook somewhat of the nature and likeness of both. Thus was the red man created; for these children were the first Indians.

All the other grizzlies throughout the black forests, even down to the sea, were very proud and very kind, and met together, and, with their united strength, built for the lovely little red princess a wigwam close to that of her father, the Great Spirit. This is what is now called "Little Mount Shasta."

After many years, the old mother Grizzly felt that she soon must die, and, fearing that she had done wrong in detaining the child of the Great Spirit, she could not rest till she had seen him and restored to him his long-lost treasure and asked his forgiveness.

With this object in view, she gathered together all the

61

grizzlies at the new and magnificent lodge built for the princess and her children, and then sent her eldest grandson to the summit of Mount Shasta in a cloud, to speak to the Great Spirit and tell him where he could find his long-lost daughter.

When the Great Spirit heard this, he was so glad that he ran down the mountain side on the south so fast and strong that the snow was melted off in places, and the tokens of his steps remain to this day. The grizzlies went out to meet him by thousands; and as he approached they stood apart in two great lines, with their clubs under their arms, and so opened a lane through which he passed in great state to the lodge where his daughter sat with her children.

But when he saw the children, and learned how the grizzlies that he had created had betrayed him into the creation of a new race, he was very wroth, and frowned on the old mother Grizzly till she died on the spot. At this, the grizzlies all set up a dreadful howl; but he took his daughter on his shoulder and, turning to all the grizzlies, bade them hold their tongues, get down on their hands and knees and so remain till he returned. They did as they were bid, and he closed the door of the lodge after him, drove all the children out into the world, passed out and up the mountain and never returned to the timber any more.

So the grizzlies could not rise up any more, or make a noise, or use their clubs, but ever since have had to go on all-fours, much like other beasts, except when they have to fight for their lives; then the Great Spirit permits them to stand up and fight with their fists like men.

That is why the Indians about Mount Shasta will never kill or interfere in any way with a grizzly. Whenever one of their number is killed by one of these kings of the forest, he is burned on the spot, and all who pass that way for years cast a stone on the place till a great pile is thrown up. Fortunately, however, grizzlies are not now plentiful about the mountain.

In proof of the story that the grizzly once stood and walked erect and was much like a man, they show that he has scarcely any tail, and that his arms are a great deal shorter then his legs, and that they are more like a man than any other animal.

AS A HUMORIST

Not long ago, about the time a party of Americans were setting out for India to hunt the tiger, a young banker from New York came to California to hunt what he rightly considered the nobler beast.

He chartered a small steamer in San Francisco Bay and taking with him a party of friends, as well as a great-grandson of Daniel Boone, a famous hunter, for a guide, he sailed up the coast to the redwood wilderness of Humboldt. Here he camped on the bank of a small stream in a madrona thicket and began to hunt for his bear. He found his bear, an old female with young cubs. As Boone was naturally in advance when the beast was suddenly stumbled upon, he had to do the fighting, and this gave the banker from the States a chance to scramble up a small madrona. Of course he dropped his gun. They always do drop their guns, by some singularly sad combination of accidents, when they start up a tree with two rows of big teeth in the rear, and it is hardly fair to expect the young bear-hunter from New York to prove an exception. Poor Boone was severely maltreated by the savage old mother grizzly in defense of her young. There was a crashing of brush and a crushing of bones, and then all was still.

Suddenly the bear seemed to remember that there was a second party who had been in earnest search for a bear, and looking back down the trail and up in the boughs of a small tree, she saw a pair of boots. She left poor Boone senseless on the ground and went for those boots. Coming forward, she reared up under the tree and began to claw for the capitalist. He told me that she seemed to him, as she stood there, to be about fifty feet high. Then she laid hold of the tree.

Fortunately this madrona tree is of a hard and unyielding nature, and with all her strength she could neither break nor bend it. But she kept thrusting up her long nose and longer claws, laying hold first of his boots, which she pulled off, one after the other, with her teeth, then with her claws she took hold of one garment and then another till the man of money had hardly a shred, and his legs were streaming with blood. Fearing that he should faint from loss of blood, he lashed himself to the small trunk of the tree by his belt and then began to scream with all his might for his friends.

When the bear became weary of clawing up at the dangling legs she went back and began to turn poor Boone over to see if he showed any signs of life. Then she came back and again clawed a while at the screaming man up the madrona tree. It was great fun for the bear!

To cut a thrilling story short, the party in camp on the other side of the creek finally came in hail, when the old bear gathered up her babies and made safe exit up a gulch. Boone, now in Arizona, was so badly crushed and bitten that his life was long despaired of, but he finally got well. The bear, he informed me, showed no disposition to eat him while turning him over and tapping him with her foot and thrusting her nose into his bleeding face to see if he still breathed.

Story after story of this character could be told to prove that the grizzly at home is not entirely brutal and savage; but rather a good-natured lover of his family and fond of his sly joke.

THE GRIZZLY AS FREMONT
FOUND HIM

General Fremont found this powerful brute to be a gregarious and confiding creature, fond of his family and not given to disturbing those who did not disturb him. In his report to the government — 1847 — he tells of finding a large family of grizzly bears gathering acorns very much as the native Indians gathered them, and this not far from a small Mexican town. He says that riding at the head of his troops he saw, on reaching the brow of a little grassy hill set with oaks, a great commotion in the boughs of one of the largest trees, and, halting to cautiously reconnoiter, he noticed that there were grouped about the base of the tree and under its wide boughs, several huge grizzlies, employed in gathering and eating the acorns which the baby grizzlies threw down from the thick branches overhead. More than this, he reports that the baby bears, on seeing him, became frightened, and attempted to descend to the ground and run away, but the older bears, which had not yet discovered the explorers, beat the young ones and drove them back up the tree, and compelled them to go on with their work, as if they had been children.

In the early '50s, I myself, saw the grizzlies feeding together in numbers under the trees, far up the Sacramento Valley, as tranquilly as a flock of sheep. A serene, dignified and very decent old beast was the full-grown grizzly as Fremont and others found him here at home. This king of the continent, who is quietly abdicating his throne, has never been understood. The grizzly was not only every inch a king, but he had, in his undisputed dominion, a pretty fair sense of justice. He

66

was never a roaring lion. He was never a man-eater. He is indebted for his character for ferocity almost entirely to tradition, but, in some degree, to the female bear when seeking to protect her young. Of course, the grizzlies are good fighters, when forced to it; but as for lying in wait for anyone, like the lion, or creeping, cat-like, as the tiger does, into camp to carry off someone for supper, such a thing was never heard of in connection with the grizzly.

The grizzly went out as the American rifle came in. I do not think he retreated. He was a lover of home and family, and so fell where he was born. For he is still found here and there, all up and down the land, as the Indian is still found, but he is no longer the majestic and serene king of the world. His whole life has been disturbed, broken up; and his temper ruined. He is a cattle thief now, and even a sheep thief. In old age, he keeps close to his canyon by day, deep in the impenetrable chaparral, and at night shuffles down hill to some hog-pen, perfectly careless of dogs or shots, and, tearing out a whole side of the pen, feeds his fill on the inmates.

One of the interior counties kept a standing reward for the capture of an old grizzly of this character for several years. But he defied everything and he escaped everything but old age. Some hunters finally crept in to where the old king lay, nearly blind and dying of old age, and dispatched him with a volley from several Winchester rifles. It was found that he was almost toothless, his paws had been terribly mutilated by numerous steel traps, and it is said that his kingly old carcass had received nearly lead enough to sink a small ship. There were no means of ascertaining his exact weight, but it was claimed that skin, bone and bullets, as he was found, he would have weighed well nigh a ton.

BILL CROSS AND HIS PET BEAR

When my father settled down at the foot of the Oregon Sierras with his little family, long, long years ago, it was about forty miles from our place to the nearest civilized settlement.

People were very scarce in those days, and bears, as said before, were very plenty. We also had wolves, wild-cats, wild cattle, wild hogs, and a good many long-tailed and big-headed yellow Californian lions.

The wild cattle, brought there from Spanish Mexico, next to the bear, were most to be feared. They had long, sharp horns and keen, sharp hoofs. Nature had gradually helped them out in these weapons of defense. They had grown to be slim and trim in body, and were as supple and swift as deer. They were the deadly enemies of all wild beasts; because all wild beasts devoured their young.

When fat and saucy, in warm summer weather, these cattle would hover along the foothills in bands, hiding in the hollows, and would begin to bellow whenever they saw a bear or a wolf, or even a man or boy, if on foot, crossing the wide valley of grass and blue camas blossoms. Then there would be music! They would start up, with heads and tails in the air, and, broadening out, left and right, they would draw a long bent line, completely shutting off their victim from all approach to the foothills. If the unfortunate victim were a man or boy on foot, he generally made escape up one of the small ash trees that dotted the valley in groves here and there, and the cattle would then soon give up the chase. But if it were a wolf or any other wild beast that could not get up a tree, the case was different. Far away, on the other side of the valley, where dense woods lined the banks of the

68

winding Willamette river, the wild, bellowing herd would be answered. Out from the edge of the woods would stream, right and left, two long, corresponding, surging lines, bellowing and plunging forward now and then, their heads to the ground, their tails always in the air and their eyes aflame, as if they would set fire to the long gray grass. With the precision and discipline of a well-ordered army, they would close in upon the wild beast, too terrified now to either fight or fly, and, leaping upon him, one after another with their long, sharp hoofs, he would, in a little time, be crushed into an unrecognizable mass. Not a bone would be left unbroken. It is a mistake to suppose that they ever used their long, sharp horns in attack. These were used only in defense, the same as elk or deer, falling on the knees and receiving the enemy on their horns, much as the Old Guard received the French in the last terrible struggle at Waterloo.

Bill Cross was a "tender foot" at the time of which I write, and a sailor, at that. Now, the old pilgrims who had dared the plains in those days of '49, when cowards did not venture and the weak died on the way, had not the greatest respect for the courage or endurance of those who had reached Oregon by ship. But here was this man, a sailor by trade, settling down in the interior of Oregon, and, strangely enough, pretending to know more about everything in general and bears in particular than either my father or any of his boys!

He had taken up a piece of land down in the pretty Camas Valley where the grass grew long and strong and waved in the wind, mobile and beautiful as the mobile sea.

The good-natured and self-complacent old sailor liked to watch the waving grass. It reminded him of the sea, I reckon. He would sometimes sit on our little porch as the sun went down and tell us boys strange, wild sea stories. He had traveled far and seen much, as much as any man can see on water, and maybe was not a very big liar, for a sailor, after all. We liked his tales. He would not work, and so he paid his way with stories of the sea. The only thing about him that we did not like, outside of his

69

chronic idleness, was his exalted opinion of himself and his unconcealed contempt for everybody's opinion but his own.

"Bill," said my father one day, "those black Spanish cattle will get after that red sash and sailor jacket of yours some day when you go down in the valley to your claim, and they won't leave a grease spot. Better go horseback, or at least take a gun, when you go down next time."

"Pshaw! Squire. I wish I had as many dollars as I ain't afeard of all the black Spanish cattle in Oregon. Why, if they're so blasted dangerous, how did your missionaries ever manage to drive them up here from Mexico anyhow?"

Still, for all that, the very next time that he saw the old sailor setting out at his snail pace for his ranch below, slow and indolent as if on the deck of a ship, my father insisted that he should go on horseback, or at least take a gun.

"Pooh, pooh! I wouldn't be bothered with a horse or a gun. Say, I'm goin' to bring your boys a pet bear some day."

And so, cocking his little hat down over his right eye and thrusting his big hands into his deep pockets almost to the elbows, he slowly and lazily whistled himself down the gradual slope of the foothills, waist deep in the waving grass and delicious wild flowers, and soon was lost to sight in the great waving sea.

Two things may be here written down. He wouldn't ride a horse because he couldn't, and for the same reason he wouldn't use a gun. Again let it be written down, that the reason he was going away that warm autumn afternoon was that there was some work to do. These facts were clear to my kind and indulgent father; but of course we boys never thought of it, and laid our little shoulders to the hard work of helping father lift up the long, heavy poles that were to complete the corral around our pioneer log cabin, and we really hoped and half believed that he might bring home a little pet bear.

This stout log corral had become an absolute necessity. It was high and strong, and made of poles or small logs stood on end in a trench, after the fashion of a primitive fort or stout stockade. There was but one opening, and that was a very narrow one in front of the cabin door. Here it was proposed to put up a gate. We also had talked about port-holes in the corners of the corral, but neither gate nor port-holes were yet made. In fact, as said before, the serene and indolent man of the sea always slowly walked away down through the grass toward his untracked claim whenever there was anything said about port-holes, posts or gates.

Father and we three little boys had only got the last post set and solidly "tamped" in the ground as the sun was going down.

Suddenly we heard a yell; then a yelling, then a bellowing. The yelling was heard in the high grass in the Camas Valley below, and the bellowing of cattle came from the woody river banks far beyond.

Then up on the brown hills of the Oregon Sierras above us came the wild answer of the wild black cattle of the hills, and a moment later, right and left, the long black lines began to widen out; then down they came, like a whirlwind, toward the black and surging line in the grass below. We were now almost in the center of what would, in a little time, be a complete circle and cyclone of furious Spanish cattle.

And now, here is something curious to relate. Our own cows, poor, weary, immigrant cows of only a year before, tossed their tails in the air, pawed the ground, bellowed and fairly went wild in the splendid excitement and tumult. One touch of nature made the whole cow world kin!

Father clambered up on a "buck-horse" and looked out over the stockade; and then he shouted and shook his hat and laughed as I had never heard him laugh before. For there, breathless, coatless, hatless, came William Cross, Esq., two small wolves and a very small black bear! They were all making good time, anywhere, anyway, to escape the frantic cattle. Father used to say afterwards, when telling about this little incident, that "it was nip and tuck between the four, and hard to say which was ahead." The cattle had made quite a "round-up."

They all four straggled in at the narrow little gate at

71

about the same time, the great big, lazy sailor in a hurry, for the first time in his life.

But think of the coolness of the man, as he turned to us children with his first gasp of breath, and said, "Bo — bo — boys, I've bro — bro — brought you a little bear!"

The wolves were the little chicken thieves known as coyotes, quite harmless, as a rule, so far as man is concerned, but the cattle hated them and they were terrified nearly to death.

The cattle stopped a few rods from the stockade. We let the coyotes go, but we kept the little bear and named him Bill Cross. Yet he was never a bit cross, despite his name.

TREEING A BEAR

Away back in the "fifties" bears were as numerous on the banks of the Willamette River, in Oregon, as are hogs in the hickory woods of Kentucky in nut time, and that is saying that bears were mighty plenty in Oregon about forty years ago.

You see, after the missionaries established their great cattle ranches in Oregon and gathered the Indians from the wilderness and set them to work and fed them on beef and bread, the bears had it all their own way, till they literally overran the land. And this gave a great chance for sport to the sons of missionaries and the sons of new settlers "where rolls the Oregon."

And it was not perilous sport, either, for the grizzly was rarely encountered here. His home was further to the south. Neither was the large and clumsy cinnamon bear abundant on the banks of the beautiful Willamette in those dear old days, when you might ride from sun to sun, belly deep in wild flowers, and never see a house. But the small black bear, as indicated before, was on deck in great force, at all times and in nearly all places.

It was the custom in those days for boys to take this bear with the lasso, usually on horseback.

We would ride along close to the dense woods that grew by the river bank, and, getting between him and his base of retreat, would as soon as we sighted a bear feeding out in the open plain, swing our lassos and charge him with whoop and yell. His habit of rearing up and standing erect and looking about to see what was the matter made him an easy prey to the lasso. And then the fun of taking him home through the long, strong grass!

As a rule, he did not show fight when once in the toils

73

of the lasso; but in a few hours, making the best of the situation like a little philosopher, he would lead along like a dog.

There were, of course, exceptions to this exemplary conduct.

On one occasion particularly, Ed Parish, the son of a celebrated missionary, came near losing his life by counting too confidently on the docility of a bear which he had taken with a lasso and was leading home.

His bear suddenly stoppped, stood up and began to haul in the rope, hand over hand, just like a sailor. And as the other end of the rope was fastened tightly to the big Spanish pommel of the saddle, why of course the distance between the bear and the horse soon grew perilously short, and Ed Parish slid from his horse's back and took to the brush, leaving horse and bear to fight it out as best they could.

When he came back, with some boys to help him, the horse was dead and the bear was gone, having cut the rope with his teeth.

After having lost his horse in this way, poor little Ed Parish had to do his hunting on foot, and, as my people were immigrants and very poor, why we, that is my brother and I, were on foot also. This kept us three boys together a great deal, and many a peculiar adventure we had in those dear days "when all the world was young."

Ed Parish was nearly always the hero of our achievements, for he was a bold, enterprising fellow, who feared nothing at all. In fact, he finally lost his life from his very great love of adventure. But this is too sad to tell now, and we must be content with the story about how he treed a bear for the present.

We three boys had gone bear hunting up a wooded canyon near his father's ranch late one warm summer afternoon. Ed had a gun, but as I said before, my people were very poor, so neither brother nor I as yet had any other arms or implements than the inseparable lasso.

Ed, who was always the captain in such cases, chose the center of the dense, deep canyon for himself, and, putting my brother on the hillside to his right and myself on the hillside to his left, ordered a simultaneous "Forward march."

After a time we heard him shout. Then there was a long silence.

Then suddenly, high and wild, his voice rang out through the tree tops down in the deep canyon.

"Come down! Come quick! I've treed a bear! Come and help me catch him; come quick! Oh, Moses! come quick, and—and—and catch him!"

My brother came tearing down the steep hill on his side of the canyon as I descended from my side. We got down about the same time, but the trees in their dense foliage, together with the compact underbrush, concealed everything. We could see neither bear nor boy.

This Oregon is a damp country, warm and wet; nearly always moist and humid, and so the trees are covered with moss. Long, gray, sweeping moss swings from the broad, drooping boughs of fir and pine and cedar and nearly every bit of sunlight is shut out in these canyons from one year's end to the other. And it rains here nearly half of the year; and then these densely wooded canyons are as dark as caverns. I know of nothing so grandly gloomy as these dense Oregon woods in this long rainy season.

I laid my ear to the ground after I got a glimpse of my brother on the other side of the canyon, but could hear nothing at all but the beating of my heart.

Suddenly there was a wild yell away up in the dense boughs of a big mossy maple tree that leaned over toward my side of the canyon. I looked and looked with eagerness, but could see nothing whatever.

Then again came the yell from the top of the big leaning maple. Then there was a moment of silence; and then the cry: "Oh, Moses! Why don't you come, I say, and help me catch him?" By this time I could see the leaves rustling. And I could see the boy rustling, too.

And just behind him was a bear. He had treed the bear, sure enough!

My eyes gradually grew accustomed to the gloom and density, and I now saw the red mouth of the bear amid the green foliage high overhead. The bear had already pulled off one of Ed's boots and was about making a bootjack of his big red mouth for the other.

"Why don't you come on, I say, and help me catch him?"

He kicked at the bear, and at the same time hitched himself a little further along up the leaning trunk, and in doing so kicked his remaining boot into the bear's mouth.

"Oh, Moses, Moses! Why don't you come? I've got a bear, I tell you."

"Where is it, Ed?" shouted my brother on the other side.

But Ed did not tell him, for he had not yet got his foot from the bear's mouth, and was now too busy to do anything else but yell and cry "Oh, Moses!"

Then my brother and I shouted out to Ed at the same time. This gave him great courage. He said something like "Confound you!" to the bear, and getting his foot loose without losing the boot he kicked the bear right on the nose. This brought things to a standstill. Ed hitched along a little higher up, and as the leaning trunk of the tree was already bending under his own and the bear's weight, the infuriated brute did not seem disposed to go further. Besides, as he had been mortally wounded, he was probably growing too weak to do much now.

My brother got to the bottom of the canyon and brought Ed's gun to where I stood. But, as we had no powder or bullets, and as Ed could not get them to us, even if he would have been willing to risk our shooting at the bear, it was hard to decide what to do. It was already dusk and we could not stay there all night.

"Boys," shouted Ed, at last, as he steadied himself in the forks of a leaning and overhanging bough, "I'm going to come down on my laz rope. There, take that end of it, tie your laz ropes to it and scramble up the hill."

We obeyed him to the letter, and as we did so, he fastened his lasso firmly to the leaning bough and descended like a spider to where we had stood a moment before. We all scrambled up out of the canyon together and as quickly as possible.

When we went back next day to get our ropes we found the bear dead near the root of the old mossy maple. The skin was a splendid one, and Ed insisted that my brother and I should have it, and we gladly accepted it.

My brother, who was older and wiser than I, said that he made us take the skin so that we would not be disposed to tell how he had "Treed a bear." But I trust not, for he was a very generous-hearted fellow. Anyhow, we never told the story while he lived.

A RIDE THROUGH OREGON

They sat opposite me, leaning heavily from each other, and looking sour and sullen. By these signs I knew they were man and wife.

"My dear, I hope you are comfortable." The man who said this was short, dark, heavy, and black-bearded, with a niche in the side of his nose. He looked straight at my boots as he spoke, and did not deign to even lift his heavy brows in her direction. We had sat in the stage silent for hours. When he spoke, she merely dusted her threadbare silk with a large, gloved hand, half straightening, as if adjusting her spinal column, coughed slightly, and subsided into statuary.

"I hope you are comfortable, my dear," he spoke again, in the same tone and manner — a tone and manner as cold and false as an epitaph. No answer from the statuary, not even a ruffle; and, whatever may have been the hopes of the short, dark man, as to the comfort of the tall, fair woman, it was very evident that he was not altogether comfortable himself. After awhile, she impatiently drew off her glove, and I saw that there were no finger-nails on her right-hand. How fortunate, thought I, for her husband! Finally, I saw that she wanted to "blow him up;" and not having the slightest objection, I took the first opportunity to get a seat outside.

"Who are they?" said I, twisting my head inquiringly toward the pair in the coach.

The driver snapped his silk under the leaders' heels, and, from under the stiff hat that rested on his nose, answered:

"Webfeet."

A well-known, but not popular writer, as far as the will

78

of Oregon goes, once wrote, when on the tour of the Pacific, that California ended and Oregon began where white sugar failed, and a brown, Kanaka article was substituted. This is, perhaps, fiction; but it is safe to say that even the Chinese wall does not divide two more distinct peoples than did the Siskiyou Mountains, until within a very few years. And, even now, after the infusion of the new life, the original Chinook or Cayuse Orgeonian — a transplanted cross of Pike and Posey County — remains, as uninformed and unaffected as the Chinaman, after twenty years' contact with the Yankee.

These people held, by donation of the Government, all the best portions of the State; every head of a family holding 640 acres, as a rule. They put up log-cabins, fenced in a calf-pasture and a cabbage-patch, turned their stock loose on the native meadows, and, living on the increase of the same, reared as idle and worthless a generation as ever the sun went down upon. The old men trapped, traded in stock, ate, smoked, and slept, were very hospitable in their way, and, no doubt, were happy. The young men wore long hair, rode spotted Cayuse horses; in fact, lived mostly on horseback, and mixed largely with the Indians. True, there were many men of enterprise, education, and all that, in this coun- try — skilled mechanics, fine farmers, good lawyers, and sound men generally, who held and still hold high places in the State; but, as a rule, the old Oregonian was and is a distinct and singular individual. This is the manner of man I found on the Wallamet, twenty years ago.

Twenty years ago, the old Oregonian, with his cattle on a hundred hills, had neither butter nor milk on his table, save that which he bought of his neighbor, the newly arrived immigrant. He is the same to-day — improvident and uncivilized. The first one you encounter is on the Oregon side of the Siskiyou Mountains. He stands in the door as the stage passes, with his hands in his pockets, patches on his knees, and with three or four blue-haired children clinging to his legs and staring at the great stage-coach. He wears a broad, slouch hat, long hair, and looks as though he had just got out of bed, and is only half awake. But what will attract your attention at this

79

first house in Oregon, is the immense sign that stretches across the toll-road. We pass under it as under a great gate-way on entering an ancient city. The letters are so large and prominent that they suggest a popular text in Holy Writ:

"T-O-L-E R-O-A-D."

"What does that mean?" Charley Robinson, who held the lines at my elbow, again snapped the silk at his leaders, and, lifting his head to the Great Rogue River Valley before us, said, "That means that we are in Oregon."

Oregon is an anomaly. With a population made up largely of such people, she has always had some man in Congress who was, in his day, a power in the land.

Here you pass a house that stands in a little pen, mossy with age. In it a generation has been born and raised, yet it has never had a window. Get into the house, if you can for the dogs and deer-skins under your feet, and there you find an order of things not much above the simple *siwash*. The next house you pass, perhaps, will be a model of architecture and rural ornamentation, with people polite and progressive. And so it goes. Oregon is wonderfully mixed. The best and the worst of men; the sunniest and wettest of weather, and the first and most worthless live stock in the world. Rogue River Valley, which mainly lies away from that stream to the south, on Bear River, is a staid, sweet place. Rains are less frequent here than farther on, and many accept it as a compromise between the droughts of California and the great rains of the Wallamet, and are not to be allured away, although it is now the most isolated portion of the State. This is the only part of Oregon that has a military history. Away down the valley, not unlike a magnificent castle in appearance, stands Table Rock, the old fortress of Captain John, the famous Chief of the Rogue River Indians. Here were fought some sharp skirmishes; and here General Lane, "the Marion of Mexico," received wounds and won laurels in the capture of the battlement. The brave old Chief and his son, who burnt and butchered successfully up and down this lovely valley for many years, are even now, I believe, prisoners of war at

Alcatraz. He fought to the last, and even when on the ship on the way to his military prison, the reckless old savage, with his son, rose against the officers one night, and fought till they were both shot down. But bad Indians die hard; and, I believe, they both recovered, though the old warrior lost a leg in this his last battle. He is now nearly forgotten, and his wild and bloody history unwritten.

Umpqua Valley is really no valley at all, but a succession of little hills, with dimples and depressions along the crooked, rocky Umpqua and its tributaries. Roseburg is a little, peaceful-looking town of a thousand souls or more, but it is no baby, and has a bloody record. Here, on this rickety old bridge, a howling mob hung its victim; and there, in that dusty, dog-fennel street, last summer, the editors of the two rival little papers had a lively six-shooter war-dance, and, when the ball closed, three editors were found fearfully wounded. The cold, cold world may learn with a possible tinge of regret that not one of the three has, so far, died of his wounds. Back yonder, on the banks of the Umpqua, one night, at a little country ball, a misunderstanding arose, and, in a moment, more than half a dozen strong, fine young men lay dead or dying on the floor.

Roseburg is the home of the Lanes—once the political power of the State—and up this creek, that comes pitching down between the great oak-topped hills, three miles in an easterly direction, and four miles perpendicular, as his son had it, lives General Joseph Lane—soldier, Governor, Senator, and at last candidate for the Vice-Presidency. Very old is the General now, and quite retired, but the same as of old. His quiet, unpretending fireside and frugal meal are shared by the hermit the same now as when he was not poor, but strong and well-to-do, a great politician, and a power in the land.

Boats do not reach Roseburg; but down the rocky Umpqua, at Scotsburg, was once a lively trade, and many steamers decked the river—a river rich in scenery, deep and dark from rugged cliffs in many places, and then overshadowed by the spicy myrtle. Two hours' ride from this little town, through rolling hills of oak, and we touch

81

the advance of Holladay's railroad army. Farther on, we pass a town of tents. Thousands of men, it seems—and mostly Chinamen—are at work, like beavers, sweeping away the great fir-forest, that shuts out the sun the whole year through. Two hundred miles from Portland, and three hundred miles from the sea, by the line of travel, we take the cars. At present, the gap between the California and Oregon sections, that the traveler has to cross by coach, is three days' hard travel; but it is safe to say that, in another year, somewhere up about the Siskiyou Mountains, the last spike will be driven. The Oregon section has the heavier force employed, is displaying the greater energy, and will probably first reach the junction.

We are now in the matchless and magnificent Wallamet Valley, fifty miles wide, one hundred and fifty long, watered and timbered like a park, and capable of being turned into one unbroken field of grain. The cold, clear river, with its fringe of balsam and fir, winds directly through its length; while, on either hand, far back in the clouds loom mountains, black in their forests of eternal green. Here, if a man sows, he shall surely reap; while many even reap who do not sow at all, for a succession of volunteer crops is no new thing. Here the seasons never fail. That reliable individual, known as the oldest inhabitant—who, I believe, makes his home in Oregon—fails to remember a time, in the last half-century, when this prolific valley failed the husbandman. Here, on the river, at the head of navigation, is Eugene City—a dear, delightful town among the oaks, but slow and badly "hide-bound." It needs a good shaking up; wants some one who had the courage, and is enough its friend, to tell it of its sins. Here are six great church-buildings—never half filled—and hardly two decent school-houses. Here is a great army of boys growing up, proficient chiefly in the mysteries of "kissing-bees" and country-dances. No trades, no professions, no education to speak of; nothing but helpless dependence on the "old man." This is a representative interior town. After awhile, the keen, cultivated Yankee will come along, and push these young men off the track, out of their homes, back into the mountains; and they will murmur some, and wonder how it is, but should not complain.

Here, too, is an army of men at war with the railroad. Men, whose land has been trebled in value by the location of this line, are fighting every foot of its advance. While some men, awake to the interests of the country, have generously given a right of way to the enterprise, the sleepy Webfoot, who is afraid his cow will be run over and his grass burnt up by the railroad, is suing for damages, and displaying an energy in his opposition that he has never shown in any thing else. If Holladay had undertaken to pass through the lines of the Apache Indians, he could not have encountered more trouble than this class of people have given him in Oregon.

A little way from here is the junction of the East Side and West Side lines, both owned by Holladay. The "West Side," with its southern terminus now in the city of Portland, but which will be carried to Astoria, runs all the way up the west side of the Wallamet; while the "East Side" keeps up the other side, and makes its crossing just below the forks of the river, to the junction; thus giving this valley railroad advantages equal to any in the Union. In fact, it is safe to say, that, at the end of the present year, Oregon will have more railroad, according to its population, than any State you can name.

Be sure and stop at Albany, a little wide-spread town on the east bank of the Wallamet; for this is the heart of the valley. Ten and twenty miles, in many directions, you see only level fields, farm-houses, and orchards. It looks much like Illinois. Wheat is the great production. It never fails. No floods, no droughts, no grasshoppers, no weevil; nothing that can make the farmer feel less secure than if insured. Here are fields, I am told, that for twenty successive years have brought forth their unfailing crops of wheat, without fallow or manure. However, we must know that such is not the rule, and, at best, is only a shiftless Webfoot way of getting on that no farmer should boast of. Still, if there is a soil under the sun that can endure such culture, this is surely the soil. Go down to the river, and see where it has cut through its banks of fifteen feet of loam and black alluvial bottom, and you will agree

83

with me. Yet, with these broad and matchless fields, all kinds of produce are high and scarce. All along the stage-line through the southern part of the State, the drivers stated they could not get oats at even $1 a bushel, and had to feed wheat to a great extent. This is remarkable. Labor is needed here. I have taken pains to look into this, and write advisedly. Nearly twenty years' residence in the State, and then recent observations abroad, where I could make comparisons, enable me to speak truly, as well as plainly; and I think it safe to say that no country presents nearly so many attractions to settlers, either with or without means, as this. There are some who complain of the climate of this valley—and it is certainly not attractive during the winter months—yet it is almost exactly like that of England, with the advantage of temperature on the side of Oregon. That of England is a little more cold and crisp, while this is the more damp and humid of the two, but not excessively so.

Salem, the Capital (how one tires of these old Eastern names all through this country. Why not, like California, have given pretty local names to their towns? Name them after the old Indian chiefs, for instance, who wore feathers in their hair and quills in their noses, and were well up in the art of tomahawking missionaries), is in the woods, on the banks of the Wallamet. This is the Boston of Oregon: famous for its schools and churches. The city is magnificent in dimensions; is, in fact, rather thickly settled for the country: yet, far too thinly settled for a city.

A little while ago, this State was called a northern county of California. This infant commonwealth then stood holding on to her apron-strings, and looking up into her face helpless and pleading-like, much as a barefooted country girl to a big, proud sister just back from boarding-school. Then you may remember, also, that California frowned a little, looked wise, talked patronizingly, and put on many airs. Now, Oregon is her rival. She has a city, railroads, commerce, and wealth. Yet she is still tied up by the old "Webfoot" laws. A county can not incur a debt in excess of $5,000, while the State is almost powerless to contract under the present

Constitution. And what can be said of the laws of a State where a legislator receives the same pay as a Chinese day-laborer? However, a new order of things is here, and this will soon pass away. Oregon, in the last year, has become thoroughly wakened from her twenty years' sleep, and she now wears a new face. Holladay has galvanized her into a real life, vigor, and energy that will last.

I do not say that this man built the city, or brought all the wealth and ready money that now floods the State; but I do venture to say that he has done more in that direction than any other individual. His ships go directly from the Wallamet to Liverpool, laden with grain, and they return with iron. The English eat the bread of the Wallamet on the Thames, and Oregon is thus made rich with English money. It is safe to add that money is more plentiful in this new State to-day, and more readily earned, than in any other part of the world. Holladay having had a great part in bringing about this recent prosperity, he is, as a matter of course, an object of jealousy, and receives the guerilla attacks of the Webfoot portion of the Oregon press, already famous for personal onslaught. He is treated as a sort of fearful earthquake, that is finally to swallow up Oregon, Mount Hood, Webfeet, and all. The great sin with which he now stands charged is that of having designs on the Senate; while the truth is, he is not even a citizen of the State. His residence is in New York—that is, if a ten-thousand-acre farm, and a home that cost half a million, can be considered a residence. This Pacific Caesar may have ambition, but it does not lie in the direction of the United States Senate; certainly not from Orgon. This splendid specimen of American energy and Western manhood was born in Bourbon County, Kentucky, and is now just fifty. His family resides in Paris. With his twenty years of stormy life on the Pacific, he looks to be only in his prime. I pronounce him one of the finest types of manhood the West can boast of.[11]

Portland is split in two by the Wallamet, not far from its confluence with the Columbia, with the larger half on the right bank. This is now, by far, the most prosperous town on the Pacific. It is, in many senses of the word, a city, though its bankers and merchants—mostly home-made, or "valley-tan"—still show traces of their weak pin-feathers, and decline to take any great flights in speculation or outside commerce. This place has singular attractions of scenery. Here is a sort of blended savage and civilized life, that is encountered nowhere else. The town is in the heart of a forest deeper than the Black Woods of Germany. May be it is these woods that give it the sense of newness, and make it seem as if built but yesterday. On every hill-side the trees press hard on the town, and in some places over-shadow the new, white houses. The contrast of color is rich. In some places you see great stumps of trees in the streets: the town has grown so fast, they have not had time to decay.

To see the town and forest well, and enjoy the wild and the tame, the natural and the artificial, go back on the fir-topped hills, a mile west of the river, and turn your face toward sunrise and Mount Hood. Here, with your back jammed up against a wood, dense, deep, and magnificent, you have a mile of city at your feet; then a tide-river, with many ships, and not unlike the Thames; then a mile of open town; then firs, tall, taller, deep, dense, and black as Erebus, in the distance; then hills forest-crowned, of course; then grander hills, still black with forests, but nearly hidden in the clouds—rolling clouds, that sometimes sweep like seas, then drift, and lazily drag themselves through the tree-tops; higher up are peaks, crags, clouds; then Mount Hood, rugged, scarred, and broken, matchless and magnificent, and white forever, as the throne of God.

Grand and lovely, beyond the touch of words, are these steep and stupendous peaks of snow in Oregon, when flashing under a summer sun. Hood is only an elder brother of a well-raised family. Under skies that are less intensely blue, they might not thrill you so. Did they stand as in other lands, only as additions to and extensions of other mountains, gray, barren, and colorless, the effect then might not be so great. But here, the shining pyramids of white, starting sudden and solitary from the great black sea of firs, standing as supporting pillars to the dome of intense blue sky, startle, thrill, and delight you, though you have stood unmoved before the sublimest scenes on earth.

It is an hour or so from Portland to where the Wallamet joins hands with the cold Columbia, and a full day's sail down that river to the sea. The first thing you do on this day's journey is to take out your book for notes, and write: "What splendid forests! Green! black! boundless!" Then you turn a point in the river, pass a fleet of clouds laden with rain for the upper valley, and write again, "Forests! black! billowy and magnificent;" and so on, all day, till you almost tire of the splendor and majesty of the scene. The woods come down to the waters' edge, and all day long, neither on the Washington Territory nor Oregon side do you see open land enough to turn a four-in-hand. But the soil is very rich, I know from observations of old, and though the face of the ground is broken, it will admit of many farms. Now and then the Columbia is miles in width, is never narrow, and has many islands, thick with forests of ash, and balsam, and maple.

Many lumber-mills are along the river's edge, with little towns building about them; but they have hardly made a dimple in the exhaustless sea of timber. In places, ash and maple fringe the river, instead of fir; and now and then a black, basaltic cliff, not much unlike the Hudson Palisades, hangs above us. But, as a rule, the river is wide and shallow, with alluvial shores.

Astoria, the oldest town in the State, has a Historical Society and a historian. It is a sweet, but not a thriving place at all, and clings helplessly to a humid hillside that seems to want to slide into the great, bay-like river. Above the town are low, broken, timbered hills, fallen trees, burnt black, and tumbled up and down and across; then sturdy firs up the river away, stately black in their intense green, impenetrable! Clouds drag lazily through their tops, and are tangled there, like floss. Sometimes you see the hill-tops bursting through the clouds, with the fir-trees tossing in the wind; and that is very grand. Across the river, some miles away, you see some cliffs of rock, a little town or two, and a steamer stealing around the points that run out into the river. The scenery here is all natural—wild, but peaceful, splendid, and impressive! The stillness is marked and imposing. Even the petrels and the sea-doves that blow about in flocks are still as ghosts. When you look above the fleets of snow clouds that come silently in from the stormy ocean, to the cliffs and firs across the river—the ships, and clouds, and birds, and all things seeming to drift in dreamy silence—it is passing grand, and, after all, you are thankful for Oregon, the great cloud-land, her matchless forests, and her mountains.

Although this little town of the Astors is twelve miles from the open sea, the ocean steamers touch land no more in Oregon, after casting loose from this. When we had descended to dinner, and were seated at the table—which, by the way, was about the best I had seen since leaving San Francisco—I saw what I took to be the blonde companion of the black man I had encountered in the coach when crossing the Siskiyou Mountains. She seemed supremely happy now, and leaned warmly toward a brown-whiskered man, in a miner's overshirt, with six-shooter in his belt, who sat, all attention, at her side. He bombarded her with all manner of dishes and delicacies as they talked in a low, cooing tone, and seemed oblivious to every thing save each other, and their hash! Finally, she raised her right-hand in a sort of affectionate gesture to the brown-bearded man at her side, and then I knew that I was not mistaken.

"Just married," said the Captain, nudging at me with his left elbow, as he winked at the happy pair and looked straight down in his plate.

"Just married! just divorced, I should say!" chipped in a little, old maid, in black, who sat up close to the Captain's right; and she said it in a bitter, spiteful way, too, as if she was grating her teeth and trying to stick pins into somebody's back. A queer, little, sour, dried-up apple was she, whom I took to be a disappointed and dyspeptic strong-minded importation from the East yet one who knew every body and every thing, and had a ready opinion for all occasions and on all affairs. She wore glasses, and, I should say, had drank strong Bohea tea till she was as tough and tawny as a Chinaman.

"They are just divorced—that is, a portion of them—the female portion;" and here the wise and ancient virgin settled the glasses on her nose, and looked as though she believed in herself thoroughly, and felt that she had said a really clever thing.

Very true," answered the Captain, gently; "divorced yesterday, married to-day, and now off to California for their honey-moon. What adds to the interest of the situation, her former husband—a short, black man, in black— is with us, a passenger in the steerage."

"Is it possible!"

" 'Possible!' All things in that line are possible in Oregon."

"Softly, there," chimed in an old Oregonian, who was jammed up against the old maid's right elbow. "Oregon is not responsible for all the vagabonds that cross her lines. These people, I happen to know, are from down the coast—California—your own State, Captain. This lady down at the other end of the avenue, started first to Chicago to get divorced, but when that matrimonial Eden went up the flume, she switched off and came to Oregon, as the next best place in the Union for her purpose."

This man was a firm believer in his new State; and, as we arose from the table, sauntered out on deck, and stood in the clouds that came driving in from the sea, he declared that he would not allow it to be traduced, even in such a trifling matter as divorces!

Here we are at the bar. The ship begins to roll and lurch. One feels nervous and uneasy, and something worse than snakes seems creeping up and down the spine. Passengers look at each other, and turn pale. Now they turn and lean, and look into the sea for whales and pretty mermaids!

Mercy! The savage old Columbia pitches us out of her mouth into the sea, as if glad to get rid of us—as if we were a sort of Jonah. A stormy sea is this; and in this, the winter season, one of the roughest in the world. Here are indeed the seas the poet would adore;

> "The seas full of wonder and peril,
> Blown white round the capes of the North."

89

THE NEW AND THE OLD

The careless and happy Indians who used to ride in a long bright line up and down the land and past the door, laughing at our little fence as they leaped their ponies over the few rails that cost us so much labor, now ride only on the ghostly clouds. There is not one left now in all the land.

The vàst level valley before us at the base of this long and lonely ridge of flowers and fruit and sunny water, is a waving wheatfield now, and houses, little palaces of peace and refinement, even of splendor, dot the land as thick as stars in heaven at night under the strangely perfect skies. And the thousand square miles of hyacinth blossoms that made blue like the skies this whole valley for months together, have given place to a shield of gold on our mother's breast.

And so the world goes on. The wheels of progress have rolled over the graves of the pioneers and they are level as the fields of golden grain. And it is well. Even the marble tombs of the strange and strong new people—paving their way with gold where we came long ago with toil and peril—even these will be levelled, as our graves are levelled, and give place to others. The world is round. Let us look forward. Yet what is there that is lovely, what is there to love in this new tide of people pouring in upon us with their airs and their arrogance? They despise us and our primitive ways. Yet their hard examples give us little encouragement to abandon our ways and accept theirs. Nothing ever happened so disastrous to the Pacific States as the building of the Pacific Railroad. It became at once a sort of syphon, which let in a stream of weak and worthless people, and gave the brave young States here all the vanities and vices of the East, with none of the virtues.

The isolation of this country, the valor, the virtues, and the unusual wealth of the people—all these gave it an elevation and splendor that no land in so short a time ever attained. Even the literature began to have a flavor and individuality all its own. But all this became neutralized, passed away and perished, when men came and went so easily to and from the Pacific States.

Monopolists came and laid hands on the lands, the mines, the cattle—indeed, all things; and made, or attempted to make the men, gray and grizzled old pioneers, hewers of wood and drawers of water.

Even our seaport, which ought to be a great commercial city, is sick and gloomy and sad. She looks like a ship at half-mast.

It is not the immigration of Chinamen; for the Chinaman is not in any sense of the word an immigrant. He does not come to stay. I think it would be much better for the country if he did. If the Chinese could be treated so that their better class would come, and bring money, and remain, instead of having their laborers only come, to get hold of a few dollars and then return, I think the Chinese question would be satisfactorily solved.

But the real trouble began in gambling. When the railroad brought Wall Street it brought that which was tenfold more fatal than any plague ever brought us from an infected port. This spirit of speculation led honest men from their work in the mines to the cities. Nine men out of ten of them perished—either financially, morally, or physically. Perhaps the tenth man—the coarsest, the grossest, and hardest—held out, got hold of millions and became a king.

But Oregon proper is a sort of nut—a nut with a sweet, rich kernel, but also with a bitter bark and rind—through which you have to gnaw in order to reach the kernel. Portland is the bark or rind. The rich heart of the richest young State in the Union lies nearly two hundred miles in the interior. Portland sits at the seadoor—the very gates of the State—taking toll of him that comes and him that goes. The Orient has met the Occident here in this westmost town. One of these new men, speculator in town lots and land, who was clad in a slouch hat and

91

enormous mud-boots reaching almost to the knees, approached me in Portland. He carried an umbrella thrust up under his arm, while his two forefingers hooked and wrestled resolutely together as he stood before me. He chewed tobacco violently, and now and then fired a brown stream far up and down the new pine sidewalk.

"Can't you put this city into poetry? Yes, you kin. What's poetry good for, if it can't rize the price of land? Jist tell 'em we never had a shake. Yes, an' tell 'em that the old men never die; but jist git kivered with moss and blow away. An' tell 'em—yes, tell 'em that the timber grows so tall that it takes a man an' two small boys to see to the top of a tree! Yes, an' tell 'em that we have to tie poles to the cows' horns, to let the wrinkles run out on. Yes, biggest country, richest country an' dogondest healthiest country this side of Jericho! Yes, it is."

Drip! drip! drip! The rain put a stop to the man's speech. But he shall not be forgotten, for I had sketched him, from his prodigious boots to the very tobacco-stained beard, long before he gave his last testimony of the health and wealth of his chosen home.

Drip! drip! drip! Slop! slop! slop! incessantly and all the time, for an uninterrupted half a year, here in this mossy, mouldy town of Portland. Rain! rain! rain! until the trees grow out of the cracks and roofs of the houses, and until, tradition says, Mother Nature comes to the aid of the inhabitants and makes them web-footed, like the water-fowl. And even then, and in the face of all this, this man stood up before me with the water fairly bending his umbrella from the weight of the rain—the rain running down his nose, his head, his hair—and there he smilingly bowed and protested that it did not really rain much in Portland; but that down about the mouth of the Columbia, at Astoria, it did "sometimes rain a-right smart."

No, I don't like the new money-getting strangers. But the pioneers here were giants. Look at a piece of their gold! These men fashioned their own coin, as no other part of this Republic ever did. They coined it our of pure gold, without alloy, and stamped on its face the figure of a beaver and sheaves of wheat, the signs of industry and plenty. Its device of toil and harvest heralded it. Its intrinsic worth and solid value placed it above the need of any other indorsement. The wars, the trials, and the achievements of these men mark a shining bit of history. There is nothing nobler in the annals of the bravest and oldest States in the Union than the achievements of this State of Oregon.

IN THE LAND OF CLOUDS

Months ago we steamed away from San Francisco for the wild and savage coast of Oregon. A rugged coast is hers; a hard and almost impenetrable hull like a walnut's, and with a kernel quite as sweet then once you get inside. Almost a thousand miles, as the sea runs, and hardly a single inviting harbor.

But once inside her white sea-shores, and a world so grand, so sublime and vast, so entirely new, is. yours, that you stand uncovered, as if you had entered the home of the eternal.

The Indians tell you that giants dwelt here of old; that they fought for this peerless land, fought for it to the death, and that these seventeen peaks of everlasting snow are their monuments, which they built above their dead.

Well, whatever be the traditions, or the truths, it is something to have seen this land when it came first from the Creator's hand to the possession of man. It is sweet to have loved it first, last, and always. So sweet to have set the cross of song on its everlasting summits, and so sit down and wait for stronger and better and more cunning minstrels to come and subdue it to their dominion.

Yet on the proudest of these peaks I tried to set something more than a song. There are footprints on its topmost limits, for frowning and cloud-roofed Mount Hood is not at all unapproachable; but even woman, if she loves him well and has the daring and audacity of some English travellers I have known, may conquer him, put him under her pretty feet, easily.

Here lifts the land of clouds! The mantled forms,
Made white with everlasting snow, look down
Through mists of many cañons, and the storms

94

That stretch from Autumn-time until they drown
The yellow hem of Spring. The cedars frown,
Dark-brow'd through banner'd clouds that stretch and stream
Above the sea from snowy mountain crown.
The heavens roll, and all things drift or seem
To drift about and drive like some majestic dream.

Mount Hood stands about sixty miles from the great Pacific, as the crow flies, and about two hundred miles up the Columbia River, as it is navigated. The Columbia is tranquil here—mild and calm and dreamy as Lake Como. But twenty miles higher, past the awful over-hanging snow-peak that looks as if it might blow over on us as we sail up under it, the grand old river is all torrent and foam and fearful cataract.

Mount Hood stands utterly alone. And yet he is not at all alone. He is only a brother, a bigger and taller brother, of a well-raised family of seven snow-peaks.

At any season of the year, you can stand on almost any little eminence within two hundred miles of Mount Hood and count seven snow-cones, clad in eternal winter, piercing the clouds. There is no scene so sublime as this in all the world.

The mountains of Europe are only hills in comparison. Although some of them are quite as high as those of Oregon and Washington Territory, yet they lie far inland, and are so set on the top of other hills that they lose much of their majesty. Those of Oregon start up sudden and solitary, and almost out of the sea, as it were. So that while they are really not much higher than the mountain peaks of the Alps, they seem to be about twice as high. And being all in the form of pyramids or cones, they are much more imposing and beautiful than those of either Asia or Europe.

But that which adds most of all to the beauty and sublimity of the mountain scenery of Mount hood and his environs is the marvellous cloud effects that encompass him.

In the first place, you must understand that all this region here is one black mass of matchless and magnificent forests. From the water's edge up to the snowline, clamber and cling the dark green fir, pine, cedar, tamarack, yew, and juniper. Some of the pines are heavy with great cones as long as your arms; some of the yew trees are scarlet with berries; and now and then you see a burly juniper bending under a load of blue and bitter fruit. And nearly all of these trees are mantled in garments of moss. This moss trails and swings lazily in the wind, and sometimes droops to the length of a hundred feet.

In these dark forests is a dense undergrowth of vine-maple, hazel, mountain ash, marsh ash, willow, and brier bushes. Tangled in with all this is the rank and ever-present and imperishable fern. This fern, which is the terror of the Oregon farmer, stands so rank and so thick on the ground in the forests that oftentimes you cannot see two yards before you, and your feet can hardly touch the ground. Through this jungle, with the great dark trees towering hundreds of feet above, prowl the black bear, the panther, the catamount, and the California lion.

Up and through and over all this darkness of forests, drift and drag and lazily creep the most weird and wonderful clouds in all this world. They move in great caravans. They seem literally to be alive. They rise with the morning sun, like the countless millions of snow-white geese, swans and other water-fowl that frequent the rivers of Oregon, and slowly ascend the mountain sides, dragging themselves through and over the tops of the trees, heading straight for the sea, or hovering about the mountain peaks, as if they were mighty white-winged birds, weary of flight and wanting to rest.

They are white as snow, these clouds of Oregon, fleecy, and rarely, if ever, still. Constantly moving in contrast with the black forests, these clouds are strangely, sadly sympathetic to one who worships nature.

Of course, in the rainy season, which is nearly half the year here, these cloud effects are absent. At such times the whole land is one vast rain-cloud, dark and dreary and full of thunder.

To see a snow-peak in all its sublimity, you must see it above the clouds. It is not necessary that you should climb the peak to do this, but ascend some neighboring hill and have the white clouds creep up or down the valley, through and over the black forest, between you and the snowy summit that pricks the blue home of stars. What color! Movement! Miraculous life!

A few months ago, I met a party of English travellers who were completing the circuit of the world by way of San Franciso. I was on my way to Oregon, and this party decided to sail up the coast with me, and, if possible, ascend Mount Hood.

The party consisted of a gentleman and his wife, his wife's sister and brother, besides their little child of about ten years, a pale little cripple on crutches. The journey around the world had been undertaken, I was told, in the hope of restoring her to health. So she was humored in every way, and everything possible done to please and amuse her.

We sailed pleasantly up the barren, rocky, and mountainous coast of Oregon for two days, and all the way we watched the long, moving lines of white clouds clinging about the mountain-tops, creeping through the mountain passes in long, unbroken lines, or hovering wearily around some snowy summit and the English travellers counted it all strangely beautiful.

Not a sail in sight all these two days. And the waters of this, the vastest of all seas, as still and as blue as the blue skies above us.

Whales kept spouting about us, and dolphins tumbled like circus men before us; and the pale little cripple, sitting on the deck on a soft chair made of shreds of cane or rattan by the cunning Chinamen, seemed very happy. She had a lapdog, of which she was amazingly fond. The dog, however, did not seem so fond of her. He was a very active fellow, full of battle, and much preferred to lying in her lap the more active amusement of running and barking at the sailors and passengers.

After some ugly bumps on the sand-bars at the mouth of the Columbia — a place strewn with skeletons of ships — we at length entered this noble river. It is nearly ten miles wide here, and many little islands, covered with tangled woods from water's edge to summit, dot the wide and tranquil harbor.

97

Half a day's hard steaming up the river, with here and there a little village nestling in the dense wood on the water's edge at the base of the mighty mountains on either side, and we were in Portland and preparing to ascend Mount Hood.

It seems incredible, but, unlike all other mountains of importance, this one has no regular guides. We had to hunt up and make an entire outfit of our own.

Of course the little cripple was left behind, with her nurse and dog, when we five gayly mounted and rode down to the ferry to cross the Willamette River, which lies at the edge of the town and between our hotel and Mount Hood.

As the boat pushed off, the little cripple's frolicsome dog, Vixey, leaped in with us from the shore, barking and bounding with delight, to think he was to escape being nursed and was to make one of the expedition.

We rode hard through the tangled woods, with rank ferns and brier bushes and thimbleberry bushes in our faces. We climbed up almost entirely unfrequented roads and trails for half a day. Then we dismounted by a dark, treacherous, sandy stream, and lunched.

Mounting again, we pushed on in single file, following our guides as fast as we could up steep banks, over stones and fallen logs, and through almost impenetrable tangles of fern and vine-maple. There were three guides. One, an Indian, kept far ahead on foot, blazing out the way with a tomahawk, and shouting back and yelling to the other guides till he made the solemn forest ring.

The two ladies kept the saddle and clung to the horses' manes. But the men often dismounted and led their tired horses by the bridle.

The yelping dog had gone astray a dozen times, chasing squirrels, deer, and even birds, and I heartily hoped he would get lost entirely, for I abhor poodles. But the parents of the little cripple, when he would get lost, would not go on without him. So this kept us back, and we did not reach the snow-line till dusk.

The guides had shot a deer, two grouse, and many gray squirrels; so that, when we had made a roaring fire of pine knots, and had fed and rubbed down our worn-out horses, we sat there in the light of our great fire by the snow border, and feasted famously. For oh, we were hungry!

Then we laid down. But it seemed to me we were hardly well asleep before the guides were again boiling coffee, and shouting to each other about the work of the new day. How tired we all were still! All but that dog. That noisy and nervous little poodle seemed to be as eager as the guides to get us up and on before the sun had softened the snow.

In the gray dawn, after a solid breakfast, each with a pike in hand and hobnailed shoes on the feet, we were in line, lifting our faces in the sharp, frosty air for the summit of Mount Hood.

The snow was full of holes. Now and then a man would sink to his waist. We strangers would laugh at this. But observing that the guides took such mishaps seriously, we inquired the reason. When they told us that some of these holes were bottomless, we too became serious, and took hold of the long rope which they carried, and never let go. The ladies brought up the rear, and like all English ladies, endured the fatigue wonderfully. That tireless little dog yelped and bounded, now in the face of this man, now in the face of that, and seemed by his omnipresence to belong to flank and rear and van.

Before noon we came to a great crack, or chasm, or cleft, in the mountain side, for which the guides could give no reason. Their only idea of it appeared to be one of terror—their only object to escape it. They all fastened the rope to their belts, so that, in the event of one falling in, the others could draw him back.

As we advanced we found the mountain precipitous, but in nowise perilous, if we except these treacherous cracks and holes referred to.

Now and then we would lean on our pikes and turn our heads to the world below. Beautiful! Beautiful! Rivers of silver! Cities, like birds' nests, dotted down in the wilderness beneath. But no one spoke, when speaking could be avoided. The air was so rare that we were all the time out of breath.

As we neared the summit, one of the guides fell down,

bleeding at the mouth and senseless. One of the gentlemen forced some brandy down his throat, when he sat up and feebly beckoned us to go on.

Ten minutes more of hard climbing and five Saxons stuck their pikes in the summit and stood there together, five or six feet higher than the highest mountain in all that mountainous region of North America.

The wind blew hard, and the little woolly dog lay down and curled up in a knot, for fear lest he should be blown away. He did not bark or take any kind of delight now. The fact is, he did not like it at all, and was pretty badly frightened. It is safe to say that he was quietly making up his mind that, if he ever got back to that little basket with its blue ribbons about the borders and the cosey little bed inside, he would be willing to take a nap and stay with the lonesome little cripple.

The ladies' lips and noses were blue with the cold, and their hair was making all kinds of banners and streamers in the biting wind. The guides seemed dull and indifferent to everything. They lay flat down a few feet from the summit, pointing out the highest place to us, and took no interest in anything further, not even in their companion, whom we could see doubled up a little way below on the steep side of the snow.

We men moved on down over the summit on the Columbia side a few yards, in the hope of getting a glimpse of the great river which we knew rolled almost under us. But the whole world seemed to be one mass of clouds on that side; and we hastened back to the ladies, resolved to now descend as soon as possible.

One of the ladies, meantime, had gone down to the guides and got a little bundle, consisting of a British and an American flag and a Bible, with all our names in it. And the two were now trying to fasten the flags on a small iron pipe. But the wind, which had been getting stronger every minute since we came, was now so furious that we felt it was perilous to keep the ladies longer on the summit. So one of our party started with them down the mountain, while we other two took charge of the tokens of our achievement, which we hoped to leave here to tell others who might come that we had been before them.

Flutter! flutter! flap! snap! phew! Away went the British and American flags together. And before we knew it, the Bible, now lying on the snow, blew open and started after them. The gallant Briton at my side threw out his long leg and tried to stop its flight with his foot. But it bounded over the snow like a rabbit, and was gone.

The little dog lying there on his breast was terribly tempted to start after it, and if he had, there would have been no further interest in this sketch. But he seemed to have lots of sense, and lay perfectly still till the last one of us started down the mountain. Then he bounded up and on down after us, and his joy seemed without limit.

As we hastily descended, we found the stricken guide already on his feet and ready to lead in the descent. The ladies, too, had thawed out a little, and did not look so blue.

We began to talk too, now, and to congratulate ourselves and each other on the success of our enterprise. We were in splendid spirits, and the matchless scenery before us filled us with exultation.

The guides, however, cautioned us at every step as we neared the holes, and all held stoutly on to the rope. The little dog leaped ahead over the hard snow, and seemed the happiest of all the happy party. He advanced down the mountain backward. That is, he would somehow leap downward tail first, looking all the time in our faces—looking up with his red mouth open, and his white, fat little body bounding like a rubber ball over the snow. Suddenly the head guide cried out in terror. The dog had disappeared!

We all looked at each other, horror on every face. We were on the edge of a fissure, and the dog had been swallowed up. Whose turn next?

The wind did not blow here, for we had descended very fast and were now not far from the timber line. We had all driven our pikes hard in the snow and fallen on our knees, so as to be more certain of our hold, and were silent as the dead. Hark!

Away down, deep in the chasm, almost under us somewhere, we heard the poor dog calling for help. After a while, one of the guides answered him. The dog called back, so far off, so pitiful! This was repeated two or three times. But as the little brute seemed swallowed up forever, and as we lay there shivering on the brink and could not help him out, we obeyed the first law of nature, and cautiously crept back and around the ugly gorge. Soon we were once more safe with our horses, and drinking coffee by the warm fire as before.

We reached the city without further accident. But the very first thing the little cripple did on our return was to lift her pale face from her crutch and eagerly inquire for her dog. No one could answer. The parents exchanged glances. Then, for the first time, as the child still entreated for her pet, they seemed to realize their loss. They refused to tell her what had become of the dog at first. But, little by little, as we sat at dinner together, she got the whole truth. Then she left the table, crying as though her heart would break.

There was no dinner that day for any of us, after that. The father had strong, fresh horses brought, and on the next day we men, with the guides, set out to find the dog. At the last moment, as we mounted and were riding away, the child brought her little dog's basket, with its blue ribbons and its soft bed. For, as we assured her the dog would be found, she said he would be cold and sleepy, and so we should take his bed along.

On the first day we came to the chasm in the snow from the lower side. But had the dog not been drowned? Had he not perished from cold and hunger? We had brought a sort of trap—in fact, it was a large kind of rat-trap. This we baited with a piece of roasted meat on the trigger. Would not the hungry little fellow enter the trap, tug at the bait, throw the trap, get caught and so be drawn up to the light, if still alive? We all heartily hoped so, at least.

Some of the shelving snow broke off and fell as we let the rope slide down with the trap. Then for the first time we heard the little rascal yelp.

I never saw a man so delighted as was that usually stolid and impassive Englishman. He could not stand still, but, handing the rope to his friend, he danced about, and shouted, and whistled, and sang to the dog away down there in his dark, ugly pit.

The dog answered back feebly. It was evident he was not in the best of spirits. Perhaps he was too feeble to even enter the trap. Anyway, he did not enter it.

We drew it up time and again, but no sign of the dog. The stout Englishman prepared himself to descend the pit. But when the guide explained the danger of the whole side shelving off, and imperilling the lives of others, as well as his own life, that last hope was abandoned.

The father of the little cripple, after all was packed up and ready for the return, picked up the basket with the blue ribbons and soft bed inside. He looked at it sadly. Tears were in his eyes. Should he take the basket back? The sight of it would only make the cripple more sad. I could read all this in his face as he stood there irresolute, with the basket in his hand and tears streaming down his face. He at length made a motion as if to throw the little basket, with its blue ribbons and soft bed inside, down into the pit with the dog.

"No, we will let him have his little bed to die in in good shape. Here, fasten this on a rope, and lower it down there where you last heard him cry," said the kind-hearted Englishman.

In a few moments one of the guides had unloosened a rope which he had packed up to take back; and the basket was soon being lowered into the dark pit, over the hanging wall of snow.

The dog began to whimper, to whine, then to bark as he had not barked that day.

As the basket struck the bottom it was caught as a fish-line is caught, and the rope almost jerked out of the hands of the guide.

The father of the little cripple clutched the rope from the guide, and drew it up hand over hand as fast as possible. Then the bright black eyes of the dog danced and laughed at him as he jerked the basket up over the treacherous wall of snow.

The poor shivering little fellow would not leave the basket. There he lay all the time as we hurried on down

103

and mounted horse. The happy Englishman carried it back to the city on his arm. And he carried it carefully, too, as if it had been a basket of eggs and he on his way to market.

And the little girl?   Well, now, it was worth all the work and bother we had to see her happy face as she came hobbling out on her crutch to take the little basket, with its blue border and the dog curled up in his bed inside.

ROUGH TIMES IN IDAHO

Lewiston, built of boards and canvas, looking sickly and discouraged, stood shivering in the wind of October, 1862, and wincing under volleys of pebbles that struck the sounding houses with such force you might have thought an unseen army was bombarding them. The town looked as if it had started down from the mines in the mountains above, ragged and discouraged, and, getting to where it then was, had sat down in the forks of the river to wait for the ferry. The town looked as if it ought to go on — as if it wanted to go on — as if it really would go on, if the wind kept blowing and the unseen army kept up the cannonade.

On your left, as you looked down the course of the Columbia, sixty miles away, the Snake River came tumbling down, as if glad to get away from the clouds of dust, sage-brush, and savages. On the other hand, the Clear Water came on peacefully from the woody region of Pen d'Oreille, and joined company for the Columbia. Up this stream a little way stood the old *adobe* wintering quarters of Lewis and Clarke, exploring here under President Jefferson, in 1803; and a few rods beyond, the broad camp of the Nez Perces Indians flapped and fluttered in the wind — while the sombre lock of a Blackfoot warrior streamed from the war-chief's tent.

There is something insufferably mean in a windy day in the northern Territories. The whole country is a cloud of alkali dust — you are half-suffocated and wholly blinded — you shut your eyes and compress your lips — you hold your hat with both hands, lean resolutely against the wind, and bravely wait for it to go by. But it will not go by; it increases in fierceness; it fills your hair and your nostrils with dust; it discharges volleys of little pebbles, flints, and quartz into your face till it smarts and bleeds, and then, all suddenly, goes down with the setting sun.

The mines thus far found in the north had proved of but little account; and the miners were pouring back, as from a Waterloo. I had run a fierce opposition to Wells, Fargo & Co.; and as a result, sat alone in my office, trying to think, calmly as I could, how many of the best years of my life it would take to settle the costs, when the most ragged and wretched-looking individual I ever beheld, looking back stealthily over his shoulder, entered, and took a seat silently in the farther corner. He had a round, heavy head, covered with a shaggy coat of half-gray hair, which an Indian the least expert could have lifted without the trouble of removing his patched apology for a hat. He had an enormous chin, that looked like a deformity. He seemed to sit behind it and look at me there, as you would sit behind a redoubt in a rifle-pit, watching an enemy. His right hand stuck stubbornly to his pocket, while his left clutched the bowl of his pipe, which he smoked furiously, driving the smoke fiercely through his nostrils like steam through twin-valves. I think his tattered duck-pants were stuck in the tops of his boots; but after the lapse of nearly eight years I do not remember distinctly. However, this is not so important. He looked up at me, pulled busily at his pipe, then dropped his head and deliberately fired a double-barreled volley of smoke at his toes, that looked up wistfully from the gable-ends of his boots. Then he arose, glanced at the door, and being sure that we were alone, shuffled up to the counter, and drew out a purse from his right pocket, half the length of my arm.

"Ned," he cried, in a harsh, cracked voice, "don't you know me? That's gold; and I know where there's bushels of it."

"What! Baboon?—beg pardon, Mr. Bablaine."

"No! Baboon. Old Baboon; that's my name. Old Baboon."

As this man was the real finder of that vast gold-field, including Salmon, Warren's, Boise, Owyhee, and Blackfoot, it is but right that the world should have a brief of his history, as well as his photograph.

Peter Bablaine, Esq., of Easton, Northampton County, Pennsylvania, reached San Francisco in 1849, as refined and intelligent a gentleman as could be found. A few weeks of luckless ventures, however, left him unable to respond to his landlady's bill. She said, fiercely, "You are no gentleman." He answered, quietly,"neither are you, Mrs. Flanagan;" and quietly left the house. He felt that he had lost or left something behind him. He had. The "Esq." had been knocked from his name as easily as you would wish to kick a hat from the pavement on the first day of April.

Another week of wandering about the town in dirty linen, and his acquaintances treated the tail-end of his Christian name as Alcibiades did the celebrated dog of Athens. He was now simply "Pete Bablaine," and thus set out for the mines. A few months of hard usage, and he found the whole front of his name ripped off and lost. "Bablaine" was all that was left.

Ten years now passed. Ten terrible years, in which this brave and resolute man had dared more than Caesar, had endured more than Ney; and he found that the entire end of his father's name had been, somewhere in the Sierras, worn or torn away, and hid or covered up forever in the tailings. He was now nothing but "Bab." Here, while ground-sluicing one night on Big Humbug, and possibly wondering what other deduction could be made and not leave him nameless, he was caught in a cave, sluiced out, and carried head-first through the flume. This last venture wore him down to about the condition of an old quarter-coin, where neither date, name, nor nationality can be deciphered. His jaws were crushed, and limbs broken, till they lay in every direction, like the claws of a sea-crab. They took him to the County Hospital, and there they called him "Old Bab." It was a year before he got about; and then he came leaning on a staff, with a frightful face. He had lost all spirit. He sat moodily about the hospital, and sometimes said bitter things. One day he said of Grasshopper Jim, who was a great talker: "That man must necessarily lie. There is not truth enough in the United States to keep his tongue going forever as it does."

107

One evening a young candidate told him he was going to make a speech, and very patronizingly asked him to come out and hear him. Old Bab looked straight at the wall, as if counting the stripes on the paper, then said, half to himself, "The fact of Balaam's ass making a speech has had a more demoralizing influence than any other event told in the Holy Bible; for ever since that time, every lineal descendant seems determined to follow his example." His face was never relieved by a smile, and his chin stuck out fearfully; so that one day, when Snapping Andy, who was licensed by the miners to be the champion growler of the camp, called him "Old Baboon," it was as complete as a baptismal, and he was known by no other name.

"The sorrowful know the sorrowful." I was then a helpless, sensitive, white-headed boy, and so found refuge and relief in the irony of Old Baboon, and, like the Captain, "made a note of it."

Some women visited him one evening: fallen angels — women with the trail of the serpent all over them — women that at that day lived their fierce, swift lives through in a single lustrum, and at the same time did deeds of mercy that put their purer sisters to the blush. They gave him gifts and money, and, above all, words of encouragement and kindness. He received it all in silence; but I saw when they had gone that the coldness of his face had tempered down, like a wintry hill-side under a day of sun. He moodily filled the meerschaum they had brought him, and after driving a volume of smoke through his nose, looked quietly at me and said: "Society is wrong. These women are not bad women. For my part, I begin to find so much that is evil in that which the world calls good, and so much that is good in what the world calls evil, that I refuse to draw a distinction where God has not." Then he fired a double-barreled volley at society through his nose, and throwing out volume after volume of smoke as a sort of redoubt between himself and the world he hated, drifted silently into a tropical, golden land of dreams.

This was the man who now stood before me with gold enough to buy the town.

"There are nine of us," he went on, "all sworn not to tell. Of course, being sworn, they have all taken the first opportunity tell their friends and send word to their relatives. Therefore, I will tell you."

This is briefly his account of the discovery. When it reached California that gold had been found in the great watershed of the Columbia River, the miners waited for none of the details as to the wealth of the mines, their extent, or the dangers and hardships to be endured. They poured over the northern mountain-walls of Nevada-California, dreaming the dreams of '49. He fretted to go, and being able to travel, the fallen angels again fluttered around the friendless man, and his outfit was as complete as the camp could afford. Arrived north, the mines were found a failure, and a party of prospectors attempted to reach the Shoshone Falls through the densely timbered mountains from Elk City. He was of the number. They made but little headway; and the party of forty, in a few weeks, was reduced to nine. Then some became worn-out and discouraged, and being reduced to half-rations, attempted to return by what they thought a shorter route. After nine days' struggle through dense undergrowth and fallen timber, they came out on a little prairie. Here they found signs of game, and being entirely out of provisions, they determined to turn out their horses on the grass and replenish with their rifles. Baboon was left to keep camp. Their blankets were spread by a little spring stream that hugged a dense growth of tamarack at the edge of the prairie. The prairie lay near the centre of an immense, snow-crested, horseshoe opening to the south, of about thirty miles in diameter. A farm on the Ohio could have produced as many "indications" to the California gold-hunter as the site of this camp; but as the day wore on and the hunters delayed return, Baboon, to kill time, took up a pan, stepped to where a fallen tamarack had thrown up the earth, filled it, and carelessly washed it out. Marshall, in the mill-race, could not have been more astonished. Half a handful of gold—rough, rugged little specimens, about the size of wheat-grains, and of very poor quality, as it afterward proved, being worth but $11 an ounce—lay in the pan; and the great gold belt, which embraced Salmon, Warren's, Boise, Owyhee, and Blackfoot, was found!

I said, "Thank you, Mr. Bablaine." He looked at me with blended pride and pain, and deliberately firing a double-barreled volley of smoke at my breast, told me to make the best use of the discovery, gave me a written direction of the course and locality, and went out. In less than a week I was in the new mines with a cargo that sold for a dollar a pound before it was unpacked.

Baboon Gulch—a little indention of not more than a hundred yards in length, dipping down the prairie to a larger gulch—was perhaps the richest spot of earth ever found. The gold lay beneath a thin turf, or peat, on a soft, granite bed-rock in a stratum of but one or two inches thick, and but a few inches wide. This stratum was often half gold. The oath of Baboon could be had to-day, showing that the lightest day's yield was fourteen pounds of gold dust.

Having been the butt of the party, and having but little love or respect for his companions, when he left me at Lewiston he went into the streets, and, depending entirely on his interpretation of faces, made up a party of his own—all poor men—and before sunrise was on his return. I found, when I entered the camp, that he had one evening laid off a town and given it the name of the writer; but the next morning, those who had not procured lots, not feeling disposed to pay from $1,000 to $5,000 when there was so much vacant ground adjoining, went a few hundred yards farther on, and there, under the direction of Dr. Furber, formerly of Cincinnati, and author of "Twelve Months a Volunteer," laid off a town and named it Florence, after the Doctor's oldest daughter. The town laid out by my friend never received the distinction of a single building. However, with a singular tenacity, it retained its place in the maps of Idaho, and there, at least, is as large and flourishing as its rival.

On the 3rd day of December, in the fierce storm we read the prophecy of the fearful winter of 1862-3. Thousands of homeless and helpless men began to pour out over the horseshoe in the direction of Lewiston. Going into the camp late one night with the express, I met Baboon and his party quietly making their way over the mountain. Each man had a horse loaded with gold. Promising to return and overtake them, I rode on, and soon met a party headed by the notorious Dave English and Nelse Scott. They were all well-known robbers, and down on the books of the Expressmen as the worst of men; but, as there was not a shadow of civil law, and Vigilantes had not yet asserted themselves, these men moved about as freely as the best in camp. Only a few days before had occurred an incident which gave rise to a new and still popular name for their Order. Scott and English had reached a station on the road with their horses badly jaded. They were unknown to the keeper of the station, who had the Express-horses in charge; and not wishing to do violence to get a change of horses, resorted to strategy. They talked loudly to each other concerning the merits of their stock, and quietly telling the keeper they were connected with the Express, and were stocking the road — acting as road agents — ordered him to saddle the two best horses at the station, and take the best possible care of theirs till their return. He did so, and when the Express arrived that night for its relays, the innocent keeper told the rider the "road agents" had taken them.

English was a thick-set, powerful man, with black beard and commanding manner. One of his gray eyes appeared to be askew, but, other than that, he was a fine-looking man. He was usually good-natured; but when roused, was terrible. Scott was tall, slim, brown-haired, and had a face fine and delicate as a woman's. Both men, as well as their four followers — one of whom was once well known to circus-goers of California as Billy Peoples — were young.

Knowing their object, I asked them if Old Baboon had left camp.

They answered, "Yes, they thought he had." They then halted, and I rode by uninterruptedly. I reached camp, got a fresh horse, returned, and before dawn overtook Baboon and party. Six days, or rather nights, of travel, and we reached Lewiston, now a sea of canvas. The next

111

day English and party also entered. The river was full of ice, and the steamers tied up for the winter. Even the ferry was impassable for thirteen days. It was a little over one hundred miles to Walla Walla, and the snow deep and still falling. We had hardly got over the ferry, when English and party followed. But as we had been joined by three resolute men, and were now nine, while they were but six, we kept on. We knew their business, and when they passed us soon, chatting gayly, they must have felt, from our compact manner of travel and silence, that they were understood. I observed that they were splendidly mounted and armed.

It was twenty-four miles to Petalia — the nearest station. The days were short, and the snow deep. With the best of fortune, we did not expect to make it till night. At noon we left the Alpowa, and rode to a vast plateau without stone, stake, or sign to point the way to Petalia, twelve miles distant. Here the snow was deeper, more difficult; besides, a furious wind had set in, which blinded and discouraged our horses. It was intensely cold. We had not been an hour on this high plain before each man's face was a mass of ice, and our horses white with frost. The sun, which all day had been but dim, now faded in the storm like a star of morning drowned in a flood of dawn, and I began to experience grave fears. Still English and party kept on — not so cheerful, not so fast as before, it is true — but still kept on as if they felt secure. Once I saw them stop, consult, look back, and then in a little while silently move on. I managed to turn my head a moment in the terrible storm, and saw that our trail was obliterated the moment we passed. Return was impossible — even had it been possible to recross the river, if we had reached it. Again they halted, huddled together, looked back, then slowly struggled on again; sometimes Scott, sometimes English, and then Wabash or Peoples in the lead; but most of the time that iron-man English silently and stubbornly kept ahead. I did not speak to Baboon — it was almost impossible to be heard; besides, it was useless. I now knew we were in deadly peril — not from the robbers, but from the storm. Again they halted; again grouped together, gesticulating in the storm, shielding their faces against the sheets of ice. Our trail had closed like a grave behind us, and our horses were now floundering helplessly in the snow. Again English struggled on; but at three in the evening, standing up to the waist in the snow beside his prostrate horse, he shouted for us to approach. We did so, but could scarcely see each other's faces as we pushed against the storm. We held our heads bowed and necks bent, as you have seen cattle at such times in a barnyard.

"H————'s to pay, boys! I tell you, h————'s to pay; and if we don't keep our heads level, we'll go up the flume like a spring salmon. Which way do you think is the station?" said English.

Most of the party did not answer, but of those who did, scarcely two agreed. It was deplorable—pitiful. To add to our consternation, the three men who had joined us at Lewiston did not come up. We called, but no answer. We never saw them again. In the spring following some Indians brought in a notebook, which is now in my possession, with this writing: "Lost in the snow, December 19th, 1862, James A. Keel, of Macoupin County, Ill.; Wesley Dean, of St. Louis; Ed. Parker, of Boston." They, at the same time, brought in a pair of boots containing bones of human feet. The citizens went out and found the remains of three men, and also a large sum of money.

English stopped, studied a moment, and then, as if resolving to take all into his own hands, said:

"We must stick together; stick together, and follow me. I will shoot the first man who don't obey, and send him to hell a-fluking."

Again he led on. We struggled after in silence—benumbed, spiritless, helpless, half-dead. Baboon was moody, as of old. Scott seemed like a child. It grew dark soon, the most fearful darkness I ever saw. I heard English call and curse like a madman. "There is but one chance," he said; "come up here with your horses, and cut off your saddles." He got the horses together as close as possible, and shot them down—throwing away his pistols as he emptied them. Throwing the saddles on the heap, he had each man wrap his blankets around him, and all huddle together on the mass.

"No nodding, now! I'll shoot the first man who don't answer when I call him."

I truly believe he would have done so. Every man seemed to have given up all hope, save this fierce man of iron. He moved as if in his element. He made a track in the snow around us, and kept constantly moving and shouting. In less than an hour we saw the good effects of his action: the animal heat from the horses warmed us as it rose.

Suddenly English ceased to shout, and uttered an oath of surprise. The storm had lifted like a curtain; and away in the north, as it seemed to us, the full, stately moon moved on toward the east. That moon to us was as the sea to the Ten Thousand. We felt that we were saved. For as the moon seemed going in the wrong direction for the station, we, of course, were in the right, and could not be far from help.

When the morning sun came out, our leader bade us up and follow. It was almost impossible to rise. Baboon fell, rose, fell, and finally stood on his feet. But one of his party—a small German, named Ross—could not be roused. English returned, cursed, kicked, and rolled him over the frozen horses, and into the snow, but it was useless. I think he was already dead; at least he had not moved from the position we left him in, when found by the returning party.

At eleven in the morning English, who still resolutely led the party, gave a shout of joy, as he stood on the edge of a basaltic cliff, and looked down on the *parterre*. A long, straight pillar of white smoke rose from the station, like a column of marble supporting the blue dome above.

The dead man and money were brought in, and in a few days the trail broken.

Baboon stood leaning on the neck of his horse, and firing double-barreled discharges of smoke across it, as over a barricade. Then he called Scott and English to him; told them he knew their calling; still he liked them; that the believed a brave robber better than many legal thieves who infested the land; and offered them, or any of

114

their band, a fair start in life, to leave the mountains and go with him. Scott laughed gayly—it flattered his vanity; But English was for a moment very thoughtful. Then he threw it off, and spoke a moment to Wabash—a quiet, half-melancholy young man, born in the papaw woods of Indiana.

"Wabash has been wanting to quit and go home," said English to Baboon. "Take him—he is braver than Lucifer—and not a hair of your head shall be hurt."

Wabash then solemnly shook hands with his old companions, and rode on. English and his remaining comrades returned to Lewiston.

We reached Walla Walla safely, and I never saw Wabash or Baboon again. But a letter lies before me as I write, postmarked Easton, Northampton County, Pennsylvania, and signed "Old Baboon." This letter contains the following paragraph:

"The house stands in this wood of elms. We have two California grizzlies, and a pair of bull-dogs. Wabash keeps the dogs chained, but I let the grizzlies go free. We are not troubled with visitors."

Scott, English, and Peoples were arrested, some months later, for highway robbery, and, heavily ironed, were placed under guard, in a log-house, as a temporary jail. That night was born the first Vigilance Committee of the north. It consisted of but six men, mostly Expressmen. About midnight, under pretense of furnishing the guard with refreshments, they got hold of their arms, and told the prisoners they must die. Scott asked time to pray; English swore furiously, but Peoples was silent. Soon one of the Vigilantes approached Scott, where he was kneeling and was about to place a noose over his head.

"Hang me first,"cried English, "and let him pray."

The wonderful courage of the man appealed strongly to the Vigilantes, but they had gone too far to falter now. They had but one rope, and proceeded to execute them, one at a time. When the rope was around the neck of English, he was respectfully asked by his executioners to invoke his God. He held down his head a moment, muttered something, then straightened himself up, and turning to Scott, said:

"Nelse, pray for me a little, can't you, while I hang! D——— if I can pray."

He looked over to where Peoples sat, still as a stone, and continued, "D——— if I can pray, Billy; can you?"

Peoples died without a word or struggle. When they came to Scott, and put the rope about his neck, he was still praying most devoutly. He offered, for his life, large sums of money, which he said he had buried; but they told him he must die. Finding there was no escape, he took off his watch and rings, kissed them tenderly, and handing them to one of the Vigilantes, said, "Send these to my poor Armina," and quietly submitted. At dawn the three men, eyes aglare, lay side by side, in their irons, on the floor, rigid in death.

"IDAHHO"

The name of the great north-western gold-fields, comprising Montana and Idaho, was originally spelled I-*dah*-ho, with the accent thrown heavily on the second syllable. The word is perhaps of Shoshonee derivation, but it is found in some similar form, and with the same significance, among all Indians west of the Rocky Mountains. The Nez Perce Indians, in whose country the great black and white mountain lies which first induced the white man to the use of this name, are responsible for its application to the region of the far North-West.

The literal meaning is, "sunrise mountains." Indian children among all tribes west of the Rocky Mountains, so far as I can learn, use the word to signify the place where the sun comes from. Where these tawny people live out of doors, go to bed at dusk, and rise with the first break of day, sunrise is much to them. The place where the sun comes from is a place of marvel to the children; and, indeed, it is a sort of dial-plate to every village or ranchrea, and of consequence to all. The Shoshonee Indians, the true Bedouins of the American desert, hold the mountain where the first burst of dawn is discovered in peculiar reverence.

This roving and treacherous tribe of perfect savages, stretching from the Rocky Mountains almost to the Sierras, having no real habitation, or any regard for the habitation of others, but often invading and overlapping the lands of fellow-savages, had some gentle sentiments about sunrise. "Idahho" with them was a sacred place; and they clothed the Rocky Mountains, where the sun rose to the, with a mystic or rather a mythological sanctity.

The Shasta Indians, with whom I spent the best years
of my youth, and whose language and traditions I know
entirely, as well as those of their neighbors to the north of
them, the Modocs, always, whether in camp or in winter
quarters, had an "Idahho," or place for the sun to rise.
This was a sort of Mecca in the skies, to which every
Indian lifted his face involuntarily on rising from his rest.
I am not prepared to say that the act had any special
religion in it. I only assert that it was always done, and
done silently, and almost, if not entirely, reverently.

Yet it must be remembered that this was a very
practical affair nearly always and with all Indians. The
warpath, the hunt, the journey — all these pursuits
entered almost daily into the Indian's life, and of course
the first thing to be thought of in the morning was
"Idahho." Was the day to open propitiously? Was it to be
fair or stormy weather for the work in hand?

But I despair of impressing the importance of sunrise
on those who rarely witness it, although to the Indian it is
everything. And that is why every tribe in the mountains,
wherever it was, and whatever its object in hand, had a
Mount "Idahho." This word, notwithstanding its beauty
and pictorial significance, found no place in our books
till some twenty-one years ago, and then only in an
abbreviated and unmeaning form.

Indeed, all Indian dialects, except the "Chinook," a
conglomerate published by the Hudson Bay Company for
their own purposes, and adopted by the missionaries,
seem to have always been entirely ignored and unknown
throughout the North Pacific territory. This Chinook"
answered all purposes. It was a sort of universal jargon,
was the only dialect in which the bible was printed, or
that had a dictionary, and no one seemed to care to dig
beyond it.

And so it was that this worthless and unmeaning
"Chinook" jargon overlaid and buried our beautiful
names and traditions. They were left to perish with the
perishing people; so that now, instead of soft and
alliterative names, with pretty meanings and traditions,
we have for the most sublime mountains to be seen on
earth (those of the Oregon Sierras, miscalled the Cascade

118

Mountains) such outlandish and senseless and inappropriate appellations as Mount Hood, Mount Jefferson, Mount Washington, and Mount Raineer. Changing the name of the Oregon River, however, to that of the Columbia, is an impertinence that can plead no excuse but the bad taste of those perpetrating the folly. The mighty Shoshonee River, with its thousand miles of sand and lava beds, is being changed by these same map-makers to that of Lewis and Clarke River.

When we consider the lawless character of the roving Bedouins who once peopled this region, how snake-like and treacherous they were as they stole through the grasses and left no sign, surely we should allow this sinuous, impetuous, and savage river to bear the name which it would almost seem nature gave it, for Shoshone is the Indian name for serpent. How appropriate for this river and its once dreaded people!

The dominion of this tribe departed with the discovery of gold on a tributary of the Shoshonee River in 1860. The thousands who poured over this vast country on their way to the new gold-fields of the north swept them away almost entirely. Up to this time they had only the almost helpless and wholly exhausted immigrant to encounter, with now and then a brush with soldiers sent out to avenge some massacre. But this tribe perished, as I have said, before the Californians, and to-day it is not; except as one of the broken and dispirited remnants familiar to the wretched reservations scattered over the vast far West.

Captain Pierce, the discoverer of gold in the north, located "Pierce City" on the site of his discovery, in the dense wood away up in the wild spurs of the Bitter Root Mountains, about fifty miles from the Shoshonee River. Then "Orofino City" sprang up. Then "Elk City" was laid out. But the "cities" did not flourish. Indeed, all these "cities" were only laid out to be buried. The gold was scarce and hard to get at, and the mighty flood of miners that had overrun everything to reach the new mines began to set back in a refluent tide.

On the site of the earthworks thrown up by Lewis and Clarke, who wintered on the banks of the Shoshonee

River in 1803-04, the adventurous miners had founded a fourth and more imposing city, as they passed on their way to the mines. This they called Lewiston. It was at the head of steamboat navigation on the Shoshonee, and promised well. I remember it as an array of miles and miles of tents in the spring. In the fall, as the tide went out, there were only a few strips of tattered canvas flapping in the wind. Here and there stood a few "shake shanties," against which little pebbles rattled in a perpetual fusillade as they were driven by the winds that howled down the swift and barren Shoshonee.

"It oughter be gold-bearin' country," said a ragged miner, as he stood with hands in pockets shivering on the banks of the desolate river, looking wistfully away toward California; "it oughter be a gold-bearin' country, 'cause it's fit for nothin' else; wouldn't even grow grasshoppers."

I had left California before this rush, settled down, and been admitted to the bar by ex-Attorney-General George H. Williams, then Judge, of Oregon, and had now come, with one law-book and two six-shooters, to offer my services in the capacity of advocate to the miners. Law not being in demand, I threw away my book, bought a horse, and rode express. But even this had to be abandoned, and I, too, was being borne out with the receding tide.

Suddenly it began to be rumored that farther up the Shoshonee, and beyond a great black-white mountain, a party of miners who had attempted to cross this ugly range, and got lost, had found gold in deposits that even exceeded the palmy days of "'49."

Colonel Craig, an old pioneer, who had married an Indian woman and raised a family here, proposed to set out for the new mine. The old man had long since, through his Indians, heard of gold in this black mountain, and he was ready to believe this rumor in all its extravagance. He was rich in horses, a good man—a great-brained man, in fact—who always had his pockets full of papers, reminding one of Kit Carson in this respect; and, indeed, it was his constant thirst for news that drew him toward the "expressman," and made him his friend.

I gladly accepted his offer of a fresh horse, and the privilege of making one of his party. For reasons sufficient to the old mountaineer, we set out at night, and climbed and crossed Craig's Mountain, sparsely set with pines and covered with rich brown grass, by moonlight. As we approached the edge of Camas Prairie, then a land almost unknown, but now made famous by the battle-fields of Chief Joseph, we could see through the open pines a faint far light on the great black and white mountain beyond the valley. "Idahho!" shouted our Indian guide in the lead, as he looked back and pointed to the break of dawn on the mountain before us. "That shall be the name of the new mines," said Colonel Craig quietly, as he rode by his side.

The exclamation, its significance, the occasion, and all, conspired to excite deep pleasure, for I had already written something on this name and its poetical import, and made a sort of glossary embracing eleven dialects.

Looking over this little glossary now, I note that the root of the exclamation is *dah!* The Shasta word is *Lo-dah!* and so on. Strangely like "Look there!" or "Lo, light! is this exclamation, and with precisely that meaning.

I do not know whether this Indian guide was Nez Perce, Shoshonee, Cayuse, or from one of the many other tribes that had met and melted into this half-civilized people first named. Neither can I say certainly at this remote day whether he applied the word "Idahho" to the mountain as a permanent and established name, or used the word to point the approach of dawn. But I do know that this mountain that had become famous in a night, and was now the objective point of ten thousand pilgrims, became at once known to the world as Idahho.

Passing by the Indians' corn-fields and herds of cattle and horses, we soon crossed the Camas Valley. Here, hugging the ragged base of the mountain, we struck the stormy and craggy Salmon River, a tributary of the Shoshonee, and found ourselves in the heart of the civilized and prosperous Nez Perces' habitations. Ten miles of this tortuous and ragged stream and our guide led up the steep and stupendous mountain toward which all the prospectors were now journeying. At first it was open pines and grass, then stunted fir and tamarack, then broken lava and manzanita, then the summit and snow.

A slight descent into a broad flat basin, dark with a dense growth of spruce, with here and there a beautiful little meadow of tall marsh grass, and we were in the mines — the first really rich gold-mines that had as yet ever been found outside of California.

"Surely there is a vein for the silver, and a place for gold *where they fine it*," says the Bible — meaning that the only certain place to look for gold is where they refine it. Certainly the text never had a more apt illustration than here; for of all places for gold in the wide world this seemed the most unlikely. The old Californian miners who came pouring in after us, almost before we had pitched tent, were disgusted. "Nobody but a parcel of fools would ever have found gold here," said one, with a sneer at the long-haired Oregonian who had got lost and found the new mines. But the wheat-like grains of gold were there, and in such heaps as had never been found even in California; and so accessible — only a few inches under the turf or peat in the little meadows and little blind gulches here and there in this great black, bleak, and wintry basin that had never yet been peopled since it came fresh from the Creator's hand.

In less than a week the black basin was white with tents. Our party located a "city" where we first pitched tent, with the express-office for a nucleus. Look at your map, tracing up from Lewiston over Craig's Mountain and Camas Prairie, and you will find "Millersburg," looking as big on the map as any town in the West. Yet it did not live even the winter through. A man soon came with a family of daughters, Dr. Furber, an author of some note at the time, and settled a half mile farther on. My "city" went with and clustered about the ladies. The doctor named the rival "city" after his eldest daughter, Florence. It flourished in the now falling snow like a bay, and was at one time the capital of the Territory. There is little of it left now, however, but the populous graveyard.

And alas for the soft Indian name! The bluff miner,

with his swift speech and love of brevity, soon cut the name of the new mines down to "Idao." And so when the new gold-fields widened out during a winter of unexampled hardship and endurance into "Warren's Diggin's," "Boise City," "Bannock City," and so on, and the new Territory took upon itself a name and had a place on the map of the Republic, that name was plain, simple, and senseless Idaho. Should any one concerned in the preservation of our native and beautiful names care to know more particularly the facts here sketched, let him address Colonel Craig, of Craig's Mountain, Idaho, a well-read and the best-informed man on the subject to be found in the far West; and he is the man who found and named I-*dah*-ho.

AN OLD OREGONIAN IN
THE SNOW

I was once, when riding express, "snowed under" with a famous old pioneer in the great cañon that splits Camas Prairie in two and breaks the monotony of its vast levels.

A wild unpeopled and unknown land it was then, but it has since been made immortal by the unavailing battles of Chief Joseph for the graves of his fathers.

Joe Meek! The many books about him [12] tell you he was a savage, buckskinned delegate to Congress from the unorganized territory of Oregon, who lived with the Indians. These statements are almost all untrue. His was a plain, pastoral nature, and he shunned strife and notoriety. He had none of Kit Carson's dash about him, none of Davy Crockett's daring, nor had he Fremont's culture and capacity for putting himself well before the world; yet he ranked all these men both in the priority and the peril of his enterprises.

Indeed, before the chiefest of them was really heard of, he had called the people of the far Northwest together under the great pines by the sounding Oregon, and made solemn protest against the pretensions of England to that region. These settlers sent this man over the plains alone, a journey of more than half a year, to beg the President that they might be made or remain a portion of the United States while most of the now famous mountaineers were yet at their mother's knee. I know no figure in our history that approaches his in grandeur except that of President Houston, of the Lone Star Republic. And yet you search in vain for his name among those who sat in our Capitol in those early days. Some say he arrived at

Washington when Congress was not in session, and so did not present his credentials. Others say that he lost his papers on the way in one of his perilous passages of a stream. And then again I am told that he never had any credentials to present; that the territory had no official existence at that time, and as Congress had not then become an adept in coining States and Territories, the pioneers of the Oregon River gave him no authority to appear in Congress, but that his mission was entirely with the President.

But the spectacle of this man setting out in mid-winter to ride alone over an untracked distance of three thousand miles, the loyalty of this people, their peril form savages, as well as the cupidity of Great Britain, I count one of the finest on the page of pioneer history.

I suspect that his mission was fruitful of little, for he was, as new people came pouring in, quietly relegated to the background, and never afterward came conspicuously forward, save as an occasional leader in the wars against the Indians. But the undertaking and the accomplishment of this terrible journey alone ought to keep his memory green forever. And, indeed, had fate placed him in any other spot than isolated Oregon, he surely now would not be so nearly forgotten.

When gold was discovered in Idaho—or Id*ah*ho, an Indian word meaning, in a broad sense, mountain of light—Joe Meek, now an old man, could not resist the temptation to leave his home in the woods of Oregon and again brave the plains.

But he was no longer in any great sense a conspicuous figure. He, so far from being a leader, was even laughed at by his own people, the Oregonians, the new, young people who had journeyed into the country after his work had been done—the old story of the ingratitude of republics. And if he was laughed at by the long-haired, lank and blanketed Oregonian, he was despised by the quick, trim, sharp and energetic Californian who had now overrun Oregon on his way to the new Eldorado.

I wonder if the world would believe the half that could be written of the coarseness, the lawlessness of these unorganized armies that surged up and down the Pacific coast in search of gold a quarter of a century ago? I know of nothing like these invasions in history since the days of the Goths and Vandals.

Two wild and strong streams of humanity, one from Oregon and the other from California, had flowed on inharmoniously, tumultuously, together on their way to the mines. On Camas Prairie winter swept suddenly over them, and there, down in the deep canon that cleft the wide and wintry valley through the middle, this stream of life stopped, as a river that is frozen.

A hundred men, trying to escape the "blizzard," tumbled headlong into the cañon together, and took shelter there as best they could beside the great basalt that had tumbled from the high, steep cliffs of the cañon. They crept under the crags, anywhere to escape the bitter cold.

And how the Californian did despise the Oregonian! He named him the "webfoot" because his feet were moccasined and he came from the land of clouds and rain. The bitter enmity and the bad blood of Germany and France were here displayed in epitome and in the worst form. A wonder, indeed, if there would not be some sort of tragedy played here before the storm was over.

The Oregonians wore long hair at that date. A pair of leggings and a blanket, with his head thrust through a hole in the centre, made his chief raiment. A tall, peaked hat, with a band about it something like the brigand of the stage, crowned his long, straight, and stringy hair. Sometimes he wore an old slouch hat; he was rarely without the blanket; he was never without the leggings.

The Californian wore the traditional red shirt in that day, with rarely an exception. He always wore a pistol, often two pistols, in the great leather belt, and a bowie-knife. He generally wore duck pantaloons, tucked inside of his great long-legged leather boots. If he was "on the shoot," or "come from the shoulder" a little investigation would in many cases disclose an extra pistol or two tucked down deep in these boots. And even whiskey bottles have been known to nestle there. He rarely wore a coat. The coat interfered with his locomotion, and he despised it. If he was cold he put on

126

another shirt. And how he would howl at the long, lean, and silent Oregonian as he moved about in his moccasins and leggings, with his blanket tight about him and his hands quite hidden.

"Hello, webfoot," cried the Californian leader to old Joe Meek one day, "where's your hands? Come, show us your hands! Are you heeled?"

"Try me and see!"

The blanket flew back, two hands shot forward, and the garrulous and meddlesome Californian let the "webfoot" go, for he was "heeled."

We had but little wood here, and that was of the worst quality — willow — green and frozen. The little river gurgled and called plaintively for the first day or two as it struggled on the ground against its icy banks. But soon its lips were sealed, and the snow came down and covered the silent and dead waters as with a shroud.

The day after the little tilt between the Californian leader and quiet old Joe Meek, the Californians took occasion to walk up and down before his camp, and talk very loud and behave in a very insulting manner. The cañon was all on tiptoe. The men began to forget for a moment their miseries in the all-absorbing topic, the coming fight.

The blizzard only increased in terror. The mules and horses were freezing to death in their tracks on the snow plateau above.

It was terrible, pitiful. Death was imminent for both man and beast. The Californians outnumbered the Oregonians ten to one. They had secured the only real shelter from the storm, a sort of cavern under the over-hanging basaltic rocks, over which the snowy cyclone swept and left hanging huge masses of snow. The Californians were packed away like sardines, talking of the coming battle and firing the heart of their leader with hatred of the quiet old Oregonian, who, with his Indian sons, swung their half frozen arms or walked up and down in the vain effort to keep warm.

Suddenly the Californian came up to one of the Indian boys and slapped him in his face. There was a shout from the cave. The old man only turned, threw back his

127

blanket, tapped a pistol, pointed up to the plateau, and said:

"Them! Sunrise! Thar!"

The Californian was startled. He could not say a single word. He only nodded assent, and went back to his cave and his crowd. Never had duel been arranged so suddenly. He told his men, and they were wild, furious. A general battle was imminent.

Let us look at these silent, lean and despised Oregonians in their blankets. Comely they were not, nor graceful. They were not well read, nor had the eyes of the world been upon them as on the Californians. But be it remembered that away back before California was at all known these Oregonians had met under the pines, and most emphatically, as well as ungrammatically, proclaimed that they were a part of the United States, and not of England. They had declared war against aggressive tribes, had raised an army, maintained it in the field, and finally had coined their own money out of their own gold, paid off that army, and proclaimed peace, all on their own account. Their coin was pure gold — not a particle of alloy. The beaver on the one side of their crude coin showed the quiet industry of her pastoral people. The sheaf of wheat on the other side showed that plenty should reward the husbandman. People like that are not to be despised.

Against this record the Californian had little to exhibit. He had washed down hills and led rivers over the mountains; he had contributed much to the metallic currency of the world, but he had done little else.

The storm went down with the sun, and now how bitter cold! The moon hung high and clear right overhead. The stars stood out and sparkled in the frost-like fire. The keen, cold wind swept the plain above and threatened to fill the cañon with snow. Wolves, that had eaten only the dead horses up to this time, now began to devour the weak and dying ones. There were enough wolves gathering about us, howling, fighting, devouring our horses, to attack and eat us where we stood. But still the fight must go on. The deadly hatred must find some expression. Fortunate if it should end with this deadly duel just before us.

Clouds began to drive over the moon at midnight and stream away over toward Idaho to the east. The stars went out, as if the fierce wind had blown out the myriad lights of heaven. Then the snow began to fall again, thick and fast, massive, as the sombre Oregonians sat about their fire and talked of the coming duel. The group grew white as huddled flocks of sheep. Now and then a man would get up and shake himself, and the snow would slide off his shoulders in great avalanches. The fire began to perish under this incessant, unceasing dropping of snow. The snow simply possessed the world. The fire died out. It was dark, with a wild, a deadly darkness. They could not see each other's faces. When a man spoke it was as if some one called from deep down in a well. They groped about, feeling for each other. The Californians slept tranquilly and selfishly on in their cavern.

Snow above and snow below! The wolves howling from the hill. Snow that buried you, that lay on your shoulders like a burden, that loaded you down, that fastened upon you as if it had life and sense, and like a ghost that would never go away.

With the coming morning there came a sense of change. It was warm, warmer, sultry. The Chinook wind! But it was not light. There was only a dim, ghastly something in the air — the ghost of a dead day, and snow and snow and snow. Nothing but silence and snow!

I stop here as I write, and wonder if any one east of the Rocky Mountains knows what the "Chinook" wind is? One writes at a disadvantage here. But the world is learning. Ten years ago it would not have known what a "blizzard" or a "cyclone" meant. It knows now.

Well, this Chinook wind is a hot cyclone that leaps up from the Gulf of California, caroms from mountain-top to mountain-top toward the north, till it suddenly and savagely takes possession of the coldest and bleakest spot on the continent. It comes when the cold reaches a climax. This hot Chinook wind is born of the freezing blizzard. It is the one thing that makes this vast North-west habitable. Stick a pin here and remember.

129

This Chinook wind is the most remarkable and phenomenal thing in nature.

The Oregonians threw back their blankets, stood erect, and breathed free for the first time in all these deadly days. Puddles of water began to form at their feet. Little rivulets began to seek the frozen river in the cañon. The snow began to slip and slump in avalanches down the steep sides of the mountains. The Indian boys tightened their moccasins, and with the first sign of breaking day hurried away over the hill, pistols in hand, to look after their horses. The old pioneer calmly waited for sunrise. He stood alone by the dead firebrands.

Suddenly there was a great, dull shock. Thud! An avalanche! The whole mountain side of snow had slid into the cañon and carried with it the overhanging masses above the cavern.

The swelling river, thus suddenly brought to a standstill, began to plunge and fret and foam at his very feet. The Indian boys returned, and began to move their effects out of the cañon. They dropped their loads at the sound of a second avalanche which seemed to close the cavern, and looked at each other in the gray dawn. They were glad; wild with delight. They chuckled at first; and then a yell—such a yell of pure satisfaction was never heard before.

Their father lifted his head, looked at them hard, and then plucking me after him, hurried down to the cavern's mouth.

The Californians were on their feet, falling over each other, dazed, confused, cursing, howling. The mouth of the cave was so closed by the snow that one had to stoop to enter.

They had thrown some pitch on the embers, and as it blazed up they stared at the apparition of the old man, who stood there in their midst, in their power, and almost alone. A little white rabbit, driven in by the swelling water, came huddling at his feet. "What have you come in here for?" cried the leader, clutching a pistol.

"To save you."

"What!" And the pistol was raised to a level.

The old man did not heed or answer. He stooped and

picked up the terrified little rabbit and held it kindly, as you would hold a kitten. The men looked at each other and then out at the booming flood, foaming at the door of the cavern, and dashing in the new dawn.

I turned and ran away and up toward our camp, for there was a cry of terror on every lip. The old man led them at a run, their guns in their hands, their blankets on their shoulders.

We reached the safe eminence where the Indian boys had made our new camp, and then old Colonel Joe Meek, turning to the Californian leader and pointing to the plateau beyond, said:

"Cap'n, it's sunrise."

"Colonel Joe Meek, I begs your parding. I'm licked!" cried the Californian, as he reached his hand in token of submission and peace.

JOHN BROWN—
JOSEPH DE BLONEY

Harper's Ferry, December 8, 1883. The face of nature is frowning here forever. Dark and wrinkled, rugged and unfriendly to look upon, there is an atmosphere of hostility about this place, of savagery, of sullen defiance and impatience, that makes one willing to hasten away. Sabre-cuts in the face of the land; a fierce scowl on the face of the earth; a sullen roar in the rivers as they run angrily together; a sullen silence on the few people; dilapidation over the town—a tired, deserted, nightmare town, as if it would like to wake up and throw off some indefinable terrors; and this is Harper's Ferry, where was, in fact, fired the first gun of the greatest, the saddest, the best and the worst war that ever was.

I do not get at the heart of the best people here. I have little time, little inclination too, perhaps. A scribe wandering about alone with his own meditations, no letters of introduction, a pad and pencil in his hand and a flannel shirt on his back, is not just the man for first-class men to open either their hearts or their doors to, I admit. And then, what could they tell me that has not been told a thousand times? Besides, what does this new generation know? As for the old, it perished in the war.

But those hills have not perished. They looked down on it all. Their stony lips are set in everlasting silence. And yet they tell me that John Brown came here, climbed their heights, looked down into these rivers, measured their waters, made a thousand calculations how to advance, how to retreat, where to fight, and then to die. I think the arsenal with its store of arms had not all to do with bringing John Brown here. There was comradeship in these glorious old hills. One likes to have such friends at his back and close about him in days of desperate enterprise.

"What! A pilgrimage to Harper's Ferry to write of old John Brown? Thought you were a Democrat; thought you had your paper in Oregon suppressed for treasonable utterances durin' the wah?" A good man, a friend, said this to me, and I answered: "My friend, whether it is my love for the poor man at election, the little horse in the horse-race, or the bottom dog in the dog-fight, I do not know. I do not care. I only know that I admired, pitied, and now revere John Brown. I am going to make a pilgrimage to Harper's Ferry now on the twenty-fourth anniversary of his execution.

"But this man John Brown was a murderer—murdered my people,sah."

"Yes, but he did not murder many men; not one hundredth part as many as Sherman or Sheridan. He did not desolate the defenceless Shenandoah or burn his way through the South. He did not say, 'I have made the Shenandoah Valley so desolate that even a crow would have to carry its rations if it attempted to fly over it.' It was the man now at the head of the nation's army who said that. And yet if you were asked to dine with that man to-morrow, the chances are you would not only break bread with him, but even pocket the bill of fare as a trophy. I prefer the dead lion to the living—but why finish the biblical paraphase?"

"Then you don't like Grant?"

"As a soldier, no. The most pitiful sight to me is that of a man, any man, strutting about this earth with an implement buckled to his side for the purpose of poking some unfortunate fellow to death. We are a pastoral people in these States; keepers of sheep are we, and tillers of the soil. But right here let me tell you, while speaking of tilling the soil, that the best, the bravest, the very noblest deed that now looms up and out of and over all the desolate days and deeds of that war was done by that man Grant; and quietly and modestly done, and done in defiance, too, of all the powers at Washington. And that immortal deed, the one splendid work of the war, was expressed in these words under the apple-tree at Appomattox: 'No, General Lee, I don't want your horses. Let your men take them home. They will need them to plough with.' "

Some old, indolent mules from the country round about; greasy old wagons; a good many old and very indolent negroes shivering in the frosty weather on the corners; corner groceries that have been whittled away by jack-knives—the only sign of industry I see about or enterprise of any kind; a few seedy-looking horses hitched before the few stores; an old fortress on a winding hill where "Stonewall" Jackson pointed to the State flag of Virginia and said, "Wherever thou goest, there also will I go"—and that is Harper's Ferry as I find it, where John Brown bled, with his sons about him.

Out yonder in the middle of the river the water still plashes and leaps over and divides around the same great rock there where his black allies fell. Some ignorant, tobacco-eating idlers showed me a battered old establishment from which the old man, now sixty years old, pointed his gun and fought all night, his sons at his side, at his feet, dead, dying, fighting. Of course there is no sentiment about these men. You hear hard, and maybe not entirely undeserved, remarks from these ignorant and unsympathizing idlers.

Coming here on the anniversary of John Brown's execution—he was hung on the second of December, only a short walk away—I hoped to find something new to tell you. Not so.

But it is an impressive fact that, looking south from any other point of the Republic, this one man and his sons stand up forever before you—forever true, grand, reverend, resigned.

In the great dramas of the days to come this is the man who will walk the stage with the most majestic mien. It will not be the noisy-mouthed man of the capital; it will not be the contractor with his bloody millions; it will not be the general of the war with a million men at command, who will loom up largest and last. But it will be simple, honest, humble old John Brown, who died in pity for his helpless fellow-men.

It is a singular thing that this man, in one sense, ordered his tombstone before setting out for Harper's Ferry. At least he had his father's tombstone brought from New York to the half-savage little farm which Gerrit Smith had given him. The inscription on this stone reared to the father of John Brown of Harper's Ferry reads as follows:

"In memory of Capt. John Brown, who died at New York, Sept. ye 3, 1776, in the 42d year of his age."

Beneath this is the old hero's epitaph, and it reads:

"John Brown, born May 9, 1800; was executed at Charlestown, Va., Dec. 2, 1859."

A CALIFORNIA JOHN BROWN IN A SMALL WAY.

Joseph De Bloney, whom I first met on the head of the Sacramento River in the spring of 1855, was of the old Swiss family of that name—famous, you know, for being the first to renounce their high rank of nobility and assume a simple republican name. This was a learned man. Even in the mountains there he had many books. But I think few people ever knew his worth. Certainly but few ever sympathized with him. I believe he had first crossed the plains with Fremont. He is probably entirely forgotten now. And the world never heard of his feeble efforts to help his fellows. His ambition was to unite the Indians about the base of Mount Shasta and establish a sort of Indian republic, the prime and principal object of which was to set these Indians entirely apart from the approach of the white man, draw an impassable line, in fact, behind which the Indian would be secure in his lands, his simple life, his integrity, and his purity. Some of the many tribes were friendly; some were hostile. It was a hard undertaking at best, perilous, almost as much as a man's life was worth, to attempt to befriend an Indian in those stormy days on the border, when every gold-hunter crowding the hills in quest of precious metals counted it his privilege, if not his duty, to shoot an Indian on sight. An Indian sympathizer was more hated in those days, is still, than ever was an Abolitionist. And it was against bitter odds that this little California John Brown, even long before John Brown's raid, tried to make a stand in

135

behalf of a perishing race. He, too, failed. The plastic new land was in a chaotic state. More men than he were trying to fashion something solid and useful out of the Republic's new possessions. Walker was even trying to extend these possessions to Nicaragua. Fremont had hoisted the bear flag. It made him a prisoner. It ought to have made him President.

De Bloney gradually gathered about twenty-five men around him in the mountains, took up homes, situated his men around him, planted, dug gold, did what he could to civilize the people and subdue the savages.

Our neighbor, Captain Jack, in his lava-beds, was born of this man's endeavor. Of course his motives were miscontrued by the few who took any notice of him at all. Some suspected that we had found gold-mines of great wealth. Others, again, said we were stealing horses and hiding them away in the hearts of the mountains. And I concede that property disputes with some settlers gave some grounds for suspicion. Yet De Bloney was as honest as a sunset and as pure as the snowy mountains around us.

But he had tough elements to deal with. The most savage men were the white men. The Indians, the friendly ones, were the tamest of his people. These white men would come and go; now they would marry the Indian women and now join a prospecting party and disappear for months, even years. At one time they nearly all went off to join Walker in Nicaragua. Only two ever lived to return. I, too, wandered away from him more than once, but at last kept close and always with him. He taught me much, and was good. Once the unfriendly Indians burned his camp. He raised a company, followed and fought them. This was the battle of Castle Rocks. I was shot in the face and neck, and was nearly a year getting well. By this time there was a war on the other side of the mountain, and I was drawn into that also. This was the Pit River war. Here I got a bullet through the right arm, and was laid up for another long season.

By and by he had his plans matured, and had armed his Indians in defence against the brutal and aggressive white men. I was sent on one occasion to Shasta City for ammunition. I had made similar raids before. My horse was shot on the return. I was dreadfully bruised by a fall, and the two Indians with me took me in turns behind them. Then we got, or rather captured, a fresh horse and kept on. But I was too badly hurt to go far, and they left me with some Indians by the road. Here I was captured by the pursuing white men. This was in 1859. I was in my seventeenth[13] year, and small for my age. Of course, they had sworn to hang the renegade to the nearest tree. I was really not big enough to hang, and so they took me back to Shasta City, put me in jail, and my part in the wild attempt to found an Indian republic was rewarded with a prompt indictment for stealing horses. A long time I lay in that hot and horrible pen, more dead than alive.

God pity all prisoners, say I. Fortunately I could see and even smell some pine trees that stood on the hillside hard by. I know I should have died in those hot days, with the mercury up in the nineties, but for the friendship, the fragrance, the sense of freedom in those proud old pine trees on the hillside. Meantime, as always happens, I was left alone. All the men passed away like water through a sieve, and only the Indians remembered me. On the night of the 4th of July, while the town was carousing, they broke open the jail, threw me again on to a horse, and such a ride for freedom and fresh air was never seen before.

Poor De Bloney lost all heart and gradually sank to continued drunkenness on the border and ultimate obscurity. As for myself, I tried to inherit his high plans and spirits, and made one more attempt, for I had formed ties not to be broken. But the last venture was still more disastrous. Volumes only could tell all the dreadful story that followed — the tragedy and the comedy, the folly and the wisdom. And yet now, after a quarter of a century, I still fail to see anything but good and honesty and integrity in these bold plans for the protection of the Indians — the Indians, to whose annihilation we, as a nation, have become quite reconciled. Ah! how noble in us to be so easily reconciled to the annihilation of another race than our own! I never saw De Bloney after this final failure. I would not be taken again prisoner, and so an officer in pursuit was shot from his horse. We separated in the Sierras, and sought separate ways in life. I made my way to Washington Territory, sold my pistols, and settled down in an obscure settlement on the banks of the Columbia, near Lewis River, and taught school. And here it was that the story of John Brown, his raid, his fight, his capture, and his execution, all came to me. Do you wonder that my heart went out to him and remained with him? I, too, had been in jail. Death and disgrace were on my track, and might find me any day hiding away there under the trees in the hearts of the happy children. And so, sympathizing, I told these children over and over again the story of old John Brown there. And they, every one, loved, and honored and pitied him.

And now you can better understand why I was so resolved to make a pilgrimage to Harper's Ferry on the anniversary of his execution. However, he does not need my sympathy, or any one's sympathy. I am here simply because it is my sad pleasure to be here at this time.

It was an odd sequel to our failure to establish our Utopian Republic about the base of Mount Shasta, with the great white cone for a centre, that I should finally meet these same men who had fought and had captured me in California up in the new gold-fields of Northern Oregon. And singularly enough, they were very kind. I had received too many wounds fighting for these same men on the border of California to be quite the "renegade" they counted me once. And when the Shoshonee Indians now attacked our camp at Canyon City, Oregon, these same men chose me their captain to lead them in battle. And how they did wish for poor De Bloney now! But he had been buried away up in the golden fields of Idaho. A three-month's campaign, and I was finally beaten, leaving many dead. But, as if still to convince me of their love and confidence, when we returned to Canyon City, they elected me judge of the country, and for the four years of my administration stood truly by me, as if to try to make me forget something of the sorrow and the shame of imprisonment. Yet for all that I was in some sense an old man from the time of our failure and flight. And how wretched the few remaining Indians there now! There are only now and then in all that splendid mountain region a few miserable hovels of half-starved, dispirited beggars of the lowest sort to be met with. Captain Jack and his sixty brave rebels were the last of this race. But they made a red spot on the map which the army will long remember.

THE CALIFORNIA DIARY

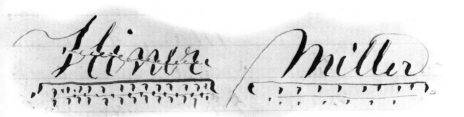

THE CALIFORNIA DIARY [14]

[*October 6, 1855*] Sat. Made $3 bought 50 lbs of flour $3 75 cents one box of sardines 75 cts
   Sun. Bought one box of yeast powder 50 cts Pork 75 cts
Mon. Made $1
Tues. I was sick
Wedensday I was sick
Thurs Made $3 50 cts Commenced building our house
Fri Made $1 bought potatoes $1
Sat Made $2 Paid for boards for house $6 Nails $1
Meat $3 Weeks work totel $14.
   Sunday Worked on house
   Mon 00
Tues Paid towards claim $4 25 cts Paid recording two claims $1
   Wedensday Paid for flour 50 lbs $4 Thread 20 cts
   Thursd Paid for house cover $3 Overhalls $1
   Friday Paid for onions 50 cts
   [*October 20, 1855*] Sat Made $5
   Sun Rested Paid for one box of Moffat Pills 75 cts
   Mon Made $4 50 cts Paid for lumber for ———— $2
for axe handle 50 cts salt 75 cts onions 25 cts for
———— 60 cts for candles 35 cts for matches 25 cts
   Tues Made 50 cts
   Wedensday Made $1 25 cts Paid for syrup 75 cts for
yeast powder 50 cts
   Thurs Made 50 cts
   Fri Made $2 worked on the Ditch Paid $5 75 cts
toward claim
   Sat Made $4 50 cts Paid for pick and handle $1.25 for
papers 50 cts writing paper 25 cts for pork 50 cts
   Sund Rested

Mon   Made $10 30 cts bought another bucket $1 Butcher knife 15 cts   pan $1   plates 50 cts   book and picture $1   fiddle string 37 cts   beens 50 cts   Gave to George 37 cts

Tues Made $9 Bought one sack of flour $4 50 onions 50 cts pork $2 mustard 75 cts candles 35 cts

Wedensday Made $5 Paid towards claim $10.50

Thurs Made $4

Friday Made $1 finished paying for claim

Sat. 00

Sun Went to texas springs.

Mon Made 00 Wrote one letter to father

[*November 6, 1855*] Tues Made $2

Wedensday Made $1 Bought one bottle of mustard 75 cts candles 50 cts

Thurs Made $1

Fri the 9th Went to Shasta City and saw A. Higgins executed for the crime of murder

Sa Made $5.75 cts Bought one shirt $2 for writing materials $1 for candy 37 cts. for straw for bed 50 cts for one sack of flour $4.50 cts beens $2 bacon $3.20 cts yeast powder $1

Su Rested light rain

Mon Made $8 little rain

Tues Made $5 Cold & cloudy

Wedensday Made $4

Thursday the 15th. Made $1 & sold my half of the claims that we took up for the sum of $85. $10 of this down & one note calling for $25 payable in two weeks & another calling for $50 payable in a year

Fri Went to Middletown. Bought fine comb 50 cts candy 25 cts. Bought one claim on Spring Gulch of Samuel Johns for the sum of $30 15 of this down, my note calling for $15 in three months

Sat Prospected Made 50 cts

Su Prospected Made 25cts Wrote one letter to Wm. Murphy Humbug Cal

Mond Prospected Made 00

Tues Prospected Made 00

[*November 21, 1855*] Wedensday Prospected Made 25 cts

Thurs Prospected Made $2.50
Frid Prospected Made 25 cts
Sat Prospected Made 00
Sund Went to texas springs
Mond Prospected Made $1
Tues Prospected Made 50 cts
Wedensday Prospected Made 50 cts
Thurs Prospected Made 50 cts
Friday Prospected Made 50 cts Bought two papers $1
Sat Prospected Made 000 Considerable Rain
Sund Rested
Mon Prospected Made $1.50 cts
Tues Prospected Made $1 Credit to Wm Johnston to one Knife $1 to one pick $3.25 cts Credit to Johnston & Climer to cash $7
Wedensday Prospected Made 000
Thurs Prospected Made 000 Bought at Middletown five sluice boxes at $4 per box. Paid towards them $14.25 $5.75 cts yet to be paid.

December the 6, 1855

Alone I sit in my cabin today
And all is quiet around
Save the rain which falls on the canvass roof
With a dull and monotinous sound.

My memory recalls the days that are past
The days ere I left my home
Ere I left my fathers fire side
In this land of gold to roam

Memory recalls the old school days
And school mates ever dear
Our little brawls and gleeish plays
Each fleeting hope and fear

But they have gone as the present will go
And the future we know not of
But the present seems to be filled with woe
And the past all peace and love

145

But see the rain no longer falls
And I to my work must go
And then with my pick and shovel
Try and banish all thoughts of woe

By Hiner Miller of O.T.
Squaw town, Shasta Co Cal

[*December 7, 1855*] Frid Prospected Made 00

Sat Prospected Rained considerable

Sun Went to Middletown. Paid for hauling sluice boxes $4 for rifles $1 Received of Wm Johnston $4

Mon Went to fixing our ditch & boxes working in company with Volney Abbey S. Covert, W. Sparks on the claim that I bought of S. Johns

Tues Got all ready to work but no watter lost at poker and debter to Wm Johnston $1 lost at poker and debter to Volney Abbey $1. Bought for $1 tobacco

Wedensday Prospected Made 000

Th. Prospected Made 00

Friday Went to Middletown. Prospected. Made 00

Sat Lost at Poker $1.50 cts.

Sun the 16th December Bought of Wm Johnston one half of a cabbin for $10 on credit of his note for $25 Went to Shasta City Bought one pencil 25cts paper 25 cts

Mond Prospected. Made 000

Tues Prospected Made $1 Paid for flour $1

Wedensday Worked half day for D. Nuning & Co Received $2 for pay

Thursday Bought of I. Melanthy one pr of shoes $2.50 cts One pr of overhalls $1 one pr of socks 75cts Paid $2.50 cts on them and the remainder on time. Won at poker 50 cts.

Fri. the 21st of December Went to Horsetown 4 miles distant to learn what the chance was to enlist in the Niquaragua expedition. found terms not very flattering and did not enlist.

Sat Set in to work on the claims that I bought of Johns & Wolcot in co with I. Werby, S. Covert, V. Abbey and I owning one share and a half I employ V Abbey who has

146

one half of a share to work my half by paying him $1.50 cts per day Made $16.75 cts.

Sun Worked Did not clean up our sluices

Mon Left the cabbin that I stopped in with V. Abbey and went to mess with I. W. Parks. V. Abbey received of the purser I. W. Parks $4 25 cts Christmas eve. Bought 1 can powder; 1 box gun caps $1.25 cts 1 box Moffat's pills 75 cts

Yes, Christmas eve of '55 has passed away and by me all most unnoticed save the loading and firing of my pistol thirty-six times and then the main spring broke and so I ceased firing

Yes the ninteenth Christmas eve has rolled over my head and as I sit in my cabbin today and look back over the past year I feel that I have not lived as I should have lived

Tues. Christmas. Wrote one letter to John D. Miller Snow fell in the night thirteen inches deep and the ground and watter froze up so that we could not work

Wedensday Did nothing Cold and windy

Thurs do

Friday do

Sat do

Sunday Rested

Mon Cleaned the ice out of our sluices New Years eve unnoticed

Tuesday Jan. 1, 1856. Yes tis fifty-six another year of my life has passed away and where or in what point have I gained In none at all save in the knowledge of my weakness failty and irresolution One year ago I was on Humbug Creek, Ciskiyou County, California and on that day I took a review of the past year '54 and I said to my self if this coming year goes no more usefully spent than the past it will be a sin and a great sin but it is so it has been uselessly spent and what can I do but resolve to do better in this new year Yes, I will do better I will leave off my follies and try and be some one. Yes, this is my resolve. time alone will determine.

Wedensday Cleaned out boxes. Had $10.80 cts.

Thurs Worked half day made $8.40 cts

Frid Went to a miners meeting held at Melanthys

where there was one hundred and thirty miners collected resolutions were passed to tear out the dams of the Texas springs ditch and lett the watter flow in its natural course for the use of the Tadpool miners. We accordingly proceeded in a company to the dams and ten of our number stood upon the hill sides with riffles as guards. The remainder tore away the dams. Worked at sluices in the afternoon Did not clean.

[*January 5, 1856*] Sat Worked half day at sluices. Cleaned had $14.50 cts. V. Abbey received of Purser $2.50 cts. Volney Abbey received of purser to pay his poll tax $4.

Sun Employed Wm Johnston to work in my place I being laid up with a pain in my side. Credit to Wm Johnston $3. S. Covert received of purser $5. Received of purser myself 25 cts to pay postage on letter.

Mon Volney Abbey received of purser $3.50 cts S Covet received of purser $4

Tuesday Bought one ———— of syrup Price $8 Worked half day Heavy rain in the night

Wedensday Worked Cleaned up had $25 Volney Abbey received of purser $7 I received of purser $7 Bought one pr of boots one shirt $7

Thursday Made $12. Gave $1 to a sick digger Indian

Friday Made $27. Finished paying for my sluices $7 received of purser $5 V. Abbey received of purser $2 Abbey & Co received of Parks 50 cts

Friday Evening had a miners meeting to see what we could do for the persons who had been arrested for tearing out the Tadpool dams the miners resolved to throw in [for] a lawyer to plead in their behalf Accordingly $50 was raised Put in $1 my self.

Sat Made $19.50 Volney Abbey received of purser $8.50

Sun 13. Rested S. Covert received of purser his week's wages settled up with W. Sparks my mess mate Paid him $26 for provisions that he had bought and I still owe him $2.87 1/2

Mon Volney Abbey sold his claim on Spring Gulch to John Criss who is a going to mess with me Made 1/11 oz. & 1/8.

Tues Made 1 oz and 1/2

Wedensday Made 1 oz and 1/16

Thurs No watter and did not work but worked in the night

Frid Cleaned our boxes had 10/16 of an oz

Sat No watter worked two hours in the night made 2/16 of an oz

Sun Rested divided our weeks work which was 4 oz & 11/16 I loaned to Volney Abbey 1/2 oz

Mon Made 11/16 & 6/10 of 1/16 of an oz

Tues Rain and did not work

Wedensday Made 1/2 oz

Thursd Moved over sluices to the lower end of our claim

Friday Made 4/16 of oz

Sat Made 5/16 of oz

Sun Made 10/16 of an oz

Monday left our claim and went prospecting with sluices Made 10/16 of oz

[*January 29, 1856*] Tues Did not work Considerable rain

Wedensday Made 2/16 of oz

Thurs did not work no watter

Friday Moved our boxes over to Maclune flat S Covert drew out from the Co

Sat Gave to an old man one dollar

Sun Received of Volney Abbey. $10. went to Oregon Gulch to buy the rifle that I got in an Indian fight on the Sacramento River (and had let it go toward a mining claim while in co with V. Abbey) But they asked me $25.00 for it and so I did not buy it Sunday night won at cards $18.00

Mon Moved our boxes further down the Gulch and took up three claims

Tues Cut a ditch and worked half day made $4.00. Settled our Co bill for the post with $15.00

Wedensday Made $10. 00

Thurs February the 7th. Made $13.00 Won at cards 50 cts

Frid No watter and did not work lost at cards 50 cts bought one box of Moffats pills at 75 cts lost at cards

$2.00 Bought one Colts revolver for $10.00 Number 35.4.81

Sat Worked half day made $4.00 Bought one ditch Paid $35. dollars this ditch is 3 1/2 mile long and heads at Smiths Reservoir and empties at Maclune flats Bought said ditch of J. Neuman Saturday night won at cards $2.00

Sun Rested lost at cards $1.

Mon 11th Worked half day at ditch Weather hot sunshine dry

Tues the 12th of Feb/56 Worked half day did not clean

Wedensday Made $9

Thurs Made $6 Hot sunshine and very dry

Friday Moved our boxes out of the Gulch no watter did not work Went to Middletown (In this journal for the past month I have not been very particular in accounts of my board bill but has been about the same that is the expense)

Sat I have also been very negligent in marking the weather the time of my writing letters etc etc in the past three weeks I have received one letter from Oregon from my parents one from Ben D. Perry

No news of interest and I have answered them. I have also wrote one letter to Wm Willoughby who came to this country with me.

Tues the weather for the past month has been very dry and very pleasant

Wedens. weather for farmers but not for miners

Thurs The last week I have just about made my board by

Friday browsing around farming out etc

Sat I have played at cards considerable the poker game and I am about two dollars and a half looser on the week

Sunday[15] Feb. the 25 or 6

Mon This day very dry no watter and no work

Tues. do

Wed. do

Thurs Friday Sat. Sun. Spring again is with us but it

has but a cool reception with the miners this year because it brought no water with it.

Mon James W Sparks my mess mate left us for french gulch where he intends to spend the spring in tending cows and selling milk dry weather dry dry dry

Wedensday Worked half night made $1.75 cts the weather is still dry and clear it is the most beautiful Spring I have ever seen that is for farmers but just the reverse for us miners

Thurs dry as ever No watter and no prospect of there ever being any Yes, this is March Winter has passed away and Spring with all her blushing modesty is ushered into our presence

Fri Sat Sun It is now verging on to six months since I first landed in Shasta Co but how different are my feelings now to what they were then Then I thought I would pass the coming winter in working a claim and take out ounce after ounce of the shining metal And I fancied that the opening of Spring would find me seated on a splendid horse with a pocket full of gold and a joyous heart a bounding away for my Oregon home and bidding forever adieu to the miners and the miners life and laying down the pick & shovel to rust forever in the gulches of California but alas how different do I find my self from my bright anticipations

I have dug and tugged starved and economized the winter through and I could not this day raise the miserable sum of twenty-five dollars

Yes here I find myself in this damed hole of Squaw town in poor health as I have been all winter without watter, no money to leave the place on and no prospect of making any

Mon I cannot tell what I shall do or where I shall go Neither do I care but such luck as I have had is enough to drive the Noblest of men to almost anything The notes that I gave to N. Walcott and S. Johns not paid up neither do I intend to for the claims were no account that I bought that is one reason that I shall not pay for them another is that I have not received pay for the claims that I sold on tadpool Creek which are paying now from eight to twenty dollars while those that I bought are not paying anything neither have they paid anything.

Thurs.

Friday No watter dry and hot

Sat No watter dry and hot

Sun. do

Mon A letter from my brother J. Miller went to Shasta saw Ben Perry Carried our sluice boxes over to flat creek to prospect in co with S. Burnie Also my partner J. Criss Made $4

Tues Made $5

Wedensday Made $1.25

Thurs Moved our boxes back to our old claim the Wolcott claim

Friday Worked half day in Co with my partner Made $10 Worked half day

Sat. Made $10.75 We got our watter from the big Shasta ditch it is second watter and we pay two dollars per day for it

Sun Cleared off some brush from our claim and set our boxes the weather today is exceedingly hot and still no prospect of rain the farmers now as well as the miners are crying out for rain

Mon George Covert came and worked with us made $12.00 Very warm

Tues Made $10.00

[*March 26, 1856*] Wedensday Made $5.50

Thurs no watter

Friday Made $6

Sat Made $5.00 Paid $13 for watter

Sun Set our boxes and cleared off brush this day the long looked for and much needed rain descended in torrents it rained as hard as I have ever saw it rain in this state

Monday I worked for Dennis Nooning this day the rain also came down in torrents mixed with snow which made it so cold and disagreeable that my partners would not work so I hired my boddy out

Tues Made $3.75 Worked for dennis Nooning for $3 per day I have such hard luck in mining for myself that I shall hire out all together until I can get a stake

Wed. April the 2/56.

Thurs   Worked for Nooning.

Friday No watter & did not work Bought some milk of a man who is going to bring it around every morning and sells it at only one tict (12 1/2) per quart this is quite a treat for me it being the first milk that I have had for almost two years

April the 4th/56

Squaw Town — Shasta Co. California

Squaw town it is of you that I would write lovely citty queen of the Universe. It is of thy goodness and thy beauty. Thy glory and thy virtues that I would speak. Ye that I would pour forth my soul in all the stirring eloquence and mighty power of a Socrates Demosthenes or a Webster.

"Many a vanquished year and age
And tempests breath and battle rage
Has swept old Squaw town, yet she stands
A fortress formed to freedom's hands
The whirlwinds wrath and tempests shock
Have left untouched her hoary rock."

It is not of thy power that I would write for though art not as yet marked among the powerful. But thou wilt be. But is it present power that makes the truly great and good. No tis honor meekness and virtue, and in these who dare stand a rival to thee Nay there is none. London, Paris, Canton — citties that for centuries back have been marked as the most powerful Now blush with shame nor dare look upon thy virtue and thy goodness I would write too of the lovely creatures that dwell within your pallaces and stately mansions. It is your ladies of their virtuous beauty and winning loveliness But no I cannot do them justice even the thoughts of them make my hand tremble and my thoughts to wander And so lovely creatures heirs of Heaven farewell. I can write of you no longer. And I would speak a few words of the sons of Squaw town. But no I will not. Already their wide spread fame and everlasting names shine out and are known oer the whole universe and are and forever will be a beacon light to lead

153

future generations on to everlasting glory   But I will refresh the memories of my people with the names and deeds of some of her most leading sons   First and most glorious and dazzling of all shines out the deeds and character of Franklin Pearce the brave and fearless leader of our gallant troops on the plains of Mexico where he won his well deserved fame and the green laurels that now deck his manly brow. Next is Thomas Hyar the pugilist and prize fighter. then there is Dick Turpin Peter Bailey Denny Craigg Dr. Gates and many other noble brave and generous spirits that I cannot now mention. But farewell glorious, noble and beautiful Squaw-town   I can write no more   This has been done by the nusence of Squaw town — Hiner Miller.

Squaw town April the 5/56

O how I wish I a goin was at home
In the valley of the old Willamette
And never again Id wish to roam
Ile seal the assertion with damn it

And if ever I get back home Ile stay
And raise fine horses and cattle
And Ile go to church and preach sing and pray
And leave the miners to fight their own battles

Yes there Ile live on foul chicken and eggs
And now and then have a fat rooster
And in place of my own use horses legs
And there act the gent as I used to

No more Ile handle the pick or pan
Or use the long tom or shovel
But go courting the girls as I well know I can
And let the miners life go to the devil

Ile not have to live on chile beans
Short beef and rusty bacon
Nor work in mud and mire and rain
And be all the time a shaken

154

But have enough to eat or drink
And best of clothes to wear sir
Ile leave the beef to rot and stink
And Ile have no chile beans out there sir

No more Ile have to bake my bread
Or mend my dirty breeches
But Ile employ some good old maid
To take up all odd stitches

No more Ile in my blankets roll
But Ile have a featherd bed sir
And I will teach my noble soul
To live as it was bred sir

But when am I to get back home
Im sure I cannot tell sir
I havent half the chance to get back there
That I have to go to hell sir

But Ile keep on trying as I have done
Though its poor prospect I meet sir
And if eer that home again Ive won
It will be all the sweeter

So fare farewell all thoughts of home
For as now I cannot go sir
For Ive not made a penny yet
I tell you it is so sir

[*April 5, 1856*] Saturday No watter & no work
Thomas Wright of Ohio died at Centerville April the 4th,
Friday evening Hols momie cultus

Sun Mondy No watter the big ditch is broke and there
being no natural watter makes it still harder on the
miners we had considerable rain last week but the
ground being so very dry it done the miners but little
good We have fair weather now and everything indicates
that our rain is over for this year

Tues Still no watter (fair weather) I sold to Kind &

co two sluice boxes for $3.00 these were boxes that I paid $5 per box last fall, But let her rip

Wedensday No watter. Hot and dry

Thurs Plenty of watter. Worked for Nooning (light rain and wind)

Frid Worked for Nooning (Rain)

Sat Worked for Nooning went to Middletown. bought one pr of boots Price $3.50

Sund rested received one from Wm Willoughby dated March[?]/56 Scotts Valley and one from John D. Miller, O. T. Lane Co

Mon Worked for Nooning

Tues. Worked for Nooning J. W. Sparks, my old Mess mate returned from french Gulch and I bought a young roan mare saddle spurs etc for the sum of ninety dollars Fifty of this I paid down and gave my note for the remaining forty to be paid when I take the mare in my possession

[*April 16, 1856*] Wedensday Worked for Nooning (weather warm & cloudy)

Thurs Worked for Nooning

Friday Worked for Nooning

Saturday Worked for Nooning

Sunday Rested (wrote a reply to the letter I received from Willoughby)

Monday Worked for Nooning

Tuesday Worked for Nooning

Wedensday Worked for Nooning

Thursday Worked for Nooning half day Unwell & did not work in the afternoon

Friday Worked for Nooning

Sat Worked for Nooning

Sunday Rested & enjoyed it too as never better for it has been a hard weeks work at work at sunrise in water up to my knees until 12 o'clock then a little snack for dinner & at it until sundown as hard as you can hit into it & this is life in the land of gold it is worse than slavery in the South

Mon Went to work

Tues Cleaned up made nothing

Wednesday Rain & did not work

Thurs   Made $9.00 two dollars per day—we pay for watter

[*May 2, 1856*] Friday   Cris was unwell   Covert and I worked   Made $17.50 cts

Sat   Worked for Emry   Paid I Melanthy $3.00

Sun   May the 5/56.[16] Went to Whiskey Creek & paid for the mare I bought of my old partner Sparks & brought her away   Bought bridle and rope for $6.00

Mondy   Rested

Tues. Worked for J. Emry. Wages two and half per day & board

Wedensdey   Worked for Emry

Thursday   May the 12/56.[17] Worked for Emry

Friday   Was unwell. lost my horse in the afternoon

May the 9/56
Squaw town, Shasta, Co.

In reading the histories or glancing over sketches written by those whose heads are crowned by the silvery locks of a good old age   How often it is we find them speaking of the happy days they spent when verging on to manhood of the time when they knew no care. When troubles courted them not in their sleep but they could quietly rest on their bed of down with naught to trouble their young minds save the visions of a bright and happy future and of coming days of bliss and happiness & now that I am of that age of which our venerable sires speak of in such glowing terms I think it but right that I should drop here in my notebook a line for fear that I too like them should I live to be an old man and will have my mind filled with vain sighs and regrets for the happy days that I passed so headless by in the springtime of life. Tis true that our minds are not weighed down with the cares of business or the hoarding of wealth (& God forbid that mine should ever be)   But then we have our cares our troubles our brawls and our battles which are all forgotten by the older men of the world   in looking back on the days of my childhood how it all seems to be a calm silvery sea of happiness and thus it is with men who have

157

passed the meridian of life in looking back upon the days of eighteen.

So mote it be
Hiner

Sat Hunted for my horse went to the American Ranch twelve miles from this place. Hired a mule to ride heard from my horse at Red Bluff This is a small though thriving town & is at the head of navigation on the Sacramento River & is thirty-five miles from this place. Following on to Tehama twelve miles from the Bluff found my horse returned to the Bluff stayed over night Bill in the morning $3.50

Sun Returned to the American house and being out of money left my pistol in pawn for the use of the mule for which the owner charged ten dollars

Mon Went to work with John Criss and George Covert

Tues. Sold my pistol to the man I hired the mule of for $15 $10 of this went towards paying for the use of the mule & as we could not make change he is to pay the remainder some other time. worked with Covert & co. We make from $1 to $2.50 per day

Wed. Worked with Covert & co

Thurs. Worked with Covert & co And when we quit work in the evening I went to get my horse but she was gone I struck her trail & followed on to Bills Ranch which is four miles distant Arrived there at dark After having some words about crossing the toll bridge (for I had not one cent of money with me) I started on for the American Ranch seven miles from Bills. Arrived at this place about eleven o'clock. All were asleep so I crept into an old stable "& in a manger laid" tired and supperless I found an old gunny sack on which I laid very comfortable until I began to get cold. I have passed worse nights in California but God knows that was bad enough

Friday Morning. May the 16/56 I arose with day break went to the landlord (whose name is Freeman) and found that the man whom I sold my pistol was not at home I then told the landlord my situation & told him that I did not ask breakfast of him but only a piece of bread at which he stuck up his arristocratic nasal organ grunted out a reply that I did not understand but I plainly saw that he did not wish to comply so I turned & left his house and struck on for Cotton wood 7 mile distant. this place I reached hungry enough. Asked the landlord for some bread He invited me into the dining room but before I had drank one cup of coffee or ate a biscuit the waiter had everything swept away. I arose from the table and left the house I first curst the whole set then I pitied them then I laughed at the affair fixed up my old slouched and torn hat tied up my patched old duck breeches that I had worn for the last six months & had patched almost every Sunday. Improved my old flannel shirt as well as I could and traveled to the prarie house 4 mile distant here I found my horse & returned to American Ranch found the man that I sold my pistol to got some money of him got my dinner left my mare on the ranch (but not with the man who refused me bread) got her pastured & insured at $4 per month returned home.

Sat Worked with Covert & co weather hot Week work to each man $7.50.

Sun Mon. No watter.

Tues. Rain Bought a rifle of Blont that I let him have on a claim last fall for $5

Wedensday Worked half day. Rain

Thurs. The miners on Jack Ass flat & Horsetown made a strike for cheaper watter—price 75 c per inch—which they the miners want three inches for a dollar So on this day they marched en masse in to Shasta City with a band of music at their head playing Hail Columbia they were about six hundred in number & marched two abreast six feet apart Several banners floated gaily oer our heads. (for I was among them) As we entered Shasta we were welcomed by the loud cheers from the citizens However but little good was effected and as yet no compromise has been made. Paid for repairing gun $3

Friday Worked

Sat Laid over weeks work per man $3

Sun. Rested. Rain. Wrote a letter to Wm Willoughby Scotts Valley Cal

Mon. Rain did not work

159

Tues. No watter (Received a letter from J. D. Miller O.T.)
Wedensday Prospected. Made 50 cts
Thurs. Prospected Made 75 cts
Friday Prospected. Made $1.50 cts

Squaw town. Shasta Co. Cal
May 31/56

Twas a calm clear morn in the month of May
And the birds their mations sung
And the dew shone bright in the sun ray glad
As it on the thorn and rose bush hung

That morn I bid a long adieu
To my Father my Mother and home
And said I go in the Siera Nevadas to view
And in her snow covered peaks to roam

But there was one who was dear to me
Oh dearer than ever life has been
She said I vow to be true to you
And you George will be the truest of men

We crossed Missouri's sluggish stream
And many a wide extending plain
Where scarce a single mile is seen
But some poor wretch to rest is lain

I gained the long sought promised land
Where the proud Sacramento rolled
Then I began with heart and hand
To dig for the shining gold

I battled on gainst ill stared fate
In hopes bright wealth to gain
Yes four years I dug both long and late
And yet no wealth is within my main

Sat. June the 1/56.[18] Prospected. Made 50 cts Light showers of rain

160

Squawtown, June 1st, 1856   One day after date I promised to pay Hiner Miller one thousand dollars for value Recd.

[signed] S. Kurov [19] [?]

Sun. Rested Rain

Mon. No watter Prospected made $1.50 cts Miners meeting at I. Melanthys store.

Tues. No watter Went up to the Reservoir and took a grand bath

Wedensdy Miners meeting at Jack Ass flat to determine on what course to pursue as regards to ditch watter. Decided to not use the water which was offered for sale at 50 cts per inch

Thurs Went to work with sluice in co with S Covert D Webster J. W. Criss. Watter 50 cts per inch

Friday Worked until 10 o'clock when the commitee came & forbid us working Cleaned our boxes had $27.12 1/2 cts

Sat Was very unwell took a bath in the Reservoir Bought a box of Moffats Pills

Sunday Was unwell (rested) Weather very hot

Monday June the 9/56. Worked alone with sluice Made 25cts

Tues Worked alone Made $2 Weather hot & dry Wrote a letter to John D. Miller of O. T. that I would be home on the 23 of Oct.

Wedensday Worked alone Made $2 Miners meeting at Horsetown

Tis the 11 day of June in the year of our Lord & Saviour Jesus Christ 1856 and I find myself sitting in the door of my old canvass cabbin in the shade of a clever old oak in company with my best and bravest friend my pipe which as Byron says has by my side a hundred battels bravely fought and yet my pipe deserts me not But darn old Byron, Moore, Shakespeare and all other poets no use for me to try to quote from any of them. But hold I have almost forgotten my subject Let me see oh yes now I savey I was going to describe the beautiful scenery I have of the surrounding world from my cabbin door Oh how beautiful. how transcendantly beautiful are yon snow

161

caped peaks of the Siere Nevadas as the sun who is sinking beneath the western horizon like a brave thought conquered ———— casts his dying gold like rays upon their majestic heads which makes them all like ———— sheathed in hot gold and silver. Golly how I would like to be up there. So it be.

Thurs. Did not work. Took a bath in the Reservoir.

Friday Did not work weather hot and sultry The miners still continue on the strike for cheaper watter Neither working themselves or allowing others to work June the 13/56 Wrote a letter to Hulings Miller of O. T. Worked in the night in co with Webster and Covert. Made $1.50

Sat Worked Saturday night Made $1.12 cts per man
Sunday Worked. Made 00
Monday Rested
Tuesday Rested
[*June 18, 1856*] Wedensday Worked in co with J Criss S Covert D Webster paid $4 per day for watter.
Thurs. Worked

By the hair on Isaacs pate
& beard on Abrahams chin
Ile slay the object of my hate
By making him go in assperity

Hiner Miller

Mans a reaper full of woes
Cuts a capar & down he goes-Anonymous

Cincinatus Hiner Miller
of Union County Indiana

Cincinatus Hiner Miller who was born in Union County Ind in the Year of our Lord 1837 on the 8th day of September Crossed the briny plains in the year 1852 and landed in Oregon on the 26th of September the same year left Oregon for California in 1854 on the 23d of Oct and is now a resident of Squawtown This the 19th of June 1856.

Friday Worked.

Saturday Worked Money to each man $13.12 1/2 cts

Sunday Hired to a man on Oregon Gulch at the rates of $60 per month and board. Yes tomorrow I shall commence operations How I shall succeed to please the great surly burly fellow I know not. Still I will do my best Time will reveal my success So mote it be

Monday Commenced work found them very agreeable boys to work for but we do not work less than 14 hrs each day and it is the hardest of work Oh this is slavery indeed but circumstances compel me to continue work

Tues No watter and was idle.

Wedensday Worked from star light to star light

Thurs No watter.

Friday No watter.

Sat. Worked half day

Sun. Went to the American Ranch after my mare was told by Freeman of the American Ranch that the man that I let have my mare had nothing to do with the ranch & to the best of his knowledge had taken my mare & gone to the states. Returned home in the evening with the conviction that my horse was lost

Mon Worked at my old place for McCoun & Collins

Tues Left off working for McCoun & saw some of the Squaw town boys who advised me to go to Freeman and tell him plainly that if he did not return my mare that they would go down in a body & have a horse at all risks. Went down and after considerable of a noise induced Freeman & Samuel Parker to come out with the truth. That was that they had had her over on Battle Creek 8 miles distant across the Sacramento River. They gave me a horse to ride after her & at sunset after a quarrel such as I hope to never see again I was mounted bareback on my horse galloping away for home. Have paid out $1.50 ferrage went without my dinner & consequently felt growly in my stomach as well as my head Freeman had made way with my rope that I had paid 2 & 50 for. Parker and Freeman are two men that will not scruple to do the darkest deeds & worst of crimes. My mare was in good order

[*July 2, 1856*] Wed. Rested

163

Thurs. Commenced work for ———— Found the work easier than at the former place would continue to work there until my departure for home if I had a safe place to keep my pony

Fri. Worked July 4/56.

Sat. Worked

Sun. Left off work to start north Paid up John Criss the money that I had from him In the evening took a bath in the reservoir There I saw Volney Abbey my old partner who seemed greatly anoyed about some poetry that had been written about him. He accused me of being the author in such a way that I could not well deny (For I was the author) I told him that if he would go to my cabbin and wait until my return he would find out I enjoyed my bath while he Abbey returned to the store of Melanthy and wrote a card accusing the writer of said poetry of everything that was wrong On my return I saw it and wrote below to the surprise of all present (I am the author, Hiner Miller) Then sat down and enjoyed the surprise of my old friends. In a few minutes the pompous advance of Abbey was noticed He carried a double-barreled shot gun and was accompanied by Gomes, J. and P. Mc. I then slipped off to my cabbin, loaded my riffle determined to meet him on equal footing but the men said I should not have my gun so I met him unarmed I told him that I was the author of the piece that amazed him so badly After talking pretty rough with him some time while he made the air blue with curses I left him set him down in my mind as a notorious coward.

The Poetry

Ye poets will open wide your eyes
Excuse me for being gabby
For I write of the renown of a man in town
By the name of Volney Abbey

Wise Dr. Gates thus speaks and prates
Though you know he is somewhat gabby
I been bereft of some flour I left
I believe by Volney Abbey

164

Monday Morning. Bid adieu to Squaw town. My debts, accounts, etc etc were as follows one joint note with Volney Abbey to N. Walcott for the sum of $28 due Christmas 1855 It is not lawful first because he failed to fill his contract One separate note to S. Johns for the sum of $15. It also is unjust I have paid Melanthy but he says I still owe him $3.30 cts I have Wm. Johnstons & Clymers note for the sum of $75 I have given Clymer a receipt. Abbey is owing me $3.75 Squaw town for the present farewell I leave thee for Yreka with a pony and rigging worth $100 rifle worth $20 & $5.25 in pocket Hurrah for little me In good health in good spirits Whats to hinder me from being happy, nothing will, nothing can The world may go as it will I will still be happy Bought in Shasta pipe and tobacco 25 cts bread 50 cts sausage —— cts strap $1.00 shirt 75 cts ——

Tues. Arrived at Portuguese Flat and I met my old partner Joe De Blony

Wed. Remained on the flat.

Thurs. Night started for the Lower Soda Spring, which place Joe was still holding on to Passed my old cabin that I had built the summer before but it was so dark that I could not see it.

Fri. Helped Joe to haul some brush for a fence with oxen they were the first oxen I had drove for nearly two years

Sat. do

Sun. Drove the oxen to ——— River 12 mile distant on the head of the Sacramento River Had a view of our old battle ground at the distance of 10 mile

[*July 14, 1856*] Mon. From this Monday up to the next I have but little to add save that we went in to Squaw Valley on the latter end of the week for we have entirely lost track of the day of the week or month.

November the 20/56
Lower Soda Spring
Shasta Co California

Sir Edward Parish

After an absence of so long a time I take my pen in

165

hand to drop you a few lines with the double purpose of hearing from and being heard from. As to my whereabouts that you will know by the caption of this epistle. And as to my proceedings since last I saw you & my present occupation I shall now proceed to give you a short sketch. You have long since heard of my awkward and unlucky manner of leaving home which was some two years ago. I reach Yreka on the 12th of Nov/54. I spent the winter mining in that vicinity in co with some Oregonians that I had formerly known I made enough to buy me a good horse a mule and a good outfit & in the spring of /55 I started for the head watters of the McCloud River as there was then a great excitement about new mines in that region. On our route we camped at this verry place which was then unsettled there we had our horses and provisions stollen by the Indians. We raised a company followed and fought them in the Devils Castle. Many of the Indians were killed and we were victorious with the loss of three killed and five wounded. I was numbered among the latter an arrow struck me fore on the left side and came out at the back of my neck it was an awful wound and I thought I would die ah it was a terrible thing Ed to lay there among the dead and the dieing of both friends and enemys. What wild and dreadful thoughts crowded through my mind But thank God I have recovered. We could get none of the horses or things that we lost & so again I was broke and obliged to stay on this the Sacramento River In September/55 I left this place for Shasta City there I mined until the first of July/56 I made money to buy me a horse saddle and rigging for one hundred and twenty-five dollars then with $5 & riffle revolver etc I started for Yreka and as this place lay on my road[20]

November the 20/56
Lower Soda

To Merinda Parish
    Yes here Merinda I will pen my thoughts My own very secret thoughts Here alone so far away from the world

166

they will never reach the eyes of mortals much less reach you then this can harm none it gives me a feeling of melancholy to recall to memory those few days of happiness so dear to me but by you alas so soon forgotten. We were young you were bright in what the world calls wealth and rich in maiden loveliness and you were proud but it seemed to me that it was that very pride that made you so beautiful it seemed that you were so far superior to me and yet you loved me Merinda you said you loved me it was your own rosy lips oer-flowing with loveliness that made the confession Ah can it be false No no it was not false you loved me then with all the ardor of a devoted heart but separation brought a change Merinda I do not blame you such is the human heart such is life as I said you were rich I was poor and I felt humbled to see the difference in our stations in life It was for that that I left my home It was for to make myself thy equal in wealth that I left my peaceful home and kind parents and came to this land where it was said a fortune was easily made I came and I was unfortunate was unwell and how I suffered Yet I battled on against it all It was for your sake Merinda You who was then the goddess of my existence my star my hope my everything. Yes had it not been that your dear memory cheered me on I would have sunk beneath my load of trouble for nearly two years it was thus when one day as I returned from my work the expressman handed me a letter it was from my brother he wrote that all was well that they hoped soon to see me at home and at the conclusion jokingly remarked that Merinda Parish was married to Samuel H——— it was an awful thought. Could there be a mistake I read the name over and over again It was too plain he had wrote the name too plain for me to cheat myself in to the belief that it was someone else.[21]

Dec. the 20 or 30th 1856. Crossed the mountains between this place and Lower Soda The snow is from 8 to 10 feet deep the snow in the valley is 5 & 6 there is a crust that will bear my weight

Numshoos Indian snow shoe, the top of the shoe is made of a bow of vine maple wood then crossed as the figure shows with braided horse hair then wrapt with buck skin to keep the hard snow from cutting the hair and the shoe is finished Squaw Valley

Jan. the 11/57 O.B. and Miller Dr to Rees & Co to 25 lbs. flour $2.50 to 2 lbs. sugar .50

December the 5/56 Hiner Miller Dr to Rees & Co to sugar 13 lbs $3.25 to 1 plug tobacco .25

Jan. the 22-30/57 Hiner Miller Dr. to Rees & Co

Jan. 22. My Indian and myself eat one meal each of bread and meat at home of Rees & Co

Jan. 23. One meal each do

24. Two meals each do

25. Indian eat one meal and went to Squaw Valley. Carried meat to McClouds house Ate 1 meal

26. Ate two meals at Rees & Co do

27. Ate one meal—went to Portuguese Flat

28. Ate one meal at Rees & Co

29. Ate two meals

30. Ate one meal. Went to Squaw Valley.

Hiner of Oregon

Feb the 4/57 McCloud Valley California Today I find the weather cloudy and some appearance of snow there is a hard crust on the snow which would almost bear up a horse the snow in the valley is about three feet deep it has been during the winter eight feet deep today I am in my cabbin with my pokona [wife] a trying to recruit up for I have had some hard times the last few months though I find it poor recruiting for it keeps me busy attending to drying the Elk meat

Feb the 5th Started to hunt for bear our——————said the Indians would show us where there was one in a tree but it was a false alarm Snow fell last night 6 in. deep it still continues snowing today.

Feb 6 Cold & Windy Light snow. Orr myself & Pokona Went prospecting two miles below in a gulch Poured out dirt got about 1 cent in all. Saw considerable otter signs on the bank of Squaw Valley.

Feb the 7 Last night was coldest night I have ever experienced in this valley

February the 8 1857 Went on Elk hunt in company with the old chief and 15 of his warriors Orr and myself making 17 in all The old chief carried a yoger as well as our selves. The snow was hard but the weather was so cold that I could not bear to breathe through my nostrils the Indians were all armed with bows and arrows & knives & clothed principally in skins the chief took the lead and his warriors followed in single file About 10 oclock we struck the McCloud River this river about 50 yards wide and very deep it is the clearest and brightest stream that I ever saw.

Is not fordable at this place in the lowest water. We however managed to cross on drift wood after an hour working, climbing and crawling through the watter up to our knees here we saw plenty of Elk signs. We followed up the bank of the river about two miles until we struck a small creek which I named Jordan the elk had taken up this stream and we followed after the signs was near a week old when we struck it but they grew fresher as we followed on. We followed up Jordan Creek about 4 miles until the elk turned up on the North Mountain side. The signs was fresh and it was likely that they had scented us By their long trot-like steps they trotted over the snow as if it had been solid earth A hasty council of war was held and it was agreed that we should continue the pursuit and on we went helter skelter rip and tear up and down hills and over the timber as fast as we could run over the hard frozen snow. I was fast falling in the rear when after about five miles we struck the head of the McCloud here

170

they formed a halt; another council was held. The word was follow we plunged into the river and crossed It was not more here than a small brook. We followed about a mile as fast as we could run and I was again falling in the rear when I saw the Indians draw their band When I came up the band was just climbing up the bank of the river and were about 50 in number I pulled on the first one that I saw but my yoger snaped. The next I aimed at was a three year old heifer that an Indian had shot. I was out of breath & shot badly as to only break its leg but this was enough I then crossed the river & followed the band. I met one acoming back I shot at it 60 yds but I was so out of breath that I could not hold my yoger steady & I missed it. I reloaded and shortly I saw a three year old standing a cross the river about 280 yds off I now determined to redeem my character so walking up to a tree I took steady aim At the shot she fell with a ball through her lights and she was my meat by this time the band had got clear out of reach and I gave up the chase and when they all had come together we found that there had been but two three year old and two one year olds the other white man killed none there was a great many shot with arrows that escaped. We then struck a camp in a valley of about 5000 acres which the Indians say is covered with beautiful meadows and teems with deer in the summer I named the valley Paradise Valley We had no blankets and we suffered with cold It was impossible to sleep.

February the 9th The Indians again followed after the elk but Orr and myself took 20 lbs of meat and started for home We gave the remainder of the meat to the Indians We reached home at sunset with no further adventure but I was very tired and moved to hunt no more until I was compelled to. The Indians returned but got no more meat.

February the 10th Cut some timber to make sluice boxes Heard that John Hale was coming with a co of men to kill the Indians Went to see the chief in the evening and while we were talking with him we heard white men talking This they thought was Hale for there had been no whites in the valley this winter except us two. They were ready for the attack in a moment but they soon found that it was Joe coming after hay the horses walked on the snow he brought my mare

Feb. the 11/57. Worked at sluice boxes. Weather cloudy with the appearance of snow

Feb. about the 25. The past two weeks have been rather eventful days. The weather was rainy for three or four days then the Indians got out of grub and danced all night for rain to stop but it still continued to rain The next night the dance was renewed I was present at the dance The Indians all having gathered in the chief took a seat in their center One lit his pipe. After smoking for some time in silence he commenced a kind of humming noise such as O a, no a, etc In this he was shortly joined by all present I among the rest Yes I the high-minded proud souled Hiner Miller join in a digger Indian dance for a change of weather Well really I must laugh and wonder at myself Yet after all what can there be wrong about it I say that it is nothing I who have been raised in a Christian country who have been taught to go weekly to the house of God and there offer up my prayers and to kneel at the family alter when the shades of evening gather round I say that in their prayers offered up to the God of their being there is more true faith more pure religion & less hypocrisy than there is in the best branch of worshipers that the Christian religion ever gave birth to

At the dance there were about 90 Indians present but 3 danced at once No one was allowed to dance but those of high family. The chief dancing all the while in the operation I lost my pipe Damn the luck

The next day it stopped raining & the next I went hunting elk in co with ten Indians (in the line of provisions I had two cakes of shorts the Indians had nothing) we traveled all day on tracks and at dusk camped on the head of Mud Creek through the day I and the Indians ate three fourths of the bread we had nothing in the morning. I divided my bread with them amounting about an ounce to each man I fared no better than the rest. A light snow fell during the night but I rested very well in the morning most of the Indians rose & striped naked waded through the snow to Mud Creek about one

172

hundred yds. distant then plunged into the water &
remained there paddling and swimming as much as five
minutes then returned to the fire and dressed the snow at
this place I figured to be a foot deep there was a crust that
would bear without snow shoes The next morning we
were on the road at day break The Indians traveled as
well as though they had dined at the Astor House but it
was very difficult for me to keep pace with them. Snow
fell thick & fast during the day at about 12 oclock we
came up on the Elk & I was soon left in the rear The
game travelled on the snow as well as any of us but they
were so harrassed by Indian dogs that the Indians
managed to slay 12 in a few hours I saw but one elk &
never fired a shot but the Indians said there was over one
hundred in the band. they appeared to continue their
course up Shasta Buttes that evening we sent for our
squaws and the next day they came here we spent two or
three days in jerking the meat and recruiting. One whole
Elk was given to me all ready dressed at the end of three
days we prepared for another hunt & I and seven Indians
took up the line of march the chief did not go when we
started there was a crust on the snow that would bear but
as we advanced up the steep hill side of the Butte this
gave way until we were obliged to put on our snow shoes
the snow after half days traveling up the mountain side
became so light that we sank to our knees it seemed as
if — but yesterday tall fir trees were covered with one solid
block of snow and as they shot up high in the air above us
like some vast pyramid of marble I could not help but
view it with admiration then the clouds came floating
past now they rode slowly past beneath our feet like some
mighty God of air and as the sun came down in her full
glory upon them they seemed to be some vast sea or ocean
studded here and there with Isles of never fading summer
Oh who could gaze upon this grand this impressive sight
& not say within his heart that it is beautiful, that it is
good & that there is a God or a creator of his being and
all beautiful world We descended in almost the same
direction that we came & shortly came upon Elk tracks
we followed these a few miles when the dogs found an old
male black bears den in the roots of an old cedar tree he

173

was induced by the noise of the dogs to come out and he was immediately pierced with arrows He would weigh about three hundred lbs and was the fattest as well as the largest I have even seen in the country I with three Indians returned to camp with the meat The others followed with the elk they were first in camp having killed two elk John my Indian killed one of these the Indians would not allow me to eat salt on the bear meat they say they will have bad luck in killing more The Indians say that in this place they are very numerous

The next day I went with my Indian to bring in the elk he had killed the next day I packed it to Squaw Valley on a horse the next day I started for Lower Soda with my mare and — mule, 200 lbs on each Could not make the trip returned, turned out the horses had a talk with Bill & he in a very friendly manner told me that he was going to do some big work on his claim that he has taken up.

March 10/57 Started from Squaw Valley for Pitt River in company with two Indians one I have had living with me for nearly a year the other is a —————— from off main Pitt river but they were both starting to the country to which I was traveling as well as myself My object in going was to learn all that I could concerning the massacre of the white settlers in Pitt River Valley and the situation of the hostile Indians I was armed with a yoger only my Indian with a yoger as well as a pistol the other Indians was armed with a bow and arrows our provisions consisted of one —————— salt sack full of elk meat all told. We started at day break and traveled on the hard snow until the snow became so soft that we were obliged to put on our snow shoes I traveled without a moments rest until the —————— of light was sinking his shield like form behind the snow covered peaks of the coast range which —————— loomed up in the far far off west —————— to be sheathed in a coat of ever shining silver and at that moment I stood on the great divide between the McCloud and Pitt River and far to the east at the foot of the divide on which I stood could be seen the smoke from the Indians camp rising high in the air and there forming & floating away into clouds and had it not been for the keen eye of my Indian I think it would have not been detected

174

by my hunt after making certain that it was smoke I determined to descend and spy out their location thinking I could reach it that night but I was mistaken as it grew dark I commenced descending the mountain (at the summit I should judge the snow was 8 feet deep for I crossed afterwards about the first of May & snow was there in places 4 feet deep) Nothing worth relating happened until about 10 oclock at night when I struck a small run as I thought which I wished to cross as we all had moccasins on and were wet to our knees I told my Indian to cross over and I would follow but he appeared to fear—so growling at his tardiness I handed him my gun and jumped in I found no bottom but I managed to climb out on the opposite bank on the brush but I was completely soaked with the ice watter from head to foot God but the air was blue with maledictions. this as I afterwards—is a good sized stream called Bear river and the place called Bear Valley and strange to say the very spot where I leaped in the river as I afterwards discovered was the place where a cattle drover by the name of Ross had been killed the summer previous The Indians crossed below on a log We went on for two hours when my Indian gave out and I was compelled to heal the Indians of soreness from travelling so long My Indian took it upon himself to act as doctor He commenced a low pow wow of a song and sucking with his mouth. In the course of half an hour he declared himself ready to travel and we set out. When I arose to continue I thought I should perish from cold my blanket and every particle of clothing that was not immediately against the skin was froze as hard as bone We continued our journey until near daylight when the river made a big bend Here we halted took off our clothes and managed to wade the stream. Daylight came and we—but after steady traveling until 10 oclock we came in sight of houses in a small valley near where Bear River empties into Pit River I passed on to the second house whose top had battered in from immense weight of snow while effecting an entrance to this I discovered a few hundred yards distant three or four Squaws they shortly after disappeared & I felt certain that we had been discovered I then went to

175

work and build scaffolds in the corners of the house upon the rubbish blocked up the doors etc & found when I had it completed that it was a place that could be defended against almost any number of Indians I then directed my two Indians to each take a corner & took two myself & calmly awaited the attack my Indians appeared eager for a fight They however did not come. perhaps we had not been discovered. as it grew dark I could see their camp fires to the north of us about half a mile distant & on the other side of Bear River I then passed out of my fort toward their camp fires (which were seven in number) to reconoitre they were camped on the banks of the river which was about thirty yards wide I found it impossible to cross the stream & so I could approach no nearer I could hear them talking very lively & my Indians said it was concerning the whites they talked the Pushoos or Pitt River language and I was unable to understand them. I calculated they were forty-five or fifty in number & their position I discovered was a strong one. Having made every discovery I thought necessary we set out on our return. My Indians advised me to go down Pitt River Valley until we came to friendly Indians where we could get some provisions as we had eat our last elk meat that afternoon we proceeded a mile or two as the Indians had advised when I began to be apprehensive of the good will towards me of the friendly Indians we were about to visit. So I determined to return the way we came It was a desperate undertaking to cross sixty miles.[22]

"He that walked with wise men shall be wise; but the companions of fools shall be destroyed," Prov, 13:20

An extract from the Journal of J Langley
Captain of the Volunteers of Yreka for Pitt River,
which Company I joined about 15 of March 1857

Attacked an Indian camp about two hundred strong April the 2d. 57 the expedition was commanded by Whitney Many arrows were discharged by the Indians but without effect. They finally fled it was uncertain how many were killed or whether any were slain or not.

Another camp was attacked on the east fork of Pitt River at a place called the Rappids the Indians were about one hundred and fifty strong. Our party was eleven in number Whitney attacked the enemy at break of day with five persons including himself While I took the remainder of our party and lay in ambush and met the enemy as they retreated fifteen of the Indians were slain and eighteen taken prisoners all of which were turned free as they were squaws and children, except one warrior which was hung.

April the 13th/57. Took 5 squaws and one buck hung the buck and freed the squaws

April the 23. Attacked two or three Indians in the hills on the Main Pitt River the expedition was commanded by Capt. Langly. the Capt was in the fight I commanded part of the attacking party thirty nine Indians were left dead on the field None of the whites were hurt a number of prisoners all of which were turned free except the children, sixteen of which were taken into the settlements by the volunteers. I remained with the Co until the close of the war.

Hiner Miller

Squaw Valley May 1857

Indulgent reader whoever you be fellow traveler down the broad stream of life come enter the grand theatre of play with me again the curtain has fell and rose again since you were here but it has arose upon a new scene I arose this morning from my bed at about 9 o'clock the sun was shining through the cracks of the cabbin. The meadow larks the swamp black birds Robin red breast as well as all the beautiful songsters of the forest were pouring forth their sweetest notes as if in praise of the great God of Day for spreading his bright rays over hill & vale & driving away the mists of night and making all look so lovely and so happy I dressed myself in my clothes washed myself combed my long hair and ate my breakfast well what did I eat now friend well as a sober fact I will tell you well it consisted of venison roots and cold water. I have not had more than this for the last three weeks I have not seen a white man in that time or tasted bread and yet I am happy Certainly how could I be otherwise when all nature in her lovliest attire and everything so gay and happy around me Yet I cannot but help feeling lonely at times a transient wish to sit down to a table of plenty as I have been raised to associate with my own kith and kin and converse in my own sweet english tongue.

This is indeed a lovely day My Indian has gone a hunting with the break of day My squaw is out digging roots my dog is lying at my feet my riffle is by my side my pipe is in my mouth a dozen or more naked Digger Indians that follow me from one place in the morning to another are lying stretched out around in the bright sunshine and I trying to pen the scene and this is the calm scene of today. You see I have chosen from my subject no desperate Indian fight with a dozen against me in mortal encounter with a Grizzley being lost in some wild fastness of the mountains where white mans foot never before has trod or living three or four days on nothing at all And such scenes as these are commoner for me to meet with than it is for me to meet a white man or to eat a piece of bread

McCloud River
May the 20/57

I'm beneath a tall and shading pine
a sitting at its foot sire
I'll take the pains to drop a line
That I might read in future

Lower Soda June 4
Amiable & intelligent self you are now seated before a writing desk & sitting in an easy & comfortable chair Your ink stand is just in the right place & if you happen to drop a pen it falls upon the clean swept floor & instead of

178

having to hunt for it half an hour among the leaves & grass you have nothing to do but to pick it up. Well well but what of such nonsense Nothing-a mere nothing only this is more pleasant than to be sitting on some old log with my book on my knee and my ink stand setting upon the ground. Hurrah for me. Day after tomorrow I am to leave this part of Gods chosen country that I have haunted so long & travel to the north yes towards my own loved Oregon then farewell diggers both friendly & unfriendly goodbye to the clear blue watters of McCloud No more upon your green grassy banks beneath the shadowing pine will I sit and smoke my pipe & watch your rippling watters as it rushes on to the deep dark sea like the mighty stream of life. What a subject to reflect upon. Farewell to your pine covered mountains and snow covered peaks never again over your craggy summits or down through your fearful chasams will I hunt the mountain lion or fight the dreaded grizzly bear Adieu my own sweet lovely valley my Paradise of peace & loveliness How can I part from you without a tear & when far far away it will be with a sigh that I ll remember you To think that no more down by the clear brooks side I will hunt the bounding deer or through the tall green grass or shadowy willows I ll trail the black bear or sitting beside a gushing spring bright as the fountain of youth, tell my tale of love your own dark eyed native maids fare thee well you clear & rushing watters with your thousand enticements Good bye you towering mountains with your scenes of daring & romance. Adieu Adieu my own bright vale my paradise of loveliness To you all inviting as you are I must say good bye but perhaps it will be only for a season So smoke the bee

Hiner Miller of the McCloud Mountains

Lower Soda Springs. Shasta Co
June the 9/57.

This is a cloudy day but pleasant I was delayed from leaving this place as I had expected but if nothing contrary turns up I shall be able to leave tomorrow morning in the few days that I have been here I have

been doing every thing and nothing in particular   I
assisted the boys in repairing their fence until I blistered
my hands. I then proposed to them if they would let me
have a horse, I would go to Squaw Valley & kill them a
deer to this they agreed so I started early in the morning
the Indian that came over with me went also my Mahala
[woman] also IIII——————the next day after I arrived, I
killed a fine buck deer & put him in sacks and so brought
him home. Old Black beard the McCloud chief is in
Squaw Valley with most of his Indians. They all appeared
glad to see me & were sorry to see me leave especially
my little Mahala who shed many a bitter tear at the idea
of my departure. So farewell my own loved mountains my
adopted home
Hiner Miller of the McCloud Mountains

[*Undated*] The father of Worrotetot or Black Beard as
he is generally called by the whites had seven wives and
was chief of a large scope of country lying to the north
south and east of Shasta Butte he was the war chief and
his warriors in their glory numbered about eighteen
hundred they had been for a long time engaged in a war
with the Narshoos as they were called (Their country lay
in & about where Shasta City now stands) They been very
successful in their wars up to the time of their glory which
was about the year 1800 but the tide of war changed the
brave old chief lost battles until he was obliged to
surrender almost one half of his country   It was the
portion of the country reaching from a few miles above
Shasta City up to the mouth of the McCloud

Indian tounge spoken on [*ms torn*] of the sacramento River

Indian	wintune	winthu.n (attributive)
white man	yapiton	ya.paytu.n
negro	chululu yapiton	čulu.li ya.paytu.n
dog	suku	suku
cat	how	ha.w "fox"
elk	cola	qu.la "elkhide"
deer	nope	no.p
Grizzly Bear	wemir	wimah (particular case) or wimay (generic case)
Black Bear	cheele	č'ił
cow	wohow	whua. (Spanish)
horse	mula	Spanish mula "mule"
fox	how	ha.w (cf. no. 5.)
kiyota [sic]	lubellas	lubeles "wolf"
birds	chil chil	č'ilčił
duck	cat cat	qa.tqat
to be mad	chillick	čileq (said of a man)
to hate	donl	danal
to love	hinma	hayna or hayhayna
to be friendly	tintin	tintin "to chat, to talk to each other"
my love	net layoure	xun-lakča˘ "to embrace, to hug" (?)
my wife	net pakona	net p'oqana
my husband	net we	netwi.h
man	mochacho	Spanish muchacho "boy"
woman	machacha	Spanish muchacha "girl"
baby	pickonina	probably from English pickaninny

181

[*ms torn*]	caroh	ca/oro-ʔ
[*ms torn*]	loop	lu·p "vagina"
[*ms torn*]	cooler	ku.li "penis"
[*ms torn*]	cewe	siwih siwiy "testicles"
[*ms torn*]	loop batler	lu·p baɫa "To have the first menstruation"
[*ms torn*]	loop doccus	lu.p doqos "semen"
[*ms torn*]	shidda	sire "to copulate"
[*ms torn*]	loop bidra	lu·p pira· "man to be sex-hungry"

head	puiyouk	phoyoq
eye	tom	tum "eyes, face"
ear	mat	ma.t
nose	sono	sono
tongue	terl	tahaɫ
teeth	ce	si.
hands	sim	sem
feet	my	may
moccasin	tommouse	t'amu.s
pants	pontotocklos	panti-t'aɫas
shirt	wenomcoddy	wenem-k'odit
hat	tackey	thaki
hair	tommoy	tamoy
blanket	checkloose	č'e.kɫoyos
water	mim	mem me.m
snow	yolla	yo.la
rain	luha	luhe· "to rain", luhes "rain"
river	mem	mem me.m
to swim (yourself)	tula	thule.
to wash	elsupona	ʔel-sopna. "to take clothes off to wash them"

to wash clothes	slosha	ɫo.sa
to make	peachuice	piyeča "to fix"
flour	chottus	č'otos "bread"
bread	chottus	č'otos
fire	po	pho.h
make fire	po duchu	pho.h· doču "make a fire!"
		pho.h duča "to make a fire"
wood	chuice	č'u.s
chop	cope	k'op "chop!"

182

ax	chomos	čaˑmis
knife	kilakila	k'elek'ele
all tool-maker	chope	k'op "chop"
frying pan	sutul pulluk	Spanish saltar "to fry" + pulu.q "container"
basket	pollok	pulu.q (cf. preceding item)
cup	collum	k'olom "cup, bucket, basket"
gun	colloul	k'ulu.l
bullets	doccus	doqos
powder	powder	this English loanword is not used by my informants
caps	caps	not used by my informants
Indian bow	colloul	k'ulu.l (cf. "gun" above)
arrow	doccus	doqos (cf. "bullets" above)
to fall down	pomondilly	pomin-dile
to fall off	condilly	ken-dile
to throw on the ground	potdilly	pat-dile
to mire down	cone harry	q'une. hare.
go ahead	tucado	tu-k'odu "go ahead!"
go farter [*probably farther*]	honharry	ho.n hare.
be quick	wittilla	witila
sit down	kentla	kinta.
spot to live	bohaw	buha "to live"
lay down	bima	bima.
sleep	bo	meant to be identical with word for "lay down"? xi.na "to sleep"
laying there	okin bea	ʔukin biya
lay it there	okin yalla	ʔukin yala.
there	okin	ʔukin
here	aiu [*or*] aiw	ʔew
when	heshen	he-sin
what	pa	pe.h
where	hecea [*or hecen?*]	heke or heke.n
what for	heshtom	hestam
who	heceat	heket
today	po	po.
tomorrow	hemir	hima.

183

day after tomorrow	uice [or *uce*] hemir	ʔus-hima .
yesterday	lendar	le . nda
day before yesterday	uice lenda	ʔus-le . nda
a few days back	lendada	lendada
a good while back	hon lendada	ho(.)n lendada
a great while back	tune hon lendada	tune ho(.)n lendada
one	cotate	kʼete . t
two	pallel	pa . lel
three	panul	panuɫ
four	clouit	ƛʼa . wit
five	chany	čʼani
comb	kryhous	kʼi . hus
lice	donos	donos
hair	tommoy	tamoy
hungry	bidra	pira .
eat	bar [*cʔ*]|	ba .
want to eat	bas boyou	ba . kuya .
want watter	mem lipada	mem lipeda "I want water, I am thirsty"
cup of watter	collim	kʼolom
give to me	duaya	duya . "to give"
give to him	dayout	doyu . t "give it to me"!
[*ms torn*]	annucada	ʔanukada "I don't want to do it, I don't like it, I don't want it"
[*ms torn*]	yole tone [*ʔ*]	yalito . na- ? "to fall or throw out"
[*ms torn*]	todaca	tede . ka "to bleed"

Parlel sas Panul sonahi 1857

Worrotatot pona [?] Charley Puakin

Umona net cotta awin hondar boha awin boha awin minel nish cotta donl yopaton bass nish cotta donl yapaton Pakon net Wintune Pakon nish hinna net pakon cotto hina ne hewahe ne cola upsha nope upsha chele wemir hewahe net upsha nope la net cotta cottera nish cotta hinna bohaw oulace

Po cotta temir yolla poeka [?] sas illohim Bill Orr y harra bass peachuice. Pakon Wintune bass harra onnucada boha awin tin Bill Orr pakona.

Lenda net tin nish donl Wintune Cote wintune nish cotta donl allce [?] widar boha awin una parlel mochache neta pakona liquet wi [?] cotate pushoos cotate numshoos lendada us us cotate numshoos cope Larkin poyouk Larkin minel depo Yopaton lidd [?][wimna [?][mochacha yopaton cota witil upshu

Parlel	sas	Panul	sonahi 1857					[Miller]
pa. lel	sas	panut	saniha					[Schlichter]
two	sun	three	to be daytime					[English translation]

Worrotatot	pona [?] Charley Puakin
woro. ta-to. t	
short (one)	

Umona	net	cotta	awin	hondar	boha	awin	boha	awin
yomoyna	net		ʔewin	honda	buha	ʔewin	buha	ʔewin
remember	my		here	long, far	live	here	live and	here

minel	nish	cotta	donl	yopaton	bass	nish	cotta	donl
minel	nis		danal	ya. paytu.	ba.s	nis		danal
dead	me		hate	white man	food	me		hate

yapaton	Pakon	net	Wintune	Pakon	nish	hinna
ya. paytu.	p'uqa / p 'uqana	net	winthu. n		nis	hayna
white man	woman / marry	my	Indian	woman?	me	love

net pakon cotto   hina   ne   hewahe ne   cola   upsha
net   [see   hayna   ni   hewehi ni   qu.le   yupča
my   above]   love   I   again I   elk   shoot

nope   upsha   chele   wemir   hewahe net   upsha   nope   la
no.p   yupča   či.r   wimay   hewehi net   yupča   no.p
deer   shoot   meat   grizzly again my   shoot   deer

net   cotta   cottera nish   cotta   hinna   bohaw   oulace
net   nis   hayna   buha   ?ule.s
my   me   love   live   as if

Po   cotta   temir | yolla | poeka [?] sas   illohim Bill Orr
                            | yalla |
po. | yo.la | sas
                            | yala |
now | snow | sun   Bill Orr
                            | to stop|

y   harra   bass   peachuice Pakon   Wintune bass
way   hare.   ba.s   piyeča   [see above] winthu.n ba.s
north   go   food   make   woman?   Indian food

harra   onnucada boha   awin   tin   Bill Orr
hare.   ?anukada buha   ?ewin   tin
go   I don't like live here say   Bill Orr

pakona.
| p'uqana |
| p uqa |
| to marry |
| woman |

Lenda   net   tin   nish   donl   Wintune Cote wintune
Le.nda   net   ti(.)n nis   danal   winthu.n ko.t winthu.n
Yesterday my   say   me   hate   Indian all Indian

nish   cotta   donl   allce [?] widar
nis   danal | wayda? |
                                      | waydal? |
me   hate | from the north |
                                      | from south to north |

186

boha   awin   una   parlel   mochache   neta/o   pakona
buha   ?ewin   pa.lel   muchacha/o   neto   p'oqana
and   here   two   woman/man   my   wife
live

liquet   wi [?]   cotate   pushoos   cotate   numshoos   lendada   us us
layk'ut?   k'ete.t puysu.s   k'ete.t   nomsu.s   lendada
younger   one   Pit River one   Trinity   long ago
  sister   Indian   Indian

cotate   numshoos   cope   Larkin   poyouk   Larkin   minel   depo
k'ete.t nomsu.s   k'upa   phoyoq   minel   tipa.
one   Trinity   chop   Larkin   head   Larkin   dead   became
         Indian

yopaton   lidd [?] wimna [?] mochacha   Yopaton   cota   witil   upshu
ya.paytu.   muchacha   ya.paytu.   witil   yupča
white man   woman   white man   fast   shoot.

187

Aug. 30
McAdams Creek

Mr. Langly
Dear Sir:
   I embrace the present opportunity of writing to you concerning my discharge of which I can get no track neather of yourself although I have called on ———— S. Berry and others who have a right to know but to no purpose If I mistake not when we parted on the head watters of the McCloud you promised to write to me as soon as you reached Yreka and send me my discharge but I have received nothing of that nature I have been at home since I saw you and now that I have returned I would be glad to get my discharge and you would oblige & accommodate me very much by sending it to me in a letter to Yreka. I would be very glad to see you and talk over our broils and battles in Pitt River So write to me soon and tell me where the boys all are and what they are doing etc
   No more at present but remaining

Yours obediently
                    Hiner Miller of the McCloud.

P.S. I think that I shall quit the mountains forever.
                    Hiner Miller

                Copied, corrected & sent to
                Mr. Capt. John Langly of
                Yreka Aug 30/57.

                McAdams Creek Siskiyou Co California
                                        Aug the 31/57
Dear ————
   I arrived at this place on the 26 in good health and excellent spirits after a pleasant though rather tedious journey I beg leave to attribute my safe arrival to your well wishes etc this is a beautiful Sabbath morning the

188

miner has laid the pick and shovel by to rest. The eternal
din of drill and sledge is hushed in respect for the
Sabbath And all man and nature seems in quiet repose
Some of the miners are seen hurrying away to the grog
shop to drown their memories and drown their purses in
well filled glasses Others seek their bunks to dream of the
happy future While a few stern & steady old fathers are
quietly wending their way to the village church. but I will
employ my leisure moments by dropping a line to my
————— I am daily in the company of your brothers
Willis & Robert besides a host of cousins all of which I
have become acquainted there is Niles Ben Bill Jim etc
all good jovial honest hearted fellows however no more of
this You perhaps are aware that they are good boys and
that is enough they are all enjoying good health and are
doing well as regards money matters Rob and I have
some famous old times together and enjoy our selves as
well as could be expected in this isolated part of Gods foot
stool

In writing the two awkwardly framed notes that I
handed you while at home it is possible that you may
think that I over-stepped the rules of decorum in
expressing my sentiments toward you If so I beg you to
reconsider the circumstances in which I was placed. My
hasty departure my uncertainty regarding matters in
which I was so deeply concerned etc. etc though God
knows that I did not falsify my own true feelings You
were frank with me — and for this I would thank you a
thousand times over and so I hope you will not be
offended at my own plainess but be as plain & frank in
turn

I did not intend when I began this letter to weary you
with anything so long and tedious but you see I have been
mistaken. Some half witted bard in writing of things of
which I think he knows nothing about says

> Write to her regarding war or win
> And drop but few brief lines within
> But let them be of witty style
> And beam with loves own beauteous smile

189

Behave with proud and pompous air
And you will win her maiden care

But I am a going to disagree with the poet in every respect. And I hope you will follow my example in writing a lengthy letter hastily and unreserved and I know you would if you only knew how often I have read the letter you handed me or how often I may still read it but indeed, cease this dull scribbling or I fear you will grow impatient When you handed me your letter you exacted secrecy of me in which I trust I have kept my promise I now ask the same of you as regards my fathers family especially
 Lady of my choice adieu. You will write to me immediately and often if you think propper (and you must think it propper) So—farewell and believe your truly and affectionate through life
Hiner Miller

Copied corrected and sent & sent to Miss Mary J. Tompkins at Willamette Forks, Oregon
Sept the 2/57
PS Write to Yreka
 Siskyou Co. Cal

McAdams Creek Siskiyou County California

Sept the 5/57

Reader who eer you are or wherever you be
You must go into fancies flight with me
Over mountain and vale in fancys flight
Now pause until half up Shastas hight
Here seat you on this throne of snow
And turn your wearied gaze below
On hill or dale or mumuring brook
And read Gods name in natures book
But look there see you just below

190

That form thats up the steep approaching
Straining climbing over the snow
And on our hermitage emerging
Tis a human form of our kind and race
For I now discern his figure and face
So I will ask what he seeks in this dreary place
Hush Ye Hark nay do not speak
Nor ask from whence or why he came
Alone hes climed this snowy peak
In search of bright immortal fame
His pistols and knife to his side are swung
A mantle over his shoulders flung
Pen ink and scroll he brings along
To paint in prose or stirring song
This mount of everlasting snow
Her thousands beauteous scenes below
On on brave bard though your limbs you break
A few steps more and on the topmost peak
Of the snowy white bright shining crown
Of Californias proudest king

Who alone can laugh at ages frown
For time with him no changes bring
The steps hes made made the hight hes now
Now downward turns his anxious eyes
As lightning through the heavens rim
He views the world that neath him lies
Glorious sight his lips declare
Then overcome with awe he kneels
Humbly bowed his head and bare
List ye what his tongue reveals

O thou almighty God of Nature
God of all we are and see
Creator of every land and creature
Oh lend a listening ear to me
When in Yreka my adopted home
As my companions slept and the moon rode high
Oft oft on yon low sloping mountain Ive come
To view this proud mount that seemed akin to the sky.

191

Thus for hours alone in the moon's cool light
Reverently Ive watched this monarch hight
And oh so dearly wished that I might stand
There where man had never stood before
To sollitude I pledge my hand
And smooth the mountains locks so hoar
And now almighty holy God
who dwelt on Sinia dreaded hights
And power gave to Moseses rod
So guide my pen to do its might
For I have climbed these hights alone
And nearest now the heavenly throne
High High above and far away
From the vulgar low contending world
I ask thee God my thoughts to sway
And guide my pen to truths unfurld

My noble self left my home at the Willamette on the 6 of August 1857 at which I arrived just six weeks previous and arrived at this place, McAdams Creek on the last Tuesday in August. Commenced work that afternoon of the same day. Worked four days and a half that week and six days last week.

(This the 6 day of September 1857)

Hiner Miller of the McCloud

McAdams Creek
Sept the 7/57

Honored Brown
    Most Excellent Sir
    It is with a degree of pleasure tinctured with the remembrance of old times that I devote my present space to you thanks to my usual good luck I arrived safe and sound in this part of God s quarters with the exception of a few holes that the — chicken pox made in my natural outside viz I have done well since I saw you and hope I

192

may continue the same But as I and this old world do not exactly agree as to the real meaning of doing well I will tell you wherein I have been so wondrous successful I have quit the filthy and degrading habits of smoking and swearing and by the help of God I hope to follow my good resolution Harve I have but little to write about unless I give you a sort of Autobiography of my humble self since I left —————— I ask you do you want to hear it no answer but the echo but silence gives consent so here goes. I left —————— the morning of the last Monday in August reached Yreka got my pony shod ate watermelons etc Hunted round for a job found none Stayed overnight on Greenhorn Creek Tuesday noon I reached McAdams Creek Commenced looking around for a job but a few hours served to convince me that search was in vain. I tell you, sir, you have no idea of the dullness of the times hell and thunder I don t really believe that a man can work here for his board but do you think that this discouraged me You are mistaken no sir I can spin my yarns or sing my songs as gaily as ever. No Harve whenever you see the Willomette run up stream or it becomes possible for me to court a live woman then I might frown on adversity or beam one smile the less at being the victim of fortunes caprice But to continue I looked at my condition with all the gravity of a philosopher and said perhaps I have money enough by being economical to last me until I can find a job So here I am and here I will remain so thats settled I soon found a vacant cabbin and into it I moved my saddle myself and blankets My poor pony I patted her on the neck gave her a lick of salt and turned her loose to pick her living and I have not seen or heard from the damned bitch since though it has been nearly two weeks since And so thus that matter stands. I bought me some bread & syrup got my beef on credit borrowed a pan to cook it in and ate a hearty supper and went to bed to dote over my fine prospects and dream of future glory Wedesnsday arose right side up though rather late ate my breakfast and sallied forth to seek for new adventures the first thing that I noticed was hand bills stuck up in every crack and corner and upon examining them I found that they were the names of the candidates for the

193

respective offices. And here a new idea flashed upon me Why not be a politican No one will dare challenge my age the beard upon my face is half an inch long though rather white and fuzzy And sir from that moment I felt that I was a man. I have not been weighed since I left home but I really thought I weight at least 170 and I am most certain that there was a mistake in the record of my age of two or three years[24] my mind was made up to be a politician Well I choose to be a Whig for Papa is a Whig. I soon got an introduction to the principal candidates of the Whig party and on the third day I wrote two letters one to the Yreka Union the other to the Republican setting forth the characters of our candidates to the greatest possible advantage and signed them with the remarkable name of H. Miller of the McCloud and when these letters appeared in public I was famous I will show them to you in print if I ever see you again. Matters went on well but I felt the necessity of a new shirt for the one I wore away from home is worn out at the elbows and I cannot spare money to buy a new one.

Copied, corrected and sent to Mr Harvey Brown of Eugene City Oregon September the 12/57

McAdams Creek
Sept the 7/57
Siskiyou Co California

Miss Willoughby:

I regret to say that I have been unable to hear from William — later than last spring he was at that time in Scotts Valley I went to the place where William and I first started when we came to the country but at that place I could learn nothing at all. You can have but a poor idea of the difficulty that one meets with in this vast theatre in searching for one particular person. The people are changing their places of abode almost as often as the wind changes her course as a person is seldom called by his propper name you never know who to

194

enquire for. I had intended to go to Scotts Valley and see if I could not find him but as I lost my horse I had to give it up. I have written to Will and when I get an answer or any late news from him I will let you know. Give my respects to your parents and little brothers.

— respectfully yours

Hiner Miller, Adieu

Copied, corrected and mailed on the 20 of Sept. 1857 to Miss Mary Willoughby Also ten verses of poetry

McAdams Creek California September 10/1857.
To William, a friend that I have not seen for three years.

Ive seen three spring times come and go
Ive seen three summers end
Thrice seen all nature wrapped in snow
Since Ive seen you my friend

When last I took your hand in mine
And wished you well with sad adieu
I little dreamed the stream of time
Would flow so dark tween me and you

But hoped that as we journey down
This path of life with pleasures rare
We'd side by side her favors share

The hope was false twas always so
They wither when I thought them won
And cruel fate then bade me go
My journey through the world alone

Since then Ive passed oer mountains high
Through chasms deep or valleys low
To where Sierras summits reach the sky
With shroud of ever lasting snow

Since then Ive stood in battles strife
And figured too in fashions hall
Or hand to hand with deadly knife
Have answered to proud honors call

Since then alone I wandered home
And saw each spot to memory dear
The old school house where first to roam
We sallied forth nor dreamed of fear

Since then beneath your parents roof
They welcomed me it seemed with joy
But their anxious words and looks were proof
That their hearts were on their absent boy

But in mountains wild in war or peace
Or at home to quiet church attend
I found none to fit to fill your place
My only best and bravest friend

Perhaps dear Will eternal fate
Decrees we meet on earth no more
Oh then let us live that we may meet
When life is done and time is o'er

Sept. 11 1857 I am alone today. I am sitting alone at home looking over my papers and meditating upon the past, the present, and the future. But thought falls too fast for utterance. I can not write today. I can only think, wish, and wonder.

Cinncinnatus Miller

Sunday, Sept. 13/57 The weather this day is clear and, pleasant (I have now worked 16 1/2 days at this place) I sold my white pony for 25 dollars to Benjamin Baxter.

Sept. 15/57
McAdams Creek
Sisky Co., Calif.

Miss ————

It is with no little embarrassment that I through the medium of my pen shall endeavor to introduce myself to your notice and I must beg a thousand pardons for intruding this note upon you as we are entire strangers. But at the same time I must beg you to be patient and read what I have penned. I saw you some time since. I was pleased as I am a stranger to you I wont say more. And a few evenings since when I saw you again and I cannot forget you your image is forever before me Laugh and call me foolish if you will I cannot help it I have figured in the gayest circles of fashion and have ever until now been master of my own feelings. As I said I am a stranger but I trust that by giving you a glance on this sheet of my life with all the open frankness of an honest heart that you will answer this epistle. I came to this country in the year 1852 when I was but fifteen years two of the last five years I have spent in the mines one year in Oregon and two in mountains on the head-watters of the Sacramento, Pitt and McCloud Rivers. And on account of some of my maneuvers there for which the public has given me favorable credit my name is not entirely unknown but that matters not

Coppied corrected and sent to Miss M.P. Worster of Yreka Sept the 20/57

Sunday Sept the 20/57 Worked all of the last week Bought two pair of ———— of India Boots one pr for myself and one pair for Belle paid $6.50 a pr Wrote three letters to-day one to Miss Willoughby another to my brothers at home and another to Miss M.P. Worster
H.M.

Sunday Sept the 27/57

Worked all last week [25]

197

Oct. 20/57   Moneys received of Tompkins & Co.
Received at one time the amount of $5.00 At another
$1.00 At another $15.00 Total $21.00
                                    Hiner Miller of McCloud

McAdams Creek California Question for discussion on
the evening of the 3 of Nov 1857
Resolved that the acquisition of California has been
beneficial to the government.
Names of the champions is said dispute Messrs. Wright
and Gay
Names of the disputors on the side of the affirmative
Messrs. Wright Cart Montgomery Cleoner Mitchell
Names of the disputors on the side of the negative
Messrs. Gay Wilson Miller Allen Cleoner

Sunday November the 4/57 Was laid up last Monday
with a stiff neck. Worked five days in the week. Hiner
Miller of the McCloud[26]

[*Undated*]
Can gold calm passion or make reason shine?
Can we dig peace or wisdom from the mine?
Gold banished honor from the mind
And only left the name behind.

Sunday - The three hundred and sixty-first day of 1857
Columbia College, Lane Co. Eugene City, Oregon I am
alone, seated alone in this institution of learning, and ask
to God that I could describe the solemn silence that is
now resting upon all surrounding nature. That I could
here give the faintest idea of the lofty grandeur in which
all nature presents itself to my mind on this holy sabbath's
morn. That I could here pen my thoughts that I might
read them in after time   Truly spoke that master—of
his—in his apostrophe to the ocean when he remarked—

    I love not man the less but nature more
    In the Silent—in which I—

198

From all that I may be or have been before
To mingle with the universe and feel
That which I can ne'er express
Yet cannot all conceal

                                — Byron

I am alone, yet not alone. I love society and yet I hate it. I know not why it is and yet I seek not to know the reason. At times I wish me far away in some stranger land where I had no home, no friends no society. It's nothing that this cold calculating world might call lovely or enticing but there alone in the midst of death surrounded by dangers and cast upon my own resources dependent upon my own energies for the necessaries of life it seems that I might then be happy, then my restless mind would necessarily be more content yet I know by experience it would not. I have tried the dark and cheerless mine and have wasted much at times in person in spirit and purse and when this came upon me I wished me home again with all the anxious impatience of a thoughtless child. And too I've tried the exciting power of war's tumultuous Thunder. I have faced the shafts and missells of death as a — by the drifting snow, in hopes that I might forever banish this harried uneasiness of mind but all in vain. I was anxious for war yet when it came I was still restless and wished for battle and when this came I rushed like a maniac into the midst and then for the first time in life was content until struck down by the desperate foe. Then again (as I lay there midst the dying and the dead of both friend and foe covered with gore from my acheing wounds) I wished me home that madening impatience and restless disposition settled upon me with almost unresisting force. recovered from this I determined to betake myself to the mountains to quit all civilized life all society save that of the red man of the forest. Two years of the sunniest part of life thus passed in the snow covered peaks of the Sierra Nevadas far far from the din of the sledge

from OVERLAND IN A COVERED WAGON

CHAPTER I

CAMP AND CABINS

My cradle was a covered wagon, pointed west. I was born in a covered wagon, I am told, at or about the time it crossed the line dividing Indiana from Ohio, wherein my mother was born. Her people had come up from the Yadkin River country, North Carolina, whither they had gone with the Boones[27] from Berks County, Pennsylvania; devoted Quakers in quest of a newer land, where there might be less friction. Daniel Boone's mother was a most devout Quaker and tried to keep her sons content to remain in the Yadkin valleys, but Daniel, declaring that he could not live on shadows and that the deer of that land were little more than shadows, gradually led his people out beyond the Alleghenies, west. Most of them went to Kentucky, but some went to Ohio, and then into Indiana.

People built their homes near each other in the early days — danger, if not desire, made them clannish. My mother's people were Dutch, not Germans, as has been so often said, and they were the oldest Dutch in the land — the Falls and the Witts, deWitts, at home. They ferried the Ohio at Cincinnati and ascending the hill pitched tent about where the university now stands; where the venerable Mrs. Fall died and was buried.

The War of 1812 took most of these restless men into the field. General Proctor and Tecumseh came down together from Canada; and the elder Harrison was sent to oppose them. Governor Shelby of Kentucky called for 1,500 men — about all the new State, the first to enter the Union, could muster.

My grandfather Miller, of Scotch stock, from

Kentucky, was among the first of those who answered the call, and fell at Fort Meigs on the Maumee River. I have read he was an officer, but hope and believe he was of the ranks. Please let the dead patriot escape the persecution of idiots seeking an ancestry. He had left his family at Cincinnati, where my papa grew up, was educated and early became a school teacher.

In those days, the teachers, as a rule, were foreign born, mostly Scotch or Irish. The boys in a certain district, a little distance back from the Ohio River, had "turned out" their teacher, a big Scotch bully, for refusing to provide a barrel of Xmas apples, a custom of the times, and as neither pupils nor teacher would yield, the trustees sent to Cincinnati for a substitute.

My papa, then a student, answered the call. He was a most painstaking teacher. His penmanship was perfect. Years after his death, while in New York, I received a letter with the address so like that I had been in the habit of receiving from him that it startled me. It proved to be a kindly letter from the mayor of Kingston, New York, asking if I were not the son of his early teacher, and he proceeded to tell me how they had instituted the "lockout" against their Scotch teacher who had been in the habit of beating them.

Then he told me how the new teacher had called them up the first morning and said, "Boys and girls, one word before we open school: I have been sent to teach you, not to beat you. I never struck any human being a blow in my life; and I never will. I want to be kind to you and I want you to be kind to me. I need your kindness, and I think you need mine. Let us try and be friends for a week, at least, and then if you are not entirely satisfied, I will gladly go back to Cincinnati."

My very first recollection is as vivid as could be any event of yesterday. My papa was moving his little family in a covered wagon from Liberty, Union County, Indiana, to a cabin in Randolph County, where he was going to teach school; but the wagon got stalled in the quicksand of a swollen stream and he had to get out into the water, to his waist, carrying us all out, one at a time, on his back. That made the load lighter.

204

It took him and mother a long time to get the horses and wagon out and over the stream, but they were very patient and quiet about it and built a big fire and camped there for the night. It was my first camp, the first of a lifetime, mainly of camps and I was exultant with delight. The horses had hay and oats from the feed trough that hung at the back of the wagon and the rattling of the bridles and harness and the munching of the hay was as music I had heard in another world.

Then mother made supper as we dried our clothes by the roaring fire and spread a table cloth on the grass under the stars and we all sat down on the ground and papa said grace and thanked God that we were all safe across the angry waters. As the hearty meal concluded, mother went to the wagon and taking out a bottle of preserves she came and sat down by papa and slyly unrolled from tissue paper three little silver teaspoons, and handed one to each of her three little boys.

"Why, Margaret," said papa.

Then mother laid her head on his shoulder and cried. I had never seen mother cry before and it was a long time before we could eat the preserves. I never saw the little spoons any more, but wondered a thousand times why mother cried and what became of the little teaspoons. Nearly thirty years after, when the world was coming my way a little, I went back to my mother's people there, none of whom I had ever seen to remember, and told a venerable aunt of this, my earliest recollection and the incident about the teaspoons, and asked her why mother had cried.

She shook her head sadly, and then told me that after Grandpapa Witt had divided up his ample fortune with his many children that papa had aspired to be a merchant—"storekeeper" it was called then. But being too openhanded; he had the sheriff in the house in less than a year. In those days nothing was exempt—nothing, not even your bed, or tableware. But mother had saved the three teaspoons for her three little boys—a blessed deed for dear mother, but papa did not know it until then, and in the simplicity of his honest heart he felt on seeing them that the sheriff should have had the three teaspoons along with all the other things.

I recall Randolph county only as a sea of sugar trees, with here and there a little island of stumps, a cabin and a struggling little field of corn encircled with a high rail fence — too high for us little boys to climb. We, in going to school or to the sugar camp, always had a "creep hole." Gates were not known in those days. The cabin in which we found ourselves the day after we had "stalled" in the stream was one that had been abandoned by the owner of the ground.

The school house was a cabin with but one room and a huge fireplace that took up nearly the entire end of the edifice. The three big girls that came to school hung their shawls and poke bonnets on pegs behind the door. There were about a dozen big boys, and they and papa kept the big fireplace roaring and blazing. This was the only way to keep warm. The floor was the solid earth and the windows were long, narrow strips of greased paper. This gave not such a bad light as might be imagined; nor was it all primitive. I have seen in the later years of my life whole cities in the interior of China with no other windows in their finest houses than oiled paper.

These big boys would snowball, whoop, and hurrah during recess, after they had cut and carried in plenty of wood; but they were good boys and tried hard to improve. Most of them were full grown, and none of them aspired to anything beyond reading and writing. The writing desks were made of big puncheons, [28] hewn from maple logs, resting on enormous pegs driven into the wall. Papa made all the pens from goose quills brought in by the big boys and set all the "copy."

The big boys were good to papa and very good natured toward my elder brother and myself, the only little ones in school. One of these tall and ungainly big boys went to Congress, then to the Mexican war, became a famous general, then was made governor of Oregon, then Senator, and in the early sixties was chosen as candidate for Vice President on the ticket with Breckenridge, who was beaten by Abraham Lincoln. [29]

There was one big boy, Alexander, who came to school

206

entirely barefooted, although there was frost on the ground and often snow. Papa would not let him help getting in the firewood, and in return Alec would be first at school in the morning and have a roaring big fire going by the time "the master" came.

Everybody was very, very poor. The scholars had to pay their own tuition entirely; the free school had not yet penetrated the dense maple tree wilderness of that region. The only source of income was the sugar camp, supplemented by an occasional coon skin. These were "cash" at 50 cents and sugar was ready money at a round figure, for the Indians[30] who sold their sugar camps bought the sugar; but the season was short for the sugar camps at best and poverty prevailed with piteous uniformity.

At last there was a breath of spring in the tossing tops of the maple trees and gray, black and fox squirrels began to leap from branch to branch overhead and chatter and quirk their tossy tails, the crows cawed and cawed from the tallest tree tops, the blue jay jawed us from the spice and hazel bush as we passed, and school was dismissed for it was "sugar making time."

Papa and mother made their sugar camp half a mile from the cabin in the middle of a great gray maple tree grove and hung up three big iron kettles on a cross beam and against these they rolled great logs on either side, filling the space under the kettles with kindling wood and chunks. Papa had worked continually every spare hour, except Sunday when he had a Bible class at the school house, making sugar troughs and spiles.

The troughs were made by splitting short basswood logs in twain and then cutting out the inside, making a little trough about three feet long and six inches deep. The spiles were driven into auger holes, piercing at an upward angle a little notch chipped into the soft gray side of the generous maple tree. Then there were little grooves, leading down to the spiles. All the trees had been tapped from time immemorial by the Indians, and they were badly scarred by a thousand tomahawks. But they seemed to have forgiven all this when papa tapped them this early spring, and the sap ran so generously that you

207

could hear it not only dripping, but actually streaming from the spiles into the new white troughs. The Indians liked my parents, who worked not only from dawn to dusk but often till midnight boiling the sap, and bought the big forty pound cakes of sugar as fast as they could be made.

There was an ancient hollow oak near the camp which had been used by the Indians as a shelter in sugar time, and there we little boys were very happy, waking up now and then and looking through the natural door or window to see the steam surging up from the kettles out of the great cracking heaps of logs and to look and wonder at our toiling parents with love and silent reverence.

After awhile Grandpapa Witt came, with a little more dowry for mother, and with his practical good sense had plans perfected to move the family to the Miami Reservation; half of which was about to be opened to settlement. With what money he had brought and my parents had made, a good team, cow and six sheep were got together and again we "moved."

The covered wagon proceeded in the narrow rough road and we three little old, very old, prematurely old, boys, brought up behind with the cow and six fat and docile sheep.

Happy? Very, very happy, but we had heard mother crying in the night so many times during the last year, had seen papa so sad all the time in his hard and continual toil that we were like old men now, even in childhood. Instead of toys and games we took to the stock for diversion, loved the cow, rode her, "petted her" and named the sheep pet names, and taught each one to stop, turn about and even to come back to us at call, as we slowly made our exodus from the sugar camp to the Miami Reservation.

The rush of settlers for the newly opened half of the old Miami Reservation on the Massassinewa River, a broad, clear and most beautiful stream, populous with fish and banked by groves of wild flowers and ancient apple trees, was so great that we had to go about three miles down from the "settlements," as the older part of Grant County was called, before finding vacant land. This three miles was a solid wood, dense, dark and full of wonder; not a cabin, nor a "clearing," only little camps, a covered wagon and a tent or so here and there.

Papa got a good claim on the banks of Cart Creek and about a mile from the south bank of the beautiful river. The woods were dense indeed and a road had to be cut for the wagon. But the generous neighbors came from far about and opened a road, cut down trees, hewed logs with broad axes and, as I remember it now, a house was built and covered with "shakes" held in place by weight poles, for there were no nails, and a flat floor of puncheons laid, as if we had an Aladdin's lamp—so suddenly and so gently was it all done.

Bed quilts and coverlets which mother's own hand had pieced or woven, were hung up for doors, greased paper was pasted up for windows, a fireplace of stones from the creek, with broad flat rocks from the river for a hearth, and we were at home in "our own house."

We two elder boys, four and six, had been given tomahawks by the kindly Indians on setting out for this new home and now we hacked and heaped brush all about, clearing, clearing, clearing. It is very wonderful what a boy can do with a hatchet. Papa told us over and over all about George Washington; and I remember feeling very sorry that he never had had such opportunities to be happy.

A great elm, not the popular Eastern shade tree, but the rare slippery elm, the bark of which is "good medicine," stood near the house, a menace in storms, and this papa felled. What a crash! And then he measured off the first ten feet for a rail-cut and proceeded to split it. Mother was busy making Jimmy his first pants, and she, wanting to surprise him with his new dignity, had us older boys with our industrious hatchets take him out to papa.

"Splits like a ribbon," shouted papa as we came to where he, with maul and iron wedge, had opened the great elm trunk. And wild with delight he kept on making rails. I never knew a rail-cut to split so beautifully. It was as easy as if the log had been a mighty watermelon. He turned out rails almost as fast as we could count them, fragrant, perfect in fashion, as if cut with a saw and so light in weight that we two boys, one at each end, could easily lift them out of his way, while he kept on with maul and iron wedge and ax till he had more than 200. Then he hurriedly put up a fence, a beautiful, fragrant, red and yellow fence.

Then he caught up Jimmy, kissed and hugged and set him down in the corner of his fence.

"Run in and tell mother Jimmy is in a fence corner."

"Where? Where is Jimmy did you say?"

"Why out there in the fence corner. Come and see."

She hastened out, the new pants in her hand, and there she found Jimmy, a lord and emperor in his own right, in a fence corner which papa had fashioned with his own untried and not overstrong hand that very hour. And then they took off his little petticoat and put on his first pants. I can not see why they both should have cried; but they did, as they leaned over and caressed him while we bigger boys looked on silently in piteous wonder. Then they set him on the fence and laughed. At which we boys shouted and danced all about with delight.

The autumn weather was beautiful, beautiful. The woods were fragrant with the glory of the Indian summer, a sea of indescribable color; a burning bush on every hand, and the Infinite visible on the minutest tawny fiber underfoot or glittering leaf of gold overhead.

That night our heaps of brush, having been made dry and combustible from the warm winds, were set on fire by our parents as we three slept together in the cabin at the foot of their bed. The great flames lighted up the house through the improvised window panes, and we two boys starting up ran out in fear. But seeing our parents happy in their hard tasks, returned and watched them through the window.

Years ago I was asked by some ladies of that region to recall some incident touching our family at that early date, and I set down this as the first recollection in my life. And so it was on the spur of the moment, but since the death of these two brave and silent builders of the State, I have recalled not only the fashionings of the first fence of all that district, but many an earlier tender memory of these scenes and times of those two most lovable Soldiers of Civilization.

Chapter II

LIFE AMONG THE INDIANS OF INDIANA

I do not know how or even why my father was made a
magistrate [31] — maybe appointed by the governor at
request of the new settlers in the new neighborhood. I am
only certain that it was not only without his request, but
without his knowledge or consent. He was the most shy
man I have ever met in a long life of contact with my
fellow-man. But for all that he was Squire or Judge Miller
from that day till up in his seventy-third year, when he
himself passed on and up to judgment. Whenever he sat
down in his many immigrations he was elected squire,
and had to perform marriages and to hear petty troubles
and pass judgment on his neighbors.

The first trial that impressed itself on my mind was
that of some Indians. The rule established by the agent
across the river among the Indians was to the effect that
so long as they remained on the reservation they should
judge themselves and rule according to their traditions
and sense of justice; but that if they left the reservation
and went over on the white man's ground, for which they
had been paid and were still receiving generous annuities,
they must abide by the white man's judgments.

There was a bad white man named George Sparks
(there are always bad white men hovering around where
there are good Indians with good money), and he had a
"doggery" over on the other side of Pipe Creek in the edge
of the settlements. The narrow little trail over which
Indians could ride their little ponies led from the
reservation to this bad place by way of our new home.
Indians often stopped in on their way back. Once some
tall splendid fellows in their red and yellow blankets got

down at the cabin door and standing in the middle of our floor, struck some sulphur matches[32] and held them up for mother to see them burn. What a miracle! I guess they had never seen matches before. I know mother never had, and it was hard to believe that fire could be made to come out of the end of a little stick, and her surprise was sincere and deep. This delighted the simple-hearted Indians, and, with many a "haw-haw," they rode away in their long single file through the brush toward Pipe Creek.

After they had gone mother and I and the rest of us picked up the dead stumps from the floor and rubbed them hard on the hearth stone, but no fire. Papa wore one entirely out and hurt his finger on the rough stone before he gave it up. He was full of wonder that he, who knew all sorts of books, could not get fire out of a little stick as well as a blanket Indian.

On the return from one of these too frequent trips to the Pipe Creek doggery they were noisy and rode with uncertain seat. And they had a poor battered and bleeding Indian tied with a rope, led in the rear, with a rope around his neck. Four of the Indians, the oldest of a numerous band, were sober Indians at the head of the unsteady party. They tied their horses to the new fence, completed now, and selected the lowest place; led by the sober Indians they all came in and squatted in the yard around their prisoner. Then a sober old man asked for the white man to come and judge them all.

Papa stood in the door. Mother, who always had a natural dignity, gave him the only chair, and he sat down looking severely at the poor naked and badly mutilated prisoner. With a singular wisdom he beckoned the oldest Indian to rise and tell him the truth. Indians, as the patriarchs of old, always have great reverence for age.

The old Indian dropped his blanket from his shoulders and pointing to all the Indians except the three at his side, one after another, said, "Cock-kusee! Cock-kusee! Cock-kusee! Drunk, drunk, drunk."

At this papa slowly and sadly shook his head, looking first at the nearest Indian a long time and so on to the rest. Then he beckoned the first to take the rich red silk shawl which he had muffled about his neck and put it about the pitiful wretch in the middle of the group. He had been kept standing all the time with his shaggy and battered head held low on his breast. The Indian, respecting this as his part of the sentence, rose on his feet at once and not only handed over the gaudy bit of garment, but helped the poor prisoner to put it on. Then he beckoned the next one to put one of his extra blankets on his shoulders. Indians in those days generally wore all they had to wear. Wearing three shirts was no unusual thing at the date of this settlement, and they were always of the most gaudy sort and often of the richest silk. Such clothing was purchased with money paid for their land.

By this time the other Indians caught up the idea that they too must pay the penalty, and one after the other took off something and put it on the naked man till he was clothed better than the best. Then the old "sober Indian" took a rich red handkerchief from about his neck and tied it about his head, pushing back the blood-matted hair that hung down over his face, and poking him gently in the stomach with his fist, made him stand up straight and look him in the face. The name of this old Indian was Shingle-Ma-See.

Another "sober Indian," Jim-Sas-See-Grass, a mighty hunter, gave him a pair of red flannel leggins. This revealed another pair of leggins, frilled buck-skin, underneath the red ones. But with all this wealth and new dignity the mutilated little man seemed not quite satisfied, and another "sober Indian" handed over an extra old blanket.

Then one Indian after another kept handing over things till the mean little prisoner was almost smothered with clothes. He was revealing the very trait no doubt that had made him despised. The climax came when he made sign that he must have a horse to ride. There was no spare pony and no true Indian of this tribe would be seen on foot.

Who this despised Indian was no one can say at this distance of years, but from my experience I should say he had come to the tribe of Miami as a traveler or, more properly, a tramp. Indians are, or were, great travelers. They were always welcome, no matter wherefrom or when, war or peace. For, as there were no fortifications to betray or expose, they were never treated as spies or suspected of evil designs.

They paid their way by describing strange lands through which they passed, making maps or figures in the ashes of the camp fires or in little heaps of sand. But there was this difference between the Indian traveler of the old days and the white traveler of the present date — he must always tell the truth. A Marco Polo would have been disgraced and driven out of camp the first hour of his stay, or possibly have lost his scalp on the spot.

A Rocky Mountain Indian of the old days who had descended the river as far as St. Louis and seen a steamboat, tried to tell about it on his return, and described it as big as about ten canoes the first night of his narrative. The next night he spoke of it as being as big as about fifty canoes. The chief stopped him and reminded the tribe, all gathered about on his right to hear the wonderful story, that he had said ten canoes at first. The honest traveler admitted this and tendered his scalp, explaining that he was afraid to say at first how big it really was.

Then he was urged to tell how big, but he loudly protested that he was still afraid, for if they should heap all the canoes to be found in the mountain lakes and rivers together they would not have half enough to make a single steamboat. He was still urged to go on, but when he tried to make the noise of the wheels and the puff and piercing scream of the monster, he nearly took the roof off the council house, and it seemed was going to kill himself in his honest effort, when the chief thought him a maniac and made him get out.

This dismal little dusky man who stood before his judge, with the tribe squatted about, was possibly a Ute or Blackfoot; anyway, he was from some barren and blowy land. For the people as well as the trees grow close to the ground in bleak and windy countries, and they are low and dark in mind and body, as well as in stature.

Papa hesitated a long time before deciding what to do with this mass of silk and wool, old clothes and new, and then at last beckoned the last donor to take back his gift, then another, then another, then another till the beggar had only meagre raiment and an extra blanket.

Then he slowly rose up, closed his hands, bowed slowly three times to old Shingle-Ma-See, and sat down. The trial had concluded. Then the sober Indians came forward, one at a time, and reaching the right hand, said heartily: "How! How! Shake! Shake!"

Then the other Indians, all sober now, or nearly so, came up and did the same. Then the mean little dark man reached his hand, but papa did not notice it, only motioning Shingle-Ma-See to lead off. Then he made sign by closing his eyes with his head aside that the dismal man must stay with him, and stay for three moons, till well and strong. At this all the Indians were glad and excited with delight—that is, as much excited as an Indian ever allows himself to be—and again coming forward, shouted: "How! How!" and shaking hands heartily they made their way over the low place in the fence, untied their ponies, and, following their old chief in long, single file, were soon lost in the dense woods on their way home.

Our savage soon washed his face, we all sat down to dinner together, and when he had hastily eaten, got my brother's tomahawk and went for wood. He slept by the fireplace in his blanket and kept the cabin warm all night.

"My," said mother next morning as we sat together at breakfast and talked of the magistrate's first "trial." "My, but I did want that red silk shawl they tied about his legs. What became of it? I didn't see it again."

The Indian must have understood. For that day he went down to the branch, washed and dried the big bright shawl and when mother was out cutting brush he spread it over the foot of the bed. And it was cheerful!

Papa said, "Why, Margaret!"

"Hulings Miller," she replied, "you are a magistrate, the judge of all this country, and here you put in nearly the whole day deciding between these Indians and never got a cent, did you?"

"Why, Margaret, I never thought of that," he said. "I guess you have a right to the shawl if you want it."

216

I think the Indian understood and was glad, for he got wood right along all winter and cut and burned more brush than any white man could have done. But in the spring when the sap began to run he ran with it and we never saw him any more. He was still an Indian!

There was talk all the time of the land coming into market. Plenty of adventurers who had been too late to get locations, were waiting to pounce on that of those unfortunate enough not to have money in hand to purchase. Papa had no money now, but he worked hard, night and day, you may say, all winter, and with the help of a neighbor had made a loom, a big spinning wheel and a little wheel for mother; the big wheel for wool, and the little foot wheel for flax. When the frost was out of the ground he plowed the little field and put in corn and flax; mother and we lads made the garden.

A man by the name of Lorenzo Jacobs began to build a mill on our side of the Massassinewa, "the beautiful river," about a mile off, and there papa got work at 50 cents a day, boarding at home, but having his dinner with the mill hands. He was paid every Saturday night.

Mother, the first Saturday night, got an old mitten she had knit for him when we were making sugar, and sewed up the holes and put the three silver dollars in it, saying as she shook it down, "Nest egg to buy the land."

Each head of a family could locate one hundred sixty acres of land. The price was $1.25 an acre. But the land laws were primitive and pretty severe in these early days and you must not only have the money in hand at the time the land came into market, but you must have two reliable witnesses to "prove up" — that is, to prove that you had built a house and made a home in it for more than a year. As there was a feeling against greased paper for windows, you were required to prove that you had glass in the windows.

When papa stopped working at the mill, after about four months, he went to Marion, the county seat of our Grant County, and got some panes of glass. At the same time he got two little dry goods boxes and from one of these whittled out a sash. One day a good-natured old neighbor from Tennessee, by the name of Billy Fields, seeing papa whittling away at his sash, said:

"All nonsense, Squire, all a waste of time."

"But the law says we must have glass in the windows," replied papa.

"Well, what's the matter with setting an old bottle or two in your window?" he said. "There are plenty of men to swear you have got glass in your window."

The last winter had been a hard one and packs of big gray wolves had crossed the ice and come down from the north into our neighborhood. As the Indians did not hunt much any more, having plenty of money, the wolves became bold, and even dangerous. One night as papa was coming home they got after him. We boys, who had gone to meet him as usual, heard him calling for mother, and we took up the cry of terror. Mother came almost at once with a big hickory bark torch, held high as she ran, and the wolves shrank back. But poor papa was sadly broken and was ill for a long time.

He was well enough pretty soon, however, to pull and cure the flax and help pick and comb the wool for mother to card into rolls and spin for her loom. The wool in those days was awful. Burs and beggar lice stuck to the sheep that ran in the woods at will, till they were almost black. And this had to be picked out by hand. But we little fellows, all three, could pick wool now. And this we did by the light of the wood fire, where one little head after another nodded and nodded till it could hold up no longer, but sank to rest on the wool. Then some one would pick up the little sleeper and lay him gently away in the trundle bed. For we no longer slept in the big bed with our parents.

The flax was not so troublesome, nor did we have to plant it, and plough it, and hoe it, as we did corn. We had to pull it in due season, shake the earth from the roots and lay it in a swath in the sun and rain till the pith or stalk became brittle and shrunk loose from the fibre. Then we must break it in the flax brake, a handful at a time. Then we must hackle it on an iron hackle, so as to get the pith all out. Then we must comb and curry it till it was ready for the distaff of the little spinning wheel.

218

Mother had to have flax to make warp for the woof of her bolt of cloth to be made on the loom; then to be marketed at Marion, the only town then within many a mile.

Papa sold all the increase of the sheep and the two calves to the Indians and got some money for mother's "nest egg" that way and mother raised many chickens and disposed of them to the tribe. Once, when we two boys went with papa, we took too much care of the poor hens, as the day was cold and raw, and smothered three of them. Papa did not count them, so the promised four dozen fell short. But the Indians counted the dead ones all the same, and paid for them. Still, for all that could be done, it seemed almost impossible to get all the money together for the land.

In this dilemma papa got a good old Irishman, who had a big family of boys, to take sixty acres and pay him $50 for the privilege. This left us only one hundred acres; but then it left only $75 more to raise, and with what we had in hand, selling the pigs and mother's big bolt of cloth and so on, the money was all secured and he set out for Fort Wayne, the land office, with Billy Fields and Lorenzo Jacobs, who also had to "prove up," as witnesses, and so the land at last was secured.

Soon after this a big raw-boned man in a beaver hat, with a hatchet face, came to us by the way of the big State road not far away, with a load of clocks in a carriage. He had a big impertinent boy with him, and he pleaded sadly that both he and his boy were sick.

Mother was very good to them; pulled out the trundle bed to the middle of the floor, had us children get back in the bed as before, and treated them as if they had been her own blood.

But they both wailed and moaned bitterly, and begged papa to take the clocks, and at his leisure dispose of them to his neighbors. There was a whole carriage load of them, but in the double and treble assurance that he could double or treble his money on them, my confiding papa, not knowing one thing about the real price or value of such wares, signed a note and once more became a "merchant."

Let me get rid of that hatchet-faced wretch right here,

for, un-Christian as it is, I hate him yet. He came at the end of the year, exacting his money with enormous interest, although papa had not sold a single one of the old clocks. Jacobs came forward and took up the note generously, and tore it up, for mother was crying; but we were in debt again, and papa had to struggle on and teach and toil as before to make up what he had lost.

When we set out to cross the plains years later these old clocks, still on hand, all save a single one, took up more than half the wagon bed. We hauled them almost to the top of the Rocky Mountains, and then one night in a terrific snowstorm, when the wagon upset and we needed the old clocks for kindling wood, they were, brass, glass and varnish, all cremated. Peace to their sounding brass; rest to their brazen faces!

But to get back among the Indians of Indiana; papa had brought the two little dry goods boxes from Marion. One he had made into two window sashes. We boys kept wondering what he was going to do with the other. He kept it in the smoke house, and once when we found him in there all alone, when he thought we were down at the creek catching crawfish, we found him busy in there fixing rockers on the little box. We were delighted with the idea, and asking him what it was for, he timidly and with some confusion, said it was to be a cradle for little Jimmy.

But little Jimmy thrust both his hands in his pants pockets and said it was not big enough, and he added, with a pout, that baby Jimmy did not want to sleep in a cradle anyhow.

A few days before this little rebellion by the baby boy in his first pantaloons, an honest man and a pretty young girl, really the prettiest woman I had ever seen except mother, had come to papa to be married, and, as usual, where money was so scarce, brought two coon skins. And they were very fine skins, killed in the heart of winter and dressed to perfection.

To dress or tan a coon skin properly you first parflesh it with the back edge of your hunting-knife, then take the brains of the animal and, rubbing them on the flesh side, you manipulate the skin with your hands industriously, rubbing and rubbing for hours. This is, or was done, in those days at night by the cabin fire, after the day's work was done. It takes three operations to complete the task. But when it is done the skin shines and glistens as if oiled; and each particular bit of fur stands up as if alive. Not many coon skins are dressed in this way.

Mother had claimed these two beautiful skins for some special purpose of her own and put them away under her pillow, where she always kept the money, when there was any money, and she now brought out the beautiful skins, which Jimmy had also admired very much and she put them carefully and tenderly in the cradle, smoothing them down with her hands and talking gently baby talk to baby Jimmy. But he again thrust his hands deep in his pockets and turning as if in disgust, stalked away to the door and went out. No cradle for Jimmy Miller. So mother took the coon skins out, for the time at least, and the cradle was put back in the smoke house.

Soon after a good old Southern woman came from the Billy Fields settlement and sent us little folks away to Billy Fields and his house full of girls. And when the good old woman went away we were all back home and very, very happy. I led the horse that carried her and she sat astraddle, smoking a cob pipe and holding tightly before her one of those clocks, the first and only one we ever disposed of.

Chapter IV

PAPA TAKES US TO THE CIRCUS

While awaiting a favorable opportunity to start for Oregon, papa found a place further up the storied Tippecanoe River, about five miles from Rochester, and arranged to teach there the coming winter. But before going there he put us all in the wagon and went down the river near to where it flows into the Wabash, to see the old battle ground, where Harrison had so stubbornly held his own during the bloody night attack by the brother of Tecumseh. He was moved to do this out of respect for his father, who had fought here and who had fallen under the same intrepid soldier on the banks of the Maumee, at old Fort Meigs.

We camped here on the battle ground for many days, and papa led us all around by day and told us all the pitiful story of the pioneers, their hardy and honest lives and unselfish devotion to duty. He took great pride in telling about the Kentucky men with their long flint-lock squirrel guns, for his father had been one of them

The trees were many and mostly oak on this high bank, where the struggle had been hardest, and all seemed to be badly scarred. But the scars were not so big and so ugly from the bullets as from the tomahawks of hunters, and perhaps Indians also, hacking into the trees to find old bullets of the battle to melt over and mold again into bullets. It was autumn and the trees were red, so very richly red, as if the woods had been enriched by the blood shed there, as if the leaves had taken on a deeper hue from the blood of the great forgotten dead.

Going from the battle ground up the river to the little farm of eighty acres, which papa had bought, we found two fairly good cabins and all the ground fenced. The man who sold it was to remain in the older cabin while we took charge of the new one and we at once set out for school. Some of the neighbors were Yankees, some German emigrants, but some of them were "poor white trash" from down South, dreadfully given to drinking and fist fighting. These fist fights were mostly on muster days, at log rollings, or house raisings, where all the neighborhood, good and bad, met together and whiskey seemed to be almost the only sort of provisions.

The school house was a most humble affair of unhewn logs, a mile away through deep woods, and greatly over crowded.

Papa got on well with the scholars, big and little, and soon found two good big boys who were anxious to work for their board nights and mornings and Saturdays and go to school at the same time—quite a custom in these early days. And it may as well be noted here as elsewhere that this sort of student as a rule made up the Lincolns, Garfields, and Lanes of the great Middle West.

Papa was making every preparation possible for a big crop of corn. For the first time in the history of the West there was to be a way to reach points of transportation to the East. The southern end of Indiana had always had an outlet by way of the rivers away down to New Orleans, but now a canal had at last been cut making some sort of connection by way of the lakes with New York, where there was a stable market.

And a plank road (toll) had been made from Rochester, only a few miles from us, to the city of Logansport, on the canal, where a certain price, fabulously low of course, was established for all the corn that could reach this point. We must take advantage of this first market in the country, and so kept hard at work, all of us except the little baby girl, who was still in Jimmy's cradle, from daybreak till dusk made it impossible to toil later.

When school ended, the two young men still stayed with us, mother not at all complaining of the extra work, but up every morning long before dawn preparing fragrant breakfasts of ham and eggs and fried chicken, all by the light of her dim tallow dip.

One pretty spring morning when the boys were plowing, a tall dark man in buckskins came where papa and I were splitting rails, and setting the butt of his long rifle heavily on the ground and throwing his big right fist away toward the west with a sweep, shouted out, "Gold Gold! Gold! Squire, they have found gold by the wagon load in California; by the cart load, by gum! The ground is full of gold in Californy, an' I'm goin' to Californy!"

He hastened on to where the boys were plowing and followed them up in the furrow, talking and gesticulating wildly as he went. At dinner we could talk, think, eat, nothing but "Californy."

Yes, the young men would go with us. We would go to Oregon, for the section of land was sacred with us all, but the boys would leave us at the forks of the road and go right on, get loads of gold, then come to us in Oregon, "and let Californy go to the bow-wows!"

That night Fremont's maps were gone over again, more carefully than ever; all the maps were out on the table, and tallow dips were burned to the socket before even little yellow and frouzy headed Jimmy began to nod his manly little head!

We would set out next March, a good month, a name with a good meaning, for three thousand miles of marching by mountain and plain, wood and water, desert and dust, and we went to bed literally filled with glittering "Californy."

Ten months more and we must be on our way. And how the work went on. Corn was planted, hoed, hilled up and plowed deep! How beautifully and healthy and proudly it waved its lifted sabres in the sun, a sea of glistening emerald!

About midsummer Washington Harrison Peterson, a tall Kentucky boy who had been at school, came to see us and brought a big and wondrous poster of pictures which he had found on the door of the now vacant school house. There were elephants, snakes, monkeys, men standing on their heads, and bearded women swallowing big long butcher knives. There was going to be a circus in Rochester!

Papa and mother talked it over that night, while Washington Harrison Peterson, who had seen a circus, or said he had, dilated on the notable beauty of the bearded woman, the wondrous celerity of the elephant, and the beautiful and alert boa constrictor as it ate apples ravenously out of a naked man's hand in the Garden of Eden, and it was unanimously agreed, all the three boys voting in the affirmative, that papa and his lads should go to that astounding circus.

Yes, papa would take Washington Harrison Peterson along as a reward for his pointing out so perfectly and entertainingly the moral, ethical and educational advantages of the coming circus. We would take a wagon load of water melons along, sell them on the streets, get money to buy the tickets, and so be none the poorer but vastly wiser for the day's work and delight.

I remember papa saying to mother as he covered up the fire for the night: "Yes, Margaret, I think it is better that the boys should see the circus; for, of course, they will never have a circus in Oregon or California, and this will be something they ought to see here while they can. It will be a sort of education for them, and they will remember it all their lives."

The days, the great big hot and dry midsummer days, busy as they were, every one dragged by slowly, but at last the great circus day came. With the wagon bed nearly full of melons and papa and his boys in one seat, we set out for Rochester. All the neighbors of all the country round about were going our way. Jimmy remarked with a business whisper that none of the wagons but our own had water melons.

"I hope you won't try to be a merchant, Jimmy; get up there, Sorrel," said papa.

The dread of papa's life was that we boys should try to be merchants. When we came to the big State road, on the bank of the river a mile or so from town, we found quite a multitude waiting there to see if the circus would go over the high bridge or ford the stream. As the band at the head came on it struck up a lively air and led through the water. The circus followed, not daring to risk the elephants, the wonderfully painted wagons and the beautifully bearded lady on the shaky wooden bridge. Papa pushed on soon after alongside of the elephants that took to the water with a roar. The big and noisy beasts stopped in the middle of the deep stream and began to suck in and spurt water all over their backs and sides and saucily throw little streams of it over all who were near them. This made everybody shout and roar, and the elephants seemed to enjoy it to the full. Jimmy said he could see them laugh. But Jimmy always had a good and lively imagination.

At last the big elephant with a man on its neck tried to lay down and the man with an iron hook had to prod and shout and yell desperately before he could make it stand up and move on. Then the band struck up loud and shrill, and the wonderful caravan, half a mile long it seemed to me, moved on to the music of the stirring drums and horns and pipes till we entered the city of Rochester, where the thousands of boys shouted their wonder, admiration, and exultation. I even saw some of them turn hand springs and try to stand on their heads.

We boys had painted some signs on boards with red poke berries, reading, "Ripe melons, melons fip and a bit! Melons six pence apiece." That is melons a five-penny bit. Melons a half shilling or six pennies. Melons a picayune or melons, a little one. This last to suit the Southerner. We took out the tail board of the wagon and handed out melons as fast as we could hand them out. Papa went down town and on coming back in a brief time he looked on and said: "Going like hot cakes, eh? How much money have you made? Enough for us all five to go in?"

"Yes, and more, too, papa, Just count it up."

And so he took the money, counted it up and said, "Good! Now, give away all the rest and let's go!"

He again seemed even more dreadfully afraid we might want to be merchants, and unhooking the horses he brought them around to the tail of the wagon, emptied out a dozen ears of yellow corn, and taking off the bridles left them to eat while we were away like birds for the big tent.

What a whirl! What a rush and roar! The shrill music, melody surely, over and above all the clamor! And how the tumblers tumbled, the spotted horses circled and the painted clown kept the center, and the impressive ringmaster cracked his whip savagely around and over all things.

I had never dreamed that there was anything waiting along the road of my coming years so grand and so all glorious as this! How we did talk to mother and sister that night!

I nearly broke my neck the very next day after we got home tryng to ride the old plow horse, head down, and had to go to bed for a week. But that did not dull my enthusiasm. I talked circus right along, so did John D., so did Jimmy, for days and days, till at last papa gently protested, said that mother and baby sister already had heard it all over a dozen times and that we must now take up our reading again and get ready for the wonderful things we were to see on the way to Oregon.

May I take time to stick a pin here and assert with my hand on my heart that that circus was really great. At least, it has ever stood out and up and over all things in my mind as the most splendid thing ever seen, until we set out for Oregon. I have had many chances in my busy life to attend other circuses, both in the old world and in the new, but I have never yet been willing to mar the memories of that first one by trying to see a second. And I want to leave this idea with you. Let your boy go to a circus—just one good circus—and then stop for all time. The clock strikes 12 only once a day. When the two hands are pointing heavenward together and you have seen the greatest and the best, be contented, for the sun is setting to the west from that moment. I am glad as I can be that I saw that circus by the Wabash waters, but most particularly glad that I never tried to see another.

When the emerald seas of corn grew golden under the first frosts, the young men, papa, mother, and we three little boys, baby sitting in the wagon, husked out the big yellow ears and carried load after load to the cribs till the

227

generous harvest was all gathered; a tremendous crop! Then the two young men, on the second day, "came down with the ague"; then papa, and then mother.

Do you know what it is to shake and to shiver, and to burn up with fever and cry aloud for water, and not be able to drink when it is brought to you? Can you imagine how terrible you feel when you are shivering and freezing to the bone, and are only the more fearfully chilled as you sit by the fire or in the sun? That is the Indiana ague, the miserable fever and ague as it was in the old days by the waters of the Wabash. [33]

Earth resents familiarity. We had turned up too much fresh and fever-laden soil. Besides, we — at least our parents and the two young men — had toiled too hard.

With all of them down on their backs, John D. and I loaded the wagon and drove away on over the plank road to Logansport. The wagonbed was so big and we were so small that, in coming home, we had to stand up all the way, so as to look ahead and see the horses. But we got home, and, oh, the glory of laying the big silver dollars in mother's hand, and of hearing poor, shivering papa count them and clink them over and over, as his teeth chattered and chattered.

They must have spent an anxious two days, for they were worse than ever. But now their blood came back, and with a flow so warm that they soon shook only every other day, and then, at last, only every third day, and then, on our final safe return, not at all.

Jimmy went with us that last time, and as we had to come home very late we were rained on in the dark, and the next day or so we were all three down flat on our backs, with the burning fever and bone-breaking chills. Jimmy, who had nearly frozen that last night as we bigger boys stood up and he lay asleep on the empty bags, shaking the worst of all three.

However, the young men were up and about soon, and so the team kept going till all the big cribs of corn were empty and the two old mittens were once more full of money, and papa began to buy oxen, cows and wagon for the wondrous journey ahead of us. The cows had to be yoked alongside of the oxen. It would not do to try driving loose stock. We got another wagon, a carriage for mother, and, having sold the farm back to the same man, a Mr. Culver, from whom we had bought it, we were promptly ready for the long march as it had been planned for nearly a year before.

The exact day of our starting, with all the neighbors for miles around to see, was by chance the sacred 17th day of March.[34] I had insisted on having a gun. Papa gave a reluctant consent, but got me an old smooth-bore flintlock, with no flints, till I made one out of an arrowhead. And somehow this would get loose and get lost nearly all the time.

The young men who were with us did not want me to have a gun, and at this remote day with my better knowledge of the world and the ways of human nature, I think I begin to guess pretty clearly what became of my flints.

It may seem strange that papa so disliked guns, since he had been nearly all his life in the wilderness, and was now pushing away into the very heart of a land of wild beasts and wilder men. But he would not touch a gun. And during all his seventy-two years in the border he never knew how to load a gun. Please do not call him eccentric. I despise the too frequent use of the term eccentric. I should say that as his father had been killed when he was yet a babe at the breast that he somehow sucked in the terror and hate of all violence with his weeping mother's milk, sucked in maybe milk and tears together.

Well, we were off and away now. The Rubicon was behind us.

And have I bothered and wearied you with a story of trifles, details of toil, trials, and baby brothers of men? So let it be. What is writ is writ. But if you do not love, pity, cherish, and revere the memories of these mighty men of these once densely wooded States, Ohio and Indiana, these pawpaw fastnesses, these maple wood empires that gave us mothers in Israel who suckled prophets, sages, soldiers, Presidents—then please follow no further.

But I say to you, that there is nothing in the pages of history so glorious, so entirely grand, as the lives of these noble Spartan fathers and mothers of Americans, who begot and brought forth and bred the splendid giants of the generation that is now fast following the setting sun of their unselfish and all immortal lives.

UTOPIA

"UTOPIA"

The incidental mention in a rambling article recently published in THE CALIFORNIAN, of a desire to found a new city or community somewhere in the warm and roomy South-west, has brought upon me a deluge of letters.

No man who is much in earnest in this world can have either time or inclination to answer the chronic letter-writer of America. He or she is the most prolific growth of this great land. Idle-handed and empty-headed, this creature, which cheap postage and thin education has made possible, is the nuisance of the nineteenth century.

But among all these letters there are half a dozen, at least, from earnest, honest, and thoughtful people, and these letters, so far from vexing me, give the greatest encouragement—not from what they say, propose, or promise, for they are mostly merely brief inquiries, with here and there a thoughtful suggestion; yet the *fact* that so many solid minded men and women are in sympathy with an enterprise of this kind shows not only its need, but that it can succeed.

I do not count Brook Farm at all a failure. Indeed, I am almost ready to reckon it the greatest success ever achieved. I know it is the custom to say that such minds as those of Fuller, Hawthorne, Ripley, Dana, Curtis, and so on, conceived Brook Farm. I think it more correct to say that Brook Farm gave us Nathaniel Hawthorne, Margaret Fuller, George William Curtis, Dana, Ripley, and on through the catalogue of the greatest, purest, best brain of America.

There are a dozen reasons why this little community, so

233

far as the "business" of it was concerned, came to an end. Plant a pine under the shadow of an oak, and it will die, although the pine be the statelier tree of the two if it can have the sun. This new city must be planted out, by itself—far out, where there is room, and in the warm sun, and in the prolific soil of another land than New England. And in another land, not only because of the richer soil and the warmer sun, but because the cardinal points must be diametrically opposed to the one hard, dominating idea of Yankee character, if it is to flourish long and do any great good upon earth.

I respect her money-getting—her hard, cold soil and climate have crystallized it. And money-getting, up to a certain point, makes greatness. But the sinews of war are not war itself.

And it is to be admitted that in all her money-getting this little land of granite and ice has brought more renown to the Republic, and done more solid good to the world, than all the other States of the Union.

But that is not the proper line of argument. Consider, rather, if she has done so much with all her hard opportunities, what is it she might not do if she had the ample leisure which the Community proposed would afford her children?

I will now briefly set down some of the cardinal ideas involved in this new establishment. It is the briefest and best way to answer these letters. The writers of those among them stamped with sincerity will be satisfied. As for the others, it does not matter.

In the city of London there is one man in thirteen at work. It takes the other twelve to stand over and watch that one man, and keep him at work.

This is a startling statement, but if you will consult statistics you will find it is the cold, frozen truth.

The city of Paris is even less industrious than London. The population of New York is so migratory and unsettled that there is no means of finding out just how idle she is, but it is safe to say that here there is not more than one man in seven or eight at work.

So you see that in the great cities of the world there is an average of about one man in ten obeying that great primal command, that by the sweat of your brow you shall eat your bread.

But how this one man has to work! Stand by and see him down in the dirt and muck, or see him pausing wearily on the pavement. He is in rags. He is filthy. His face is dirty. His hands are hard. His heart must be hard. His face is haggard and brutal. He does not lift his eyes. He works doggedly on. This man has not had enough to eat. That little tin bucket held his dinner. His *dinner,* mark you, my Lord Mayor and ladies and gentlemen, who would be miserable at missing a hot plate of soup, hot fish, hot meat, warm delicacies, and wine at *your* dinners! And yet you have not one of you done a stroke of real work in all your worthless lives.

This laborer, look at him again! He is a brute. You have made him a brute. You keep him a brute. His children will be brutes. Sometimes he lifts his eyes to the sun. May be he has been thinking. But he shakes his shaggy head, and his eyes droop, and he clutches again the pick-handle. There is no escape, and he knows it. The master is noting him. The police are eyeing him. You are all watching him. He must keep at it, ten, twelve, fourteen hours every day. You have tied him up, chained him, bound him tighter than ever slave was bound in savage Rome. Yes, right here, in the heart of your great Christian city.

One would think this strong man would climb out of the pit he had dug in the street to fix the gas or water-pipe or pavement, and run, and run, and run, for liberty, for life. But where would he run to? Right into prison. And so he holds on to his pick. He will climb out wearily when the sun goes down, take up his dirty coat in his dirty hands, and drag himself doggedly home. Home! He will kick his wife for the wrong that you have done him—you, whom he cannot reach. Then he will get drunk as he gets older and weaker and pains creep into his marrow, for he must have something to keep up his strength. Then he will kick his wife again. And what wonder! He is desperate, reckless. He must strike something, what matters it whom or what? He will kill her finally, for this wrong that you have done him. Then you will arrest him for murder. You will put him in prison, and, for the first time in his life, give him enough to eat. Then you will try him for murder. Then you will dress him up, for the first time in his life, and hang him. And what cares he? You have only taken him out of that grave in the street, and put him into another.

But suppose some one man out of the eight idlers had gone and got down into the pit with that poor laborer, and done half his work? Suppose that *three* of them had gotten into the pit, and left the poor man but one-quarter to do? He would have been a man. He would have lived a man, and died a Christian gentleman.

Secondly: Shut a man up in prison, and the average man will walk from six to eight hours daily. He will do this year in and year out, unless he be put to work there, for he must have exercise. In other words, a man must and will have some sort of physical effort every day.

Now, what we must get at in order to bring this half civilized age out into full sunlight, where it may have some possibility of development, is to give this strength, this wasted physical force, some proper direction and application.

Statistics show us that there is only one man in seven or eight at work, so far as we can learn. Of course, in the provinces and field they are more industrious than in the populous centers, but, for the sake of the proposition, we will say about that number.

Well, physical science, as well as observation, proves that these other seven absolutely need the exercise of honest toil, and will take it in any form or action, even if fenced up in prison, to the extent of about six hours a day.

These two facts are the foundation-stones on which to build this new community. The proposition, you observe, is not at all new. It is the old problem of the distribution of labor.

I believe it is pretty generally conceded by thoughtful men that our civilization is not, with all its culture, ease, and refinement, a towering success. And men are constantly hewing off corners, in the impossible effort to fit the divine doctrines of Christ into a life of idle luxury.

A hundred thousand honest clergymen climb into their pulpits every Sunday morning, perfectly conscious of the great unevenness — yes, I think unevenness is the word — of life, as laid out before them in the present form of civilization.

They charge you that by the sweat of the brow you must earn your bread. And yet they know perfectly well that the one effort of every parishioner before them is to avoid the primal curse — to get hold of money and loaf, and let the other fellow sweat *his* brow.

And this brings us back to that other old biblical truth, that money is the root of all evil.

Now, my plan is to have no money, or, rather, to have no rich man, no poor man, no individual property; but a city — a rich city, if God should so favor it — but a city in which every man there could lift up his face and say, "I own just as much, and no more, of this city, as the richest man in it. I helped make it, and it is mine."

Would you mind inquiring for a moment why men want money? To me the bravest and the greatest man in all history is Alexander the Great, and the grandest act in his life — in fact, the one act which illuminates it like a sunrise — was his behavior at the battle, or, rather, after the battle, of the Granicus. The spoils were enough to enrich an empire, but he gave away all to his generals and his soldiers.

"And what have you kept for yourself?" asked one.

"Hope!" answered Alexander, with his face lifted toward Indus.

Now, if a man could be brave — I mean morally brave, for, after our civil war, I don't think physical bravery need ever be questioned any more among Americans — all the time, and have plenty of faith and hope, he need not have much money to be happy. But man at heart is cowardly and weak, and he grows to be afraid he will come to want. He feels that he must have money, must build a wall of gold between himself and the possibility of want. And this is particularly the case with old men. As a man gets old and weak he often becomes very mean. It cannot quite be said that all old men are misers. But it can be asserted that all misers are old men.

237

The most common excuse that a strong man in his prime gives for his desire to get money is the wish to provide for those dependent upon him. A laudable desire indeed. And no doubt the man giving this reason is perfectly honest, and believes that he has this high and unselfish motive only. But, unfortunately for the solidity of this reason, we find the man who has not one relative dependent upon him just as eager to get money, just as mean-handed in keeping it.

No, the fact is we are all moral cowards. We are not only afraid to be poor, but, under our present form of society, we are ashamed of it. We even lie, and pretend to be rich.

Well, now, let us quit our city for a moment, and imagine ourselves established in a little new-built city, on a wooded and watered slope of the Sierra.

Let us suppose that we have everything there that heart can desire; that we have helped build this city; that we are part owners of it, and shall continue to be so long as we live or choose to remain there; and then let us ask ourselves what use we would have for money.

Of course, the force of habit, the hard, vulgar custom of clutching at every cent we could snatch from our neighbor might cling to us for a time. But you can see that the backbone of the desire to plunder our fellows would be broken; and knowing that for all life we would be provided for, and our children after us — why, the soul would grow good, and strong, and unselfish; and we could turn our splendid strength to higher and holier purposes than man has known since Adam's fall.

Before considering how this city is to be built, maintained, and governed, I wish you might have to shut up your book, turn down a leaf, and first imagine the happiness of a city where the only inequality is that which God himself has given to the minds and bodies of men — an inequality which is rather a difference of color or form than inequality. Just as a man arranging a garden would have red flowers, white flowers, huge or small or fragrant or fine to see; all unlike, all unequal, but all and each in time very good and to be desired.

Oh, the heart-burnings to be escaped in such a place! Consider how the rich man's neck would unbend; how the poor man's back would straighten till he stood up, straight and tall, as God first fashioned him.

Now, is this Community possible? It is as simple as is the opening of a farm in Colorado or California. I know some people will smile. Some may mock. But the world moves!

It is idle to expect any great capitalist to embark in this. The world has plenty of philanthropists; but they seem to me to prefer building a hospital to put a man in when he gets hurt, rather than put forth a little finger to help him from getting hurt at all.

But when one constantly has all this North Pole nonsense thrust in his face, millions thrown away, sending good, live men to perish up there in the cold for the sake of an uninhabitable land and sea, while we have so much untouched land here, which half a world might be made happy on, it seems as if there might be one man in the world who has faith enough in human nature to give it a chance out in the roomy West. But perhaps not. And since the enterprise has not money for its object, it very properly ought not to ask money to begin with. Bricks without straw? May be. But when you consider how Salt Lake City sprung up in the desert, without a penny, with only a pick and shovel in the hands of its builders to begin with, and with the millstone of polygamy about its neck all the time, you ought not to despair of this enterprise if it is worthy. And it is worthy, and it will succeed, without any man's help, if only a few brave, patient, and faithful souls begin it.

I once belonged to a little association formed solely for this purpose. Nearly ten years ago we talked this over and over in London. The idea has deep root there. We used to turn our faces toward our imaginary "Utopia" and sort of mecca of the club. And then we would fall to quoting "The Ancient Mariner." For you know Coleridge very nearly came over the sea for this same purpose.

Finally, when the King of Italy confiscated the property of the Church, and offered the monasteries for sale on easy terms, all of a sudden our ideal object seemed

239

about to become a fact. Some members of our club chanced to be wintering in Rome, and one of them bought a large estate, with a city already built, down below Naples.

What a happy and hilarious party we were that rode down to take possession of the old haunted convent and half deserted city on a hill! We were going to invite all the Bohemian world. There should be no houseless wanderers any more. Here were houses enough certainly to shelter all the poets, painters, and musicians out of doors. We were going to lead a river from a neighboring mountain down through the streets of this deserted and dirty old city, and wash it clean for the first time in a thousand years.

But we soon discovered that the place was stricken with fever. And that was why it had been so long deserted. The people had died! Only a few miserable monks in brown, who rather preferred death to life, and the hideous marsh-buffalo, groaning and wallowing through the mud-lakes under the hill—these seemed to be the only satisfied inhabitants of the whole region; and finally, with the fever in every one of us, we went back to Rome and gave it up, satisfied that our only fit field of operations was in young and healthful America.

But our enterprise had created some stir in the Eternal City, and soon after our return the King gave us an audience. His Majesty was over kind, and tried to encourage us to go on. But our bright young leader was still very ill, and hardly able to get out, and we had but little heart left. He died soon after, and as the hot weather came on the others of our party scattered like birds, going whither each one's fancies or fortunes led or allowed, in search of health; for we were all suffering more or less from the malaria—and we never met any more.

A few years after, I laid my plans before the Emperor of Brazil. He was at first enthusiastic, and generously offered all the land required. At a subsequent interview, while insisting on giving a large tract of land, he quietly hinted that I had better bring all the people I wished to embark in the enterprise from my own country. I saw

240

clearly that he had little faith in the work. And perhaps he was quite right, so far as his own people are concerned. The luxurious South American certainly possesses but little of that spartan self-denial required to establish a community of this sort.

The enterprise was abandoned this time, not at all because of the Emperor's indifference, but largely because just about that time the British Government had to send out a ship to bring home certain colonists, who had, from a failure of crops and other misfortunes, become destitute and dissatisfied. Clearly, the climate and fates were against it here. Besides, as this is to be an experiment, it ought to be set up and maintained right in the current and under the eyes of the world, so that whatever good it brings forth might be made apparent and encourage other like Communities to spring up over the earth. There are to-day, scattered all over the United States, nearly half a hundred "Communities," of various kinds and qualities. But they are nearly all hampered and bound down by some sort of hard and narrow doctrinal point of religion. And then they all are devoted to getting money, just the same as are individuals. One of these Communities furnishes the canned fruits of the world, and accumulates great wealth. Another one makes the famous Shaker rocking-chair. But none of these societies make any claim to superior culture, either physical, mental, or moral. And certainly they are made up, as a rule, of very melancholy types of humanity.

Perhaps the most intelligent and deserving of all associations of a cooperative sort in America is that of New Rugby, established by Tom Hughes, M.P. But let it be borne in mind that all these Communities, whatever their tenets, pretensions, or pursuits, are all getting on well, getting wealthy—are content and happy.

Remember our object is not to make money. Our aim is solely and simply to make men. The first thing to be thought of is perfect physical development.

No man should be permitted to commit suicide. If he must kill himself he ought to do it instantly, however, and not by slow degrees, during which time he begets his kind, bequeathing his disease and his weaknesses.

241

And so no man or woman should be permitted to do one stroke of work more than is needful for the healthful development of the body. To do more is to injure God's image, and outrage heaven. But only think how many millions have to do this every day as society is now organized — or do worse. I think I have explained that every man must have a certain amount of exercise. Let this exercise be taken at the plow-handle, the carpenter's bench, or anywhere, or in any way that a man may choose to work, just so much as his health may require, and no more, and we have the solution of the whole matter. Let *every* man do four hours' work each day, instead of every eighth man doing sixteen hours' work; and see how much more work would be done! And only consider what a strong and mighty race of men would spring out of the earth!

This would be one of the cardinal aims of Utopia. We would put physical culture first, because nature has put it first.

I know the theologian who follows the pale light of his midnight lamp down to the very edge of his grave, and thinks he is doing God's service in the act, would place moral culture first. And I know that the nervous and hollow-breasted student, who forever holds a book before his eyes and shuts out the sight of heaven, would place mental culture first. But I tell you that moral culture and mental culture are only handmaids, waiting meekly and dependent entirely upon physical perfection.

Give me a perfectly healthy man who sleeps well, and I will trust him utterly. And only think of the boundless possibilities of such a culture!

Poor man! For many, many thousand years a slave to his fellow-men, and even now a slave to himself. For the past half century, the horse has had some opportunities to show the blood that is in him. But man has never had any opportunity whatever. Give him half the chance of a horse. Let him forget for half a century the slavish habit of money-getting, even in our little colony as contemplated, think of his body, his mind, and his Maker, and there would be a race of gods upon earth. For surely man

242

is as capable of culture and development as the horse, the ox, the rose bush, or the pear tree.

Of course, it is repulsive to think of training up a man's body as you do that of the lower animals. But when that training leads up through pleasant paths, by the founding of cities such as I have dimly sketched, and hewing out ways for the weaker world to come after, then the idea becomes beautiful and poetic.

And here, in this simple and unselfish life, woman, for the first time in all history, would have perfect development of soul and body, and so take that higher plane to which she was born, standing midway, as it were, between God and man.

To get back to the hard practical fact of this city-building, let us consider how poor men are to accomplish it. Simply enough. You only need to begin. And you are really more in need of *men* than money. I mean strong, broad-browed men—men full of faith and hope and charity. For I care not how much money be embarked in the enterprise, if you do not have good, patient, moral, high-minded and unselfish men and women to begin with, the undertaking will have but a brief and inglorious existence.

Some rich men proposed to me the other day that I should go out and locate this city, and they would furnish all the men and money necessary; and if the community failed of its purpose it could dissolve and become a settlement, just like any other frontier town; and they would hold the deeds to the lands thus made valuable, and so, even at the worst, secure to themselves great profit.

This smell of money is so rank! Besides, when I do embark in this, if ever, I shall burn my ship; there will be no contemplated turning back. Better to go right out, one or two or three strong, and somewhere on a green and watered slope of the mountains, remote from settlements, but not too far from railroads, build a camp-fire, mark your bounds upon the land, proclaim it yours, and so begin.

You will have a sufficient following, I think, and very soon, if you once go rightly and bravely to work. The first things to be considered must be health and beauty in the location. The great men of the earth have grown up with the mighty mountains at their back and the plains for a play-ground.

Only to think of locating a city on a high watered and wooded slope, ten thousand miles to choose from, with only health, comfort, and beauty to be considered!

Never yet has been a city located with such high privilege. They have all been built subservient to commerce, to money-getting. Every city in the world save the two theocracies, Jerusalem and Salt Lake City, has been laid out and built by some marshy and sickly boat-landing, or railroad center, to oblige commerce and to make money, without any regard to health, comfort, or beauty of location whatever. And beauty is such an ally of goodness.

Of course you must have plenty of farming land at hand, rich and well watered; mountains for sheep, and plains for cattle. And then you should have mines, where surplus, new men could be set to work to take their three or four hours' exercise daily, until they could be fitted into any other place or employment, should they prefer it.

Either by ignorance or accident, I find that about one-half the world has got into the wrong box. Just about half the people you meet are dissatisfied with the calling in which they are engaged. All this is at once to be set at rights here, and every man, woman or child is to do just what he or she chooses to do in these few hours of exercise they must take.

Our agreed plan in London was to begin with at least fifty strong, and money enough to build a few substantial houses and stock our lands with cattle, sheep, and horses, and to also plow and sow as much land as would furnish our few men their required exercise in caring for it.

We, of course, expected our members to double, treble, quadruple right along year after year, after we once got fairly to work and the world came to understand our high aims and the health, happiness, delights of our new life.

Our purpose was to admit every man, woman, or child

who came to us after we were once fairly established; though it was settled that great care would have to be shown in getting in good material for the keel and main timbers of our ship at the start, so as to maintain a high and artistic level.

Any one coming to us was to have a place at the common table at once, where we all ate together in a great hall, with music and merriment, as if each day was a gala-day. He was to have clothes if he were naked, just as good as the best of us. He was to be permitted to choose his kind of work, either cook, herder, hunter, dishwasher, or what not; and he was to take his exercise at that kind of employment, and from that moment be a part and equal owner of that city and all its property, its peace and happiness, so long as he chose to remain a part of it.

These men held that there is no really bad man on earth in his right senses. Crime, they said, came of disease of mind or body. But in our model city we would live so healthily and happily that there would be disease of neither mind nor body. And so there would be no crime.

For my own part, I am quite certain that every creature does the very best he can with the light and opportunities given him. I admit there are many great fools. But no man is wicked at heart who is healthy in mind and body.

Many of us are bent and ugly in mind and form I know. But there is all the time an effort, a feeble effort — I know sometimes, a pitiful effort — to stand up straight. Trample on a plant, throw rocks and rubbish on it, crush it; yet it will try to struggle up toward the sun; it will creep up on its broken joints, peep up through the rocks and try to get straight and look as pretty as it can. Well, man is just like that. Give him a chance. He is at least as good as the plant under your feet.

All religions were, of course, to be tolerated, even encouraged. But it was agreed that we should have but one temple of worship; that this great temple in the center of the city should be lecture hall, church, music hall, theatre, and general center for all public purposes. The question of religion was counted the hardest problem of all. But it was hoped that the various denominations would finally melt into a sort of liberal Christianity, where the services to be held regularly on Sabbath days would be composed mainly of lectures on religious subjects.

Our government, of course, was to have been that of the land. But, under and subject to this, we planned a sort of patriarchal system of directions. Yet one great object was to avoid all laws and rules as far as possible; for as we considered that laws are made only for the punishment of the vicious, we hoped to never come in contact with them.

Early marriages were to be encouraged. And we hoped to establish such a high moral sense among our people that divorces would never be required or desired. The children were to all be brought up as one happy family — all alike and equal.

The ground-plan of our city was not unlike a wagon-wheel. The temple was to be the hub, with all the streets running to this great center, like the spokes of the wheel. And all were to live inside of this city, where sociability could be kept up and encouraged; for the isolated farm-house is well known to be a melancholy place, and often the scene of selfish and unmanly tyrannies. The English, with all their boasted baronial independence, look with singular favor on the social life of the peasant just across the channel. It may not be generally known that there is not a single cottage or isolated farm-house in all France. The Frenchman is too sociable for that, and will group his home close to that of his neighbors.

Such were some of the general ideas advanced in planning this new city, in the old world, now nearly ten years. Do not quite despise them; for the best of them came from the brightest minds of that time. And all were meant for the good of man.

Emerson has said it takes a great deal of time to be polite; and yet every gentleman is by nature very polite. Well, every man ought to have time to be a gentleman. This he would have in our Utopia: time to be good and great.

It was agreed among us that nothing should be written or said on this subject till something had been done. But, alas! the years have slipped through our fingers; two of the warmest supporters of the scheme have gone on to that grander City of Rest; the others are scattered over the world; I am growing gray, and nothing at all is done. And so I give these suggestions to you, lest we all die out, and the very idea of our great enterprise, of which we all hoped so much, should die out with us.

JOAQUIN MILLER

NOTES

NOTES

1   JOAQUIN MILLER'S POEMS. 6 Vols. (San Francisco: Whitaker and
    Ray Co., 1909) Vol. I, 2.

2   Mark Twain especially...but in view of Twain's later pride and delight
    at the prospect of making fortunes producing bed clamps, historical
    puzzles, and best sellers — all lumped together in the same category — it
    seems appropriate to think of Miller in London as Twain's *alter ego*
    come to life.

3   LANE COUNTY HISTORIAN, XVI (Summer 1971), 23.

4   See Stuart Sherman's AMERICANS, his Introduction to THE
    POETICAL WORKS OF JOAQUIN MILLER, and Van Wyck
    Brooks' THE TIMES OF MELVILLE AND WHITMAN, SKETCHES
    IN CRITICISM, and THE CONFIDENT YEARS: 1885-1915.

4a A point for point comparison with Melville's early experiences with the
    aboriginals of the Marquesas and the books which resulted presents an
    interesting parallel.

5   SPECIMENS (Portland: Carter Hines, 1868).

6   "Joaquin Miller and His 'Shadow,' " WESTERN AMERICAN
    LITERATURE, XVI (May 1976), 51-59.

7   Miller at this point has found his way to Beecher's Plymouth Church in
    Brooklyn. John Hay called Henry Ward Beecher (1813-1887), "the
    greatest preacher the world has seen since St. Paul preached on Mars
    Hill." A few of his sermons are in harmony with modern psychology.
    See especially, "Physical Hindrances in Spiritual Life."

8   Turpin, Richard (1706-1739), English robber, smuggler, deer-
    stealer; finally arrested and put to death.

9   Sheppard, John (1702-1724), famous for his many dramatic escapes
    from prison.

10 Miller is referring to Artemus Ward (Charles Farrar Browne,
    1834-1867), one of America's favorite humorists before Twain. Ward's

251

sketches are best appreciated by those familiar with the social and political events surrounding the Civil War period, and there is a bawdy strain in a fair number of them. Just prior to signing the Emancipation Proclamation, Lincoln read Ward's story, "Outrage in Utica," to his cabinet.

11 Miller probably finished and polished "A Ride Through Oregon" upon his return from London, and he delivers some of his more observant criticisms of the state in this story. In view of his much more favorable attitude later on, he is probably still irritated with Oregonians — especially those people who were critical of his divorce from Theresa Dyer. His other attitudes toward Oregon are found in some articles written for the New York INDEPENDENT: "Our Great Emerald State" (August 16,1888); "Down in Oregon" (August 1,1889); and "Portland, Oregon" (August 8, 1889). A still later article, "Our Great Emerald Land," in the OVERLAND MONTHLY (December, 1896) asserts that Californians came west to seek gold, but Oregonians were seeking homes, "...and that has marked the difference between those two peoples of this coast from the first, and will to the end." In the above articles, Miller also characterizes Oregonians as being more pious and pastoral than Californians.

12 This story presents an early contrast between the despoilers from California and Oregon preservers. Joe Meek is in many ways an important figure to study in relation to Joaquin Miller.

13 Joaquin was born in 1837, so in 1859 he was twenty-one.

14 A number of the pages of the diary are missing, and the first entry is for October 6, 1855 (about four months after the Battle of Castle Crags).

Miller's CALIFORNIA DIARY actually consists of three notebooks, two smaller ones and the third, ledger-size. The larger notebook was used seldom before 1857, but Miller obviously had it with him from 1854 on. One of the smaller books contains almost all of his daily entries, and the second was used primarily for subjects of debate, poems, and letters.

In the daily entry book, there is a definite lack of order. Occasionally, Miller didn't bother to find the page on which he had made his last entry, but flipped to a back page or to the middle of the book and made a dated entry at that point. From time to time a friend named I. Perkins borrowed the notebook and did a sketch of a drunken miner. Perkins' pencil sketches are either signed or properly labeled by Miller. There are also some drawings and decorative designs by Miller himself, all undated, a number of which are presented in this volume.

Miller's notoriously bad handwriting — rather than being either very bad or just moderately bad in this earliest of his works — is actually quite legible *at times* — depending on his mood and the pen he was using.

252

The first transcription of the CALIFORNIA DIARY was done in 1935 by John S. Richards and was published by Frank McCaffrey at his Dogwood Press in 1936. The portions of the DIARY that are in pencil — many of which are no longer legible — were easier to read at that time. Richards ordered the entries chronologically and inserted letters and poems from the two other books when these seemed to belong to the period, or were actually dated.

Richards' method of editing was quite arbitrary. I have followed him in omitting the drafts of speeches to the various debating societies to which Miller belonged, because these drafts were no more than academic exercises. But Richards also deleted poems, letters, biblical quotations, two rather mild examples of profanity, four pages of Wintu vocabulary, and the perplexing "message" or "letter" in the Wintu language — all of which are published in the present volume for the first time. In some places, Richards came up against words he was not able to read; a number of these I have managed to decipher. I have included, either in the text or in the Notes, all the poems and letters in Richards' version.

Richards included only entries that were written in California. Since two or three of the Oregon entries are important to an understanding of Miller's state of mind during this period, I have included these as well.

The manuscript of the DIARY came to light in 1912, a year before Miller's death, and was sent to his lifelong friend, Ina Coolbrith, by Mrs. Lischen Miller, Joaquin's sister-in-law. She sent the following letter along with the manuscript.

Dearest Ina Coolbrith:

   The old manuscript goes to you by express today. Joaquin commanded me to burn it. If when you have looked it through, you think it should be burned, please order the cremation ceremony. One thing I am sure you will agree with me in — it is not fitting that others should see it. Indeed, if you were not the truest, best and wisest friend Joaquin has or ever had, I should not dare to send it to you. If this record of forgotten days contains anything that should be preserved you will discern it. If it does not you are generous enough to understand and forgive. Anyway, I feel so strongly that you are the one and only person who can sift the golden grain from the chaff that I cannot do otherwise than place it in your hands.

After Ina Coolbrith's death, her niece, Mrs. Finlay Cook, sold the manuscript to Willard Morse, who made it available for publication. The manuscript is now a part of the Willard Morse collection at the Honnold Library, the Claremont Colleges, Claremont, California.

15 This part of the diary is arranged by the days of the week and only occasionally are dates included. In this entry, Miller is unsure of the exact date and in one or two other entries wrong dates are given. The diary has been checked with a calendar for the years 1855 and 1856 and, except for these few cases, the dates fall on the right days of the week. [*Richards' note*]

16, 17, 18
These dates are obviously incorrect. [*Richards' note*]

19 Richards deleted this mysterious item (or joke) from the diary.

20 This letter was not completed. [*Richards' note*]

21 Immediately after this letter, the following three poems appear in the Richards version of the diary.

November the 30/56

Squaw Valley Shasta Co. California

The Indian Girl

That earlier sound of which Moore has spoke
In the east had faintly broken
When we into the camp like a whirlwind broke
And our battle to the death I did open

With Colts Revolver and deadly knife
And riffles that never erred
The shrieks and yells told the flow of life
Where our fire of death was poured

The shafts of death flew thickly round
Mid balls as thickly flying
And still the fearful fight went on
With out heed to the dead or the dying

Dec. the 5/56
Squaw Valley Shasta Co. California

Wrapt in his blankets neath a clever old oak
The wearied miner lay
His mind dwelt on scenes that was far away
I knew by the half finished words he spoke

He dreamed of her he so dearly loved

254

In his Old New England home
But since he to California came
Alas false to her lover she had proved

He dreamed he stood on his native shore
His fair young bride
Stood by his side
And his California life was oer

Im alone alone in this valley of snow
Alone in the wilderness drear
The night owls cry is all I hear
Which makes me crouch in my bed with fear
And curse the day that brought me here
So far from friend or foe

Of solitude they may write and sing
May sing it in every lay
Till each bards head is streaked with grey
I swear I swear Ill never stray
From society so far away
For twill sure repentance bring

There is snow to the north there is snow to the south
To the east as well as the west
The trees alike in snow are dressed
As if it were for some great feast
Where by the Snow God they are blessed
A blessing from this ice-cold month

The wind with groans is eddying round
Ice far down from the mountains pour
A cloud of snow she drives before
As if eternity had come and time was oer
So loud so terrible that roar
Oh that deep that wild that unearthly sound

22 This entry was not completed. The account appearing in the YREKA
UNION for February 12, 1857, shows that the Pit River Massacre
occurred the last of January. Almost six weeks later Miller starts out to
investigate. In his account of the Massacre in MEMORIE AND RIME,
Miller infers that the Indian Chief Blackbeard kept the news from
him. It is possible that Miller only learned of the Massacre when the

Indians were forced to defend themselves from the subsequent military expedition of the whites. [*Richards' note*]

23 The translation of the Wintu vocabulary and the partial translation of the "message" which follows are the work of Alice Schlichter, Department of Linguistics, the University of California, Berkeley.

24 According to his own reckoning three different times in this diary, Miller is now 20 years of age....This first uncertainty about his age may be intended to make sure of his majority. Later, perhaps for reasons not unconnected with vanity, four or five years were dropped by the expedient of advancing the date of birth to 1841 or 1842. [*Richards' note*]

25 The following poems by Miller appeared in this portion of Richards' diary.

McAdams Creek. September the 28/57

The Old School house on the Hill

I

I remember thee school house with feelings of pleasure
So oft may my memory with thoughts of thee fill
For I left much behind me I prize more than treasure
When I left the old school house that stands on the hill

2

My brothers and schoolmates were all left behind me
Though fresh in my memory their lingering still
For a thousand bright fancies still live to remind me
Of the clever old school house that stands on the hill

3

With town ball or cat our recess a whileing
These innocent sports my memory fill
Or the rougish young damsels so archly a smiling
Oh I love the old school house that stands on the hill

4

Now the school mates are scattered. Some peacefully lying
Neath the fresh growing turf yea so silent and chill
While some like myself in a strange land a sighing
For their friends and the school house that stands on the hill

256

Fare well then old school house though Ile never forget thee
Through every misfortune Ile think of thee still
And whether good luck or bad or honors attend me
Ile forget not the school house that stands on the hill

Hiner Miller

October the 18/57
McAdams Creek

We both were young and both then dwelt
Beneath your fathers roof and care
At the same sacred altar knelt
Both morn and eve in humble prayer
Twas then I traced my earliest song
But doubting of its———worth
I showed it thee but kept it long
Unknown to all but thee on earth

You praised and said tis written well
And credit on the author throws
Then bade me try the magic spell
Of song upon the summer rose
It might have been I feared my power
Or skill at song. I wrote it not
Yet deem not lady for one short hour
Your request or praise has been forgot

Merinda many years have flown
And many a smiling summers past
Full many a summers rose has blown
To perish in the winters blast
The scene has changed, we meet no more
Alone I tread a foreign land
And thee thy maiden days are oer
A stranger claims thy heart and hand
Then as I alone this sabbath morn
Reflect on scenes forever oer
A line Ill pen though—
Of a rose that blooms for me no more

Midnight

Oct the 23/57 California

The pattering rain is falling fast
The winds have lent their doleful sound
Now dreary sweeps Octobers blast
The mist and rain fast eddying round
The clock strikes ten my comrades sleep
The dying embers burning low
I alone awake my mind to steep
In scenes that passed three years ago

Three years this very night has passed
Since on lifes broad tempesteous sea
I launched my bark with prospects vast
Of riches favor and dignity
Three misspent years have swiftly flown
In mind and purse still vulgar low
With burning shame I blush to own
I was nigher fame three years ago

When all was prepared for my hasty flight
The door I had closed and on the threshold stood
With folded arms to the queen of night
I said with half prophetic mood
Three years from hence I must I shall
Be more than now a school-boy low
Perchance Ill tread some senate hall
And think what passed three years ago

And thus it is from morn of life
The day is spent and life is done
Three years at most of toil and strife
Most surely then the goal is won
Deluding hopes who does not say
With struggling signs akin to woe
The joys I hoped to gain to-day
Were nigher me three years ago

But see oerflowing on yon mount
Gay pleasures cup with tears unstained
Just filled from fames undying fount
Since three years more that cup is gained
Then on again deluded host
That cup when gained is filled with woe
Can ye not learn by what you lost
Of hopes deceived three years ago

The clock strikes twelve I must to rest

258

Though the elements are battling still
Yet the storm within my own wild breast
Is more than mortal man should feel
Three years are past forever past
By time laid in their tombs so low
Their requiem howls Octobers blast
And mocking sighs three years ago

Hiner Miller

Written while at McAdams Creek, Siskiyou County, California,
October the 30/1857 on returning a letter to Miss——.

Since you must have it so then dear Mary adieu
Although fondly I had hoped that the time should not be
When I should return this epistle to you
Though I knew you cared but little for me

Yet when fate & dame fortune had called me away
From those who professed their kind friendship to show
I relied but on thee and I cared not for they
Nor the world and its troubles while you were my friend

Since I wrote to thee Mary long long months have passed
Though I wrote to thee too in the friendliest way
My letters unanswered and lies strewn in the blast
My hopes in the future like——decay

But think not I beg you to write to me now
No I cannot subdue this unconquerable pride
Even should god himself murmer this life to bestow
Id scorn it and hate it as if twas denied

Think not then Ill murmer or of troubles complain
No misfortunes have taught tis useless to mourn
Then exult not a hope that your causing me pain
By treating me thus with indifference & scorn

Yes Im determined I must I shall be content
It will cost but an effort and my conduct shall seem
As if pride and my prospects no change underwent
But lie peaceful and quiet as in loves early dream

Yet Mary if here on this page you should trace
The marks of a tear drop that by accident fell
Forgive it I pray thee if tis not in its place
But remember Im writing my forever farewell

Hiner Miller

Nov the 1/57

Adieu then my Mary, forever Adieu—
Adieu since you must have it so
You are free from your promise
And now to be—
That were given but a few months ago

Nov. 4/57
McAdams Creek, Calif.

I am far from my home in a stranger land
And the rude winds of autumn come whistling around
Which serves not at all for to solice my mind
Which now by misfortune is nigh being downed

The sun like my hopes is with clouds orcast
And too like my hopes is as fast sinking down
But see the sun now is strong the clouds now are passed
And like the sun shall my hopes now defy fortune's frown

Yes Ill laugh at misfortune in his angriest mood
Though my friends are but few I will use books instead
And take every disaster as an omen of good
And still thank my Creator for my portion of bread

November the 4/57

List ye hear the rain a poring
Autumns blasts are gathering fast
The frosty seer will soon be here
Hear the dismal winds a roaring

Gentle summer now has left us
Her sunny day has passed away
And summer mild sweet natures child
Has of many a pleasant hour bereft us

Say summer dear what was thy haste
Why leave so soon thou precious boon
Why give winter sear thy bowers here
Which even now hes laying waste

Why is it so my gentle summer
That every year old frosty seer

Is wont to come and take your home
And you leave it all without a murmur

But such the course of time does claim
The seasons each a lesson teach
That all must learn to take its turn
Ile try and learn to do the same

Then learn a lesson from the summer
Like summer sun our race is run
Soon one and all will hear deaths call
Then let us answer without a murmur

H. Miller

26   This is the last entry from California. on December 25, 1857, Miller is writing from Columbia College in Oregon. [*Richards' note*] Richards' version of the diary ends here.

27   The Boones and the de Witts moved from Pennsylvania to North Carolina about the year 1755. There was a rather large migration of settlers to North Carolina at that time, because the Cherokee Indians, who had been hostile to the settlers, had just been driven beyond the Blue Ridge. [*Firman's note*]

28   Puncheons were made by splitting logs into thin boards or planks instead of sawing them. The surface of a puncheon was sometimes smoothed with a broad axe, but it was usually very rough and uneven. [*Firman's note*]

29   This was Joseph Lane of Oregon

30   The Indians were about the only people in the new country who had any money. They received it from the Government in installments for the land they had sold. [*Firman's note*]

31   Justice of the Peace

32   Friction matches were invented in 1832, but they were expensive at first and did not reach frontier settlements until some time later. [*Firman's note*]

33   The disease described is malaria.

34   St. Patrick's Day

First known photograph of Joaquin (Cincinnatus Hiner) Miller
(Herman and Eliza Oliver Historical Museum)

Joaquin Miller in 1872 (Honnold Library)

Miller in his late thirties (Honnold Library)

Miller at work in a mountain camp, 1903

Joaquin Miller in 1911 (Sutro Library)

Miller shortly before his death in 1913

A NOTE ON THE EDITOR

Alan Rosenus graduated Phi Beta Kappa from Brown University where he studied writing with John Hawkes. He received the Master of Arts degree in Creative Writing from San Francisco State College and studied poetry there with Robert Duncan. He has done additional graduate work at Stanford University, the University of Iowa, and received his doctorate in American Literature from the University of Oregon. His first novel, THE OLD ONE, was published under the pseudonym, David Middlebrook, in 1974. His second novel, THE MEMOIRS OF A WELL-HUSTLED APPLE-EATER, as well as a third, A TIMETABLE FOR DRAGONS, are in progress. He has taught at San Francisco State College, the College of Marin, and Coe College in Cedar Rapids.

ʊrion press

P.O. Box 2244
Eugene, Oregon 97402